A Course on Aesthetics

A Course on Aesthetics

Renato Barilli

Translated by Karen E. Pinkus

University of Minnesota Press
Minneapolis
London

Originally published as *Corso di estetica*, by Società Editrice Il Mulino. Bologna, 1989

Published by the University of Minnesota Press
2037 University Avenue Southeast, Minneapolis, MN 55455-3092
Printed in the United States of America on acid-free paper

Library of Congress Cataloging-in-Publication Data

Barilli, Renato.
   [Corso di estetica. English]
   A course on aesthetics / Renato Barilli ; translated by Karen E.
Pinkus.
      p.   cm.
   Includes bibliographical references and index.
ISBN 0-8166-2118-7 (hard : alk. paper). — ISBN 0-8166-2119-5
   (pbk. : alk. paper)
   1. Aesthetics.   I. Title.
   BH39.B35313   1993
111'.85—dc20   93-21779
                                                         CIP

Contents

Introduction

In the university context, the word "course" refers to the cycle of lessons that a teacher gives within the space of a so-called academic year, developing arguments that are more or less intrinsic to a discipline in which that teacher has a degree. The author of the following pages actually was a university teacher of aesthetics for several years, and so, in that capacity, he taught a number of sequential courses in which he had to elaborate a coherent and organic strategy for presenting his own material. He was given the opportunity to modify the criteria and content of his methods from one year to the next. The present book is meant to be a faithful reflection of that experience, which accounts for its distinctive character.

This means that the principal reader is presumed to be a "participant" in either a university or in some related institution such as an academy of fine arts. Moreover, it goes without saying that the notion of participation is to be understood in a broad context. It is not meant to be limited to those few years during which a student takes classes or absorbs the content of precisely those "courses" offered by various teachers. It is hoped, rather, that some texts will follow the student for the rest of his or her professional and cultural life in general, as indispensable instruments. Ideally, a student embarks on a sort of permanent education, which is available even to those who have not spent the requisite number of years in the classrooms of our Academies. We live in a postmodern, postindustrial society, with its obvious tendency to consume an ever greater number of artistic products and to apply an ever more acutely tuned consciousness toward its own aesthetic image. Why not then provide for the potential consumer a text that offers a general, flexible, and synthetic introduction to the various postmaterial uses and needs, as we now define them, by which the user is so often stimulated?

In seeking to fulfill these objectives, I propose in this book to adopt a plain, discursive style of writing not overly burdened by technicalities or jargon that will nevertheless maintain a certain rigor with regard to terminology. Perhaps specialists in the field, aestheticians, will complain of a lack of development, of merely approximate reconstructions and schematizations of certain polemics, or of assertions offered too rapidly, without the accompanying barrage of proof and supporting arguments. Or perhaps, on the contrary, specialists will lament the fact that I offer no clear position, no sworn statement accompanied by gestures of polemical challenge toward those who would sustain an opposing position. In fact, I have attempted to construct an "economical" undertaking here, beginning from the presupposition that the field of aesthetic doctrine is already too crowded with precisely such unilateral positions. For many, to enter into this material implies first and foremost that one must present a personal interpretation couched in a brand-new set of terms, opening a new space and fiercely overturning the arguments of one's competitors. To be "economical" means, rather, to attempt to make certain doctrines coexist that at first glance may seem far apart, but then, concretely, to show how, because they actually function in a similar mode, they constitute vast blocks or family groups. Finally, this text attempts to unify and, wherever possible, to point to linkages, affinities, and substantial correspondences, in order to clarify the broader field and offer what might almost be considered a guide for locating equivalences. The reader will be reassured to learn that in spite of their diverse origins and terminology, the dominant systems we will examine tend to lead to the same ends, and one can adopt one or the other of them with equal confidence.

Naturally, this act of leveling, of equalizing, of correlation has been performed where differences seem the least relevant, almost insignificant in functional terms. I have been much more careful in proceeding along these lines in cases where differences seem more clear-cut, and in fact, in such cases I preferred to accentuate disparity precisely so that the resulting picture might be evident, and capable of assuming responsibility for itself. In other words, I have taken a clear position on the major problems that concern aesthetics, or more generally, philosophical debate, even if in an idiosyncratic and highly personalized sense. I continue to maintain a commitment to a sense of families, by sustaining widely constituted solidarity between positions.

Let us examine, then, a few of the problems around which positions are

formed. The first of these concerns the very possibility of a global aesthetics; this undertaking is periodically considered by extremely subtle
thinkers. Obviously, the so-called dogmatic route, one convinced of its
ability to reach the truth within a certain field and to sustain the excellence
of its own responses through firm faith and solid arguments, enjoys little
credit in our century. But a counterattack might be raised, to suggest that
if everyone is wrong, everyone is also right; that if God is dead, everything
is permitted and thus it no longer makes sense to theorize. We should return to a healthy empirical praxis. Art and aesthetics are then empty ves-
sels to be filled with content from time to time, by various individuals. This
attitude of total openness resulting in a lost rigor (it would be nice if God,
that is, thought grounded on rigid and unshakable foundations, still lived)
is invoked by our culture with almost seasonal rhythm. It was manifested
during the 1930s, when, arguing against Benedetto Croce, several students
of Giovanni Gentile (Ugo Spirito, in particular) carried their teacher's position to its extreme consequences: only logical activity belongs to the present. Art, on the other hand, is always past; it lags behind us, and it cannot
claim to be illuminated by the light of reason; thus, there is no possibility
of grounding aesthetics on a solid theoretical base. Then once again this
position enjoyed a revival during the 1950s in a different climate nourished
by leftist concerns, which sought to appear laically disinterested. At this
time it also became clear how far Anglo-Saxon philosophy had come in this
direction since the 1930s, strengthened by an analytic and neopositivist
spirit, in its attempt to cultivate the so-called hygiene of language. In his
book *Processo all'estetica* (Aesthetics on trial), Armando Plebe has indicated the various phases of this debate in a most singular manner. Again,
twenty years later, we have seen the domination of "weak" thought, a philosophy that also preaches the highest deconditioning, the opening up to an
influx of every possible demonstration by professionals, but within a climate
dominated by the "fall" of the West, and thus based on an elegiac note of
resignation.

Each time, these "antiquated" positions of either processes or program-
matic weakness have been supplanted by attitudes that may not be substantially different at a practical level, but that have radical theoretical
consequences. These consequences suggest that it is inherent in humanity
in its primary manifestation—culture—not to express dogmas or a "truth"
that can be proven universally: affirmations or definitions are valuable
instruments only as long as they satisfy the needs for which they were intended; but because we may experience a legitimate need for such instruments, we must keep them on hand. They form part of a critical arsenal,

and they are not interchangeable or undifferentiated. Not all hypotheses function at all times with the same degree of plausibility. Some emerge as more valuable, efficient, or responsive, whereas others should be put aside for future use. This type of thinking informs both European phenomenology and North American pragmatism.

It is not merely coincidental that we will again encounter a convergence of the various followers of this sort of critical line. We might insist here on an order of binary solutions, which, in effect, this book both uses and abuses. These "couples" permit a dynamic response to various nodal points that traditionally recur throughout the history of philosophy and aesthetics and that form the basis for any relation with the outside world, but also with other subjects within social and interpersonal life. We might begin with the pairs "inside-outside," or "internal-external," which, in basic philosophical terminology, correspond to the classic opposition of subject and object. Of a similar nature is the opposition between signifier and signified (form and content) that suggests the same fundamental dualism but in an atmosphere of more refined expressive operation, one that assumes the use of artificial instruments. Moreover, we discover an inherent ambivalence within the context of this nodal point. It is valid in terms of the most immediate relations, precisely between the internal and the external, between that which is in us and that which remains on the side of the other, but it also opens up another vexing problematic, namely the relation between that which exists here and now, as in the physical world, and that which exists in an indefinite realm, suspended in intangible formations beyond our grasp, but which nevertheless *exists* and may somehow play an indispensable role.

From time to time several lines of thought return to favor, seeking to break up this binary style, to undo the Gordian knot by brutally cutting it apart, that is, by imposing some version of monism, perhaps including signs that are radically opposed to one another, but that are equally clear and peremptory. In several cases, it might seem that there is only one series: subject and internal-signifier. And already here, by having the courage to conjoin terms of quite disparate origins, terms preferred by a variety of different proponents, we proceed toward the conclusion that there is no insurmountable difference between idealisms (whether or not these are understood in the Crocean sense) and apparently disparate positions that purport to stick closely to clearly empirical linguistic categories, but that are ultimately quick to declare, in an equally reductive spirit, that only linguistic acts exist. We can only speak about signifiers, given that, as Vico might maintain, we ourselves create them (or we posit them out of convention). About signifieds, however, we really know nothing; or, rather, here is the illusion that signifieds can be assaulted, corroded, and diluted, so that in the end all that remains are signifiers. This was the illusion of the semiotic undertaking in a strict sense, inspired on the one hand by the analytic thought of logical positivism and on the other by the linguistics of the Dane Louis Hjelmslev, who seemed to dominate the culture of the human sciences during the mid-1960s.

Naturally, there is a monism of an apparently different sort that seeks to eliminate this "internal" series, affirming that, on the contrary, an empirically grounded lay consciousness can only recognize the existence of external, physical data, verifiable by the senses or with instruments of objective measurement.

It might seem that the various reflections proposed up to this point have remained fairly far from my main subject, namely aesthetics. But on closer examination, we find that we have outlined the premises, or advanced the opportune declarations of principle, that now permit us to justify the type of response offered in the following pages, as well as the manner and the style through which we arrived at these responses.

In one sense, this text has not been limited by the various recurring trials or invocations of "weakness" so dominant in current thought. Rather, it has proceeded to promote a program of definitions or more properly of categories to which aesthetic-artistic criteria may refer even if we must imagine that such propositions are preceded by one enormous premise that reveals their contingent, pragmatic, and utilitarian nature. If these propositions are valid for our own times, they may be revoked or improved at some later date. In the meantime, however, we must offer some response, some firm ground to that vast crowd of consumers delineated above, and this text attempts to face up to that responsibility; moreover, in the pursuit of such an objective, it does not renounce the previously mentioned goal of a certain economy. To this end, we have grouped together the work of many scholars who have advanced similar hypotheses, but from quite diverse perspectives within the larger field. Thus it is not important here to decide whether it is better to assign presentationality to aesthetics, among the definite and significant categories, as Susanne Langer and Galvano Della Volpe both maintain. What matters is to act upon such a confluence and arrive at some family of responses, offering them to a public hungry for certainties, even if they are merely hypothetical and of short duration.

As for the binary style, it will find its confirmation shortly afterward. It is not enough simply to assert that art must be seen as a question of contextuality, of globalization, and so on (according to a style of definitions linked together under a large and generous set of criteria), for that reopens the usual problematic: are the elements that make up that admirable unitary context that is aesthetic experience or the work of art internal or external? Is the work of art merely a question of signifiers or do signifieds also enter into play? In homage to the style of bipolarism, in this book I have chosen a strategy of combinations, of dialectical coexistence. There is no signifier that does not refer to a signified; there is no form or subjectivity that does not open up to the external world.

It is precisely in the nature of a style grounded in such binary couples to maintain that each one of the two faces can never be isolated in a pure state; and thus nobody will ever be able to perform a surgical operation so exact that it cuts away only the single face of the world as exteriority. In that perfect Janus that for Ferdinand de Saussure is the sign, there is no lancet so sharp or so fine that it can divide one face of the ambiguous god from the other. Imagine how illusory the claim to separate the recto of a page from the verso would seem. For once a strip is torn from the verso, immediately a portion of the surface residue would be attached, faced with the very same task of separating itself, in turn, from its own verso. The most powerful graphic rendition imaginable derives from the universe of electricity or magnetism: no one will ever be able to eliminate one of the two poles in that fundamental bipolar field in which every cosmic reality is immersed from start to finish, dominated by their conjoined interaction.

And thus, from one comparison to another, even the world, that is to say, the most vast and global entity to which we can refer, displays a bipolar character and corresponds to the exercise of the culture of humanity in its most vast and engaging aspects. These aspects, as we realize now more than ever, begin at the material-technological level, which will receive our utmost attention in the pages that follow. In general, many thinkers have been quick to highlight the implications of the Gutenberg-typographical age, or even the present age founded on the exploitation of electromagnetism, for various modifications of artistic practices or aesthetic concepts. And because we live today in an electronic galaxy, perhaps this is the source for the legitimation for a type of thought based on couples, with its bipolar schemes, that forms one of the basic choices informing this study of aesthetics. And it is also a means for framing theoretical accounts, for demonstrating that the present discourse can at least boast of coherence, that is, it appears capable of administering affirmations and denials, points of strength and well-founded declarations of renunciation. Precisely because we live in a technetronic age, it is correct to adopt bipolar terms against various sorts of monisms and intentionalisms (idealisms, frustrated physicalities, analytic rigor of a pseudomathematical flavor, or naive and bulky materialisms linked to the triumph of external data). But faith in binary terms must be colored by the knowledge that humanity has known other cultural seasons, other technological assets from which monisms or unbalanced, unilateral definitions might draw their legitimacy. Today, assisted by the force of the times, we feel authorized to reject these. And naturally we do not know our own destiny, given our own lay—and thus cultural-technological—consciousness. We must be ready for any variation of aesthetic concepts or of art itself, including the possibility that one or the other of these, or both, will meet up with the very "death" that has so often been predicted.

CHAPTER 1

Aesthetic Experience

Etymology of the Term

As in any other field of investigation, in aesthetics the first move that one must make is to examine how, when, and why its institutional title was born, the plaque that one finds over the classroom doors where this subject is taught or on the shelves where books dedicated to it are collected. It would be entirely misleading to suggest that aesthetics enjoys some inherent, stable nature outside its history. On the contrary, it is an object that typically belongs to culture, and this in turn expresses an eminently historical character, positioned along an unending line of development.

Without doubt, mobility is also a fundamental characteristic of nature itself, at least since the advent of Darwinism. Nevertheless, the development of natural objects, measured in terms of millennia, is incomparably slower than that of cultural objects, so that from the perspective of any given period one has the impression of stasis. The organization of a dog today is not appreciably different from that of its ancestors of Roman times, and this holds equally true for the human animal, if considered in biological and physiological terms. But human culture, within the same arc of time, has undergone an incalculable number of transformations, which continue to produce themselves, perhaps with an ever more accelerated rhythm, now measurable in decades.

It is thus more or less possible to establish, for aesthetics as for any other cultural object, the date of its institution. We can also predict that, just as aesthetics had at one point been "posited," so it will come to be abrogated, as soon as it fails to respond to the needs that contributed to its birth or justify its survival. Furthermore, even within a given chronological arc, it should not be taken for granted that the significance of aesthetics has been in any sense univocal or stable; rather, we must admit that it has undergone a pendular movement of progressive distance from the etymological root that also corresponds to its institutional title, only to experience, once again, a movement back toward this origin.

If, for purposes of an initial orientation, we were to survey the most common usage of "aesthetics" within academic circles, we might find that it refers to something like a "philosophy of art," just as ethics is the philosophy of morals, epistemology the philosophy of knowledge, and so on. Obviously, the most persistent or dominant opinion would suggest that aesthetics concerns art, even if not exclusively, and that it has as its goal the development of a discourse or a critically rigorous and philosophical examination of art. But if we were to ask the question of a less educated individual—one who never finished high school, for example—we might encounter a series of quite different reactions. This person might express either perplexity at a term not found in his or her lexical baggage, or recognition, but in the context of a "lower" usage of "aesthetics" as it enters common speech while still retaining a certain pretentiousness and "promotional" stimulus. For the less educated, in fact, the term is familiar from its use in the *institut d'esthétique-institut de beauté*, that is to say, that place where one goes for facials, for skin massages, for various cosmetic treatments. [In Italy, as in France, many beauty salons are known as "aesthetic institutes." Operators within these houses are referred to as "aestheticians," and in fact this is a legitimate professional title—TRANS.] Or perhaps the term might arouse associations related to the "aesthetician," by which one refers to a particular profession (and, incidentally, a fairly lucrative one) carried out in an *institut de beauté* or some similar place, specializing in any one of a series of "treatments." And perhaps the term "aesthetologue," which would be the correct way to indicate an operator concerned with aesthetic problems in a more serious "philosophical" context, would resound as meaningless or disturbing. But if we wish to refer to the etymology or to the constitutive act of the entire field, we must admit that the uninformed, the uncultured, are closer to the root of the problem. As has been noted, the term "aesthetics" was first proposed by the German philosopher Baumgarten in an eponymous work published in 1750, referring to the Greek root *aisth* (and the verb *aisthánomai*). This is linked to the idea of sensing, not with the heart or with the "sentiments," but with the senses, the network of physical perceptions. The root survives in the most direct and eloquent mode in our everyday common speech, but in a negative form.

Preceded by the so-called deprivative alpha, it appears in "an-esthesia," that is, the pharmacological procedure through which we obtain, for therapeutic ends, the dulling or, more precisely, the temporary annihilation of sensory-perceptive faculties. Aesthetics, whether in Baumgarten's institutional definition or in that commonly held in our own times, indicates exactly the contrary: a force for making our sensory reactions more acute, more pointed. Yet the etymological investigation does not at all validate the domination of the idea of "art" that has become the medium-high usage of the term. The "art" connotation stems from a totally different verbal root, even if, as we shall soon see, it is possible to effect a passage between the two registers. But for the moment it is sufficient to reveal the reciprocal distance and heterogeneity of the two lexical roots. Aesthetics, understood as a philosophy (or to use a more neutral term, as a branch of knowledge, a discipline) of art thus designates a departure from the sense of the originary foundation of this subject. This departure is clearly due to the relevance, the nobility, and the spiritual excellence that art has reached in recent centuries. But we also know that the avant-garde movements of the twentieth century, at least beginning with dadaism, have placed such excellence or nobility in doubt. Now it is common to speak of antiart, "the death of art," or of recourse to extra-artistic measures, of a passage to direct practices of aesthetic animation. Beside the figure of the artist we now also find that of the "aesthetic operator." The fact remains that the final movement sketched by the most sensitive and polemical work consists in a return to the origins, that is, to "aesthetics" understood in the sense of Baumgarten, and so also in a movement toward the low definition. As often happens, we can map a solidarity between the most sophisticated sectors of scholarly research and common or popular public opinion, to the detriment of the average cultural level that has remained a repository for the elevated and noble concept of aesthetics as practically synonymous with the notion of art theory.

"Art," "poie," "rhe"

Up to now we have treated two lexical roots, "est" and "art," both claiming to dominate the sector (even if, at the level of a label, it is clearly "est" that has succeeded: nobody, today, contests the right of our particular field of study to make use of the title aesthetics). Which one is correct? If we return to origins, there is no doubt that "art" goes further back, that it predates by several centuries its competitor "aesthetics." Indeed, it is possible to locate the precise origin of this latter term, born in 1750, which was, one might say, practically yesterday. The root "art," however, is stably fixed in Latin culture, where, among other uses, it corresponds to an even more ancient Greek word, *techne* (which survives in our word "technique"). We might immediately suppose that even in this case, it is the low, current, common term of "technique" that most fruitfully approximates the meaning of the Greek *techne* as well as the Latin *ars*. The word "art" in our culture, however, is by now irreparably contaminated by Renaissance and romantic filters that make it out to be something rare and precious. The etymological significance corresponds, however, to a notion of work, production, or certain acts that transform material through intelligence and ability. This significance is correctly preserved in the term "artisan" (an individual who balances exhausting manual labor with the proper proportion of intelligence and individual expertise), and it also survives in certain lexical residues as, for example, in the term "work of art," when by this we mean not paintings in museums, but the bridges and tunnels one finds along the highway.

It is certain that both the Latin *ars* and the Greek *techne* once stood for the primary grades of technical intervention, taken in an extremely ample and generic sense—so much so, that it very soon became necessary to introduce hierarchies of values according to a rising scale and then to reward the values of the mind over those of the hand or physical labor. Such a scale could only be constructed in accordance with a social structure, which, in the Greco-Roman world, saw the radical subdivision between slaves and free citizens: hence the distinction between the *artes serviles* (artisanal) and the *artes liberales*, those worthy of a citizen, and which today we would call "professions." These would be opposed, however, to the primary task of running the government and army. Nevertheless, even the liberal arts in the ancient world constituted a more vast and engaged sphere than that defined by more recent eras (from the Renaissance to romanticism) as the *beaux arts*; and in point of fact, even these arts will be subjected to a radical schism. Artistic practices associated with painting, music, and design have tended to fall into the category of the servile arts, perhaps because of the physical-muscular work they require or perhaps for the very lack of prestige or *gravitas* associated with their recreational ends. Or, they have come to occupy a kind of autonomous limbo, neither condemned nor truly promoted.

It is for these reasons that along with technique, the generic "production" involved in any art form, Greco-Roman culture felt the need to distinguish a decidedly more refined and spiritual production linked to the only material completely worthy of a free individual, material that can be shaped without any manual labor—language. On closer inspection, this material is not really material so much as spiritual, made, that is, from "spirit" or breath, from exhalation (or from the reduced and lightened version of the act of writing, more often reserved for a "servant" in the field we call dictation). Along with the technique-art sphere was born the more circumscribed field of *poiesis*: a "making" par excellence precisely because it does not require marble or paints, but merely the "spiritual" substance of language, even if this is, to a degree, graphic in nature. With this categorization, the noble and excellent nature of poetry came to be established. Art, which in itself does indicate a certain level of ability, albeit one of rather ordinary administration, must now find a new dimension in order to accommodate poetry. Since Plato, such a refiguration has been colored by tinges of superhuman qualities, and has corresponded, very nearly, to the descent of divine powers into the human sphere. The poet speaks as if "inspired" by the divine muses. This "divine" interpretation, however, was contested by various thinkers, including Aristotle. Meanwhile, both sides of the debate insisted on the constructive power assigned to the *poiein*, especially if one keeps sight of its etymological significance as a "making." In this case, the objects of this "making" are long-lasting, light, and immaterial, but nevertheless tangible. They exhibit a certain "physicality," as do the *poemi*. On the other hand, when Aristotle wrote the *Poetics*, a treatise that analyzes the technique by which poems are constructed, he was almost compelled to concentrate on long poems (epics, comic and tragic drama) as if they were the only forms worthy of being called poems. This is especially important because poetry, and poetics as its locus of analysis or technical instruction, is quite far from embracing in toto the extremely vast sphere of all verbal expressions. Rather, this is precisely the specific field of a technique addressed to the instruction of all operations related to "speech." And because the Greek root covering this field is "rhe," we find it developed in the powerful *ars rhetorica*, codified by Aristotle in the *Rhetoric*. To sum up, the field that we would now reserve for the literary arts was actually divided during antiquity into poetics and rhetoric. The first was concerned with technical problems such as how one constructs poetry, especially of the long variety, whereas the second was concerned with general problems of examining and teaching all aspects of speech. More particularly, rhetoric was focused on problems relating to ornament, diction, and to the quality of the verbal material used. (We must remember, moreover, that in Aristotle's time the various confines between that which would come to be stylistics and that which would come to be grammar had not yet been drawn up, so both functions were contained within rhetoric in the most ample sense.) In particular, because the problems of ornamentation and rhetorical figures are more evident in short poems (if for no other reason than the fact of their verbal density), rhetorical treatises began to occupy themselves primarily with "brief" forms (epigrams, elegies, hymns, epithalamia, and so on), leaving poetics to study the longer genres, but not without obvious areas of intersection and juxtaposition between the two fields.

Throughout antiquity, then, the various fields that today we would group together under the common rubric of aesthetics did not in fact constitute a unified totality. Instead, aesthetics was fragmented into various branches and could be characterized as an archipelago made up of various islands, even if a certain harmony or communication may have existed between them. The three fields that we have already mentioned stand out in particular: technique or art, poetics, and rhetoric. Each of these, in turn, contains many subordinate sectors: the generic group of technical treatises relevant to the arts both codifies and conveys information concerning activity strictly linked to the materials employed and often addresses questions of machinery or tools (hence the term *artes mechanicae*). This field encompasses painting, sculpture, architecture, and the "making" of art and industry in general. Poetics, as we have already seen, oversees the functional rules of the literary genres, particularly "long" works, and also assures a tie between the moment of the written text and that of its dramatization or performance (whether oral, mimetic, musical, choreographic, or regarding stage design). Rhetoric is responsible for all problems of style and ornament, but also holds a prominent place in the expression of emotions, diction, and public behavior. In line with these interests, the term "rhetoric" also touches on the problem of the sublime or strong sentiment, thus tracing the causes of the emotions and affects, of the way they are produced and controlled by orators and the public in general. Each of these sectors includes points of contact with the others; in fact, at times they tend to merge, forming large blocks within the parameters of a given sector.

This situation of coexistence and carefully coordinated links was instituted in classical antiquity and has persisted for centuries, throughout the entire Middle Ages and modernity, even up until the present (or, more precisely, until the appearance of Baumgarten's *Aesthetics*). Naturally, it was facilitated by many internal negotiations, repositionings, suppressions, and partial or temporary suspensions of given areas, compensated by the force of other complementary areas that came to contain the weaker links and take on the tasks originally assigned to the subordinated groups. For example, during the Middle Ages poetics as such was essentially absent, but its field of inquiry was taken up by the *artes rhetoricae*, which assumed the burden of tracing the internal map of the literary genres. This kind of supplantation inevitably results in a flattening of those "long" genres into the patterns of the shorter ones. Moreover, we can indicate periods in which a broad concept of technique comes to dominate without many caesurae or hierarchical articulations between the various modes (manual, mechanical, logical, poetic, rhetorical, and so on) of accomplishing it. This holds true even in the persistence of the distinction between major and minor arts, which registers in only slightly less distinct terms the ancient contrast between slave and free.

The Renaissance, however, returned to a distinction between the "high," noble technical phases that are gratifying and remunerative in terms of an elevated expressive result, and those phases that can be termed purely functional, logical, or mechanical. First, we find the full rebirth of rhetoric, understood precisely as the art that teaches a means for bringing the verbal arts to the height of their dignity and beauty (reintroducing, however, all of the distance that separates rhetoric from the heavier, baser materials). At the same time, the Renaissance witnessed the full resurgence of Aristotelian poetics and, along with this, of particular and autonomous criteria with which to construct those artificial objects that are long poems. Quite soon, poetics and rhetoric found themselves at odds, given that the former imposes a subordination of the technique of diction and ornament to the global constructive exigencies of long poems (whose cadence, in most cases, does not allow for frivolities, digression, or the precious regionalisms that make up the quicker cadence of the brief genres). But rhetoric will give rise to the baroque phase ("metaphysical poetry," conceits, elegance, and so on), insisting on the priority of figures and diction. What counts here is the particular result, its intensity, the level of "marvel" that it arouses and the increase of knowledge that it produces in its audience. Such a notion really threatens the powers of the "new science," by demonstrating that within the fields of rhetoric and poetics (or literature, as we would say today), a parallel, analogical field emerges, one that exercises a technique of thought, an *ars cogitandi* not addressed to the true or the useful, but rather to the beautiful, that is, to self-gratifying pleasure or disinterested knowledge.

It should now be eminently clear that these various detailed accounts are not offered here in order to furnish the lines of a historical development of our field through the centuries (for that we would require a great deal more time and space), but rather, in order to trace the birth of the various islands (or labels) that will be so effectively unified in Baumgarten, by removing them from a colloidal state of *concordia discors*, of alternating movements or a kind of reciprocal equilibrium, as they were construed until Baumgarten, even if the individual perspectives on these islands have tended to vary over time. Moreover, this brief summary serves to confirm the assertion made earlier, that the "ancient" picture has not undergone substantial changes, but only internal retouching. For this reason, we have attempted to demonstrate, if in a rather synthetic way, how even the instruments of the baroque age that appear to us as both new and heterodox can be found within traditional spheres such as rhetoric.

Aesthetics as a Consortium

It was the achievement of Baumgarten, then, to have responded to the need for a "unification of the field." He managed this by introducing a notion and a relative term that were totally new and untried, and that still retain all of their relevancy today. His 1750 treatise opens with a definition that could not be more clear, efficient, or exhaustive. We must examine it with the greatest attention, breaking it down into its component parts. Let us begin, then, by focusing on the subject and the predicate of this definition: "aesthetica . . . est scientia cognitionis sensitivae." We must interject the warning that the ellipsis following "aesthetica" stands for an extremely important series of appositions to which we will return later in the discussion. Here we will only note the appearance of the sensory, which had never attracted the attention it deserved until Baumgarten, and which also reflects so many of our current interests, from the "low" register expressed by the *institut d'esthétique*, to the more sophisticated resonances of recent work on "aesthetic operators." More generally, the sensory immediately demonstrates its comprehensiveness, containing within itself both technical moments (one cannot undertake manual labor without appreciating the materials with which one works, without developing agility and the capabilities of human organs), as well as poetics and rhetoric. But along with making or producing, the problem of the lived relation to the world and one's peers comes into play, and this includes the pleasures of food, clothing, and healthy physical exercise. Or, if we prefer, we can refer to "making" in a rather broad sense, extending beyond its usual limitations in the idea of producing some object of relative nobility. To sum up, in Baumgarten's aesthetics, the consumer or patron also finds a place, or, at the very least, shares an equal weight with the other moment of production we have defined.

One might ask, however, if all of this simply serves to reiterate the famous judgment of Croce, namely that aesthetics is born precisely with Baumgarten (or a few decades earlier, with Vico). In part, this is true: if we identify the German philosopher as the first to truly comprehend the notion of "unifying the field," we cannot deny that this interpretation was already suggested by Croce's peremptory remarks. But things quickly appear in a different light if we investigate the modality and the contents through which this unification is supposed to have come to pass. In his reading of Baumgarten, Croce commits several forced moves that appear unnatural and excessive. Or rather, he avails himself of what is perhaps an inevitable prerogative in every interpretive act (even we make Baumgarten conform somewhat to our present purposes). At the very least, we can support the presumption that our purposes are more present-tense than those of Croce, and if nothing else, more responsive to our present situation. And perhaps at the same time, they respect the letter of Baumgarten's text more precisely (even if such a conviction undoubtedly always includes vast margins of subjectivity).

The "unification" desired by Croce and projected retrospectively by him onto the author of the *Aesthetica*, meant that within that entire field outlined he would have to find a univocal category so forceful that it could contain and consume, without leaving a trace, every collateral manifestation of that same field, which would then be reduced to mere contingent empirical appearance. That move was strengthened by the general system within which Croce worked, namely idealism. With a single initial act, the physical dimension of aesthetics could easily be reduced to its spiritual substance. What is at stake is a philosophy that acts (as we shall soon see) by reducing, contracting, proceeding through exclusion, and finally by removing. Baumgarten, however, was clearly more concerned with a process of successive inclusions such that they would not sacrifice the intrinsic character of the various sectors that came to be grouped under a common heading. Finally, Baumgarten's operation might be best expressed not by unification—this seems too strong and peremptory—but rather by consortium, in the sense that many parts come together, mesh together their respective peculiarities, strengthening themselves in the process. But in this very act they do not actually lose their own individual virtues. This "scientia cognitionis sensitivae" is more than a unifying category; it is the "bed," the geological basis, the primary stratification that certainly allows for continuity, for linkage between the various phenomena of the consortium, but at the same time, permits each one to exercise autonomous respect for all the others, just as small deposits begin to form on a common sedimentation of bedrock (to extend the geological metaphor). These phenomena thus share a common origin, but this does not impede them from attaining or expressing specific characterizations.

We have finally reached the moment for filling in those blanks that we left between the subject and the predicate in our initial definition of Baumgarten's aesthetics. What separates them is, in fact, highly significant. It corresponds to the various voices, the various branches, ramifications, the relatively autonomous formations that the German philosopher meant to bring together in the unitary definition of aesthetics, rather than sacrificing their specific roles. At the same time, it corresponds to the various nuclei into which aesthetics had been divided, segregated, and detotalized up until that period in history. The "bedrock" of the *cognitio sensitiva* thus acts as a reassuring foundation, the springboard of continuity and of reciprocal interrelationship to the next series of autonomous historical maneuvers and great traditions. In the first place, the *theoria liberalium artium*, an eloquent formula that should be familiar from the various distinctions we drew earlier, coincides with the meaning of aesthetics now in circulation at the median level of culture, aesthetics as the philosophy of art. Along with this, we have the *analogon rationis*, derived from the baroque period, also tracing its origin to the classic distinction between logical and rhetorical forms. It is a question of the challenge that the instruments of the conceit or the baroque-metaphysical *agudeza* poses to the field of logical rationality (analysis, directed toward uncovering a truth). These instruments, on the other hand, seek their own autonomous but parallel dimension that will thus be "analogic." Here the form of logical reason will be reaffirmed, but not its precise, and basically utilitarian, ends. All of this is better served by the third nucleus of the consortium, expressed as an *ars pulcre cogitandi* in which the *pulcre cogitare* is another means of affirming the space of a rationality used only by analogy with respect to its "true" counterpart, and so ultimately directed toward the free, gratuitous end of beauty (beautiful reason). As for the term *ars*, it appears here with a fairly precise significance, freed from the tasks of technical-material work, and thus from the production of objects. Although today we are not accustomed to bringing this technical aspect into the domain of "art," by right it belongs to the field of aesthetics, understood in a broader sense.

Vico, Baumgarten, Croce

This fruitful notion of the consortium, of a conjoinment of diverse activities avoiding any crude identification that might lead to the suppression of some in favor of others, can be easily schematized in two ways. One graph would exploit the image in geological terms (the bedrock, the tectonic plate), and should thus be mapped along a vertical axis. The other avails itself of the criteria of the circle, demonstrating inclusion and exclusion on a horizontal plane where the task of bringing together, assigned to the *cognitio sensitiva*, constitutes the largest and most inclusive circle containing various smaller circles. It is important to note, however, that these subgroups are not necessarily concentric. They may reciprocally exclude one another or share only partial areas of intersection.

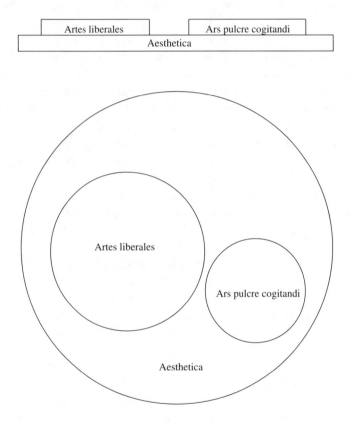

On the other hand, the Crocean system would find its graphic equivalent in a single circle where the perimeters of aesthetics and art meld together.

But this is not all. The differences we have examined up to this point have been primarily concerned with the question of "how" we should understand the process of unification, whether in terms of exclusion or inclusion. We must also confront differences of content; the *cognitio sensitiva* of Baumgarten cannot, in fact, be read as an anticipation of the romantic-idealist notion of sentiment. It should be interpreted much more literally, in its physical dimension. On close examination, it corresponds with the Greek etymon, and so it clearly legitimizes this return to origins; it is concerned with the full life of the senses, with all of their related organs and perceptual channels. Today we would be unable to retrieve this literal translation completely, given that the adjective "sensitive" has taken on an overly emotional and ambiguous connotation, not without some justification, and because it is directed toward the idea of an intense exercise, excessive but not far from certain sensible or sensory paradigms. In any case, the term *cognitio sensitiva* relates to a full appreciation of the physiological-psychological dimension of perceiving with the senses. Romantic idealism (culminating in Croce) was quick to undertake a huge cancellation of this, transforming it into a much more robust and spiritual equivalent: the sentimental, that is, affective-emotional, life in its global, tumultuous, indistinct sense, deriving from the interior and shunning the channels of exterior mediation. On the other hand, for Croce, the sensory inserts itself in all of these intermediate channels, in those snares and nets that tie the human subject to its objects of experience.

Other points of obvious difference between Baumgarten and Croce lie in the fact that for the former, aesthetics is "scientia cognitionis sensitivae," where evidently *scientia* is not philosophy (the only discipline, in Croce's mind, capable of furnishing authentic, categorical approaches). Moreover, the fact that "cognition" is given as an appositive for the activity directed to the "senses" does not sufficiently respect the categorical distance between intuition and knowledge understood in a properly logical sense. We must return to these points, since they correspond to divergences or incongruencies about the very mode of reasoning or positing problems that today we would consider more suitable or functional. Finally, the inevitable historical limitations of an eighteenth-century thinker such as Baumgarten are revealed at this moment.

Now, for the sake of fairness, we must point to an area of notable convergence between Baumgarten and the Crocean-idealist line of aesthetics. Even the German philosopher, as a product of his time and an exponent of various typical eighteenth-century conceptions, reached a certain degree of idealism. In fact, many thinkers throughout that entire century adhered to the model of a scale of values that begins with perception-cognition and ascends through acts of a sensory nature, finally reaching those of an intellectual nature. Topological characterizations were made, only to be quickly converted into hierarchical valuations. The senses clearly constitute a *gnoseologia inferior* (here the adjective should be understood in its Latin sense, as that which stands lower, and hence is of a lesser value), whereas the intellect and its contingent activities are "superior," higher, and, most important, later. Inauspicious "historicization" and diachronic undoing are among our various faculties, and this serves to guarantee their separation and disassociation (even if, as we must admit, the thinkers of the eighteenth century did not precisely intend to exhaust the possibilities of such a fracturing or to dramatize matters; rather, the expediency of this scale in their eyes must have assured the gradual passage from one moment to the next). And so, nevertheless, there is no synergic and synchronic participation of the sensory faculties in those of the intellect. This cooperation was nevertheless a given throughout antiquity and the Middle Ages, and it will seek to reestablish itself in the modern age.

This diachronic unraveling had already been presented in highly dramatic terms by Vico, who drew from it two separate ages, two noncommunicating evolutionary and psychological states that could be bridged only through the death or total destruction of the first state. Romantic idealism, with Croce as its final proponent, rendered the conflict between sentiment and intellect in even more dramatic terms and went so far as to introject it, thus creating two distinct "internal" stages in the development of the single system of the spirit. In this, Croce affirmed, resides the will to redeem the stage of feeling from its connotations of literal and figurative inferiority. Aesthetics is not worth less than logic. But this does not necessarily mean that it comes "first" (even if this is understood as a heuristic rather than as a historical or ontological precedence), or that its realization is exclusive compared with other moments of the spirit: the life of one is born from the death of the other, there is never a moment of coexistence or synchrony, but only diachrony, rupture.

From Aesthetics to Art, and Back Again

After its felicitous emergence in Baumgarten, the continent of aesthetics understood as a sensory exercise reigned for several decades, and in fact, a bit later, with Kant, enjoyed an extremely important development. As is well known, the author of the *Critique of Pure Reason* makes of aesthetics a philosophical discipline dedicated to the general study of the forms of sensory consciousness. Even earlier, many philosophers, writers, and essayists of the eighteenth century had overemphasized the field of nontechnical, preartistic, aesthetic practices directed toward an analysis of "sentiment" rather than the creation of individual works. From this was born the immense casuistry of the good and sublime in nature, of an aesthetics that resides in states of mind, in the reactions one experiences before a landscape, in the suggestions brought about by travel and geographical exploration. All of this was fertile ground for the romantic era, which then fostered the best conditions for a continuation of this discourse in terms of a general aesthetics rather than in terms of art. Nevertheless, we can point to at least two trends in romanticism: one of a Kantian derivation that remains faithful to the idea of consortium, or rather, equilibrium, of the reciprocal compensation between nature and culture, sentiment and intellect, subject and object (this passes through Schiller, Goethe, Wordsworth, and Leopardi). Another trend returns to the unfortunate conception of a scale of values, of a historical vector that leads from the base states of sentiment to the higher states of the conceptual. Moreover, this scale retroactively enlarges the powers of this latter field, leading it to consume the territory of its counterpart, thus finding itself in the lower rungs of nature and the senses where it discovers only crystallized and rigid ideals, unconscious or dormant spirit. At that point, the short circuit between the two poles, between aesthetics and art, seems inevitable. Those sensory exercises which may properly be termed aesthetic find themselves confined to a base atmosphere, subjected to reactions roused by some pseudo-object such as nature, and thus they enjoy an inferior status by definition, merely tolerated and often even prohibited. In fact, even artistic interventions find themselves deprived of their technical-material components, reduced to the spiritual essence of an emersion of the pure values of sentiment and emotion. The very concept of art becomes ever more subjected to the idea of nobility, the spiritual, elevated to its greatest distinction in the beaux arts, treated with the highest degree of solemnity, including all of the obligations imposed by the categorical definition (art as philosophy) pertaining to such a realm. Even the individual worker in this field, namely the artist, becomes the privileged vessel of such a concentration of Spirit, in order that something exceptional may be produced. This is opposed to the merely mechanical routine acts to which normal interventions of a technical-productive order are reduced, in part because by now we have reached the period of the first industrial revolution, leading to the suppression of that moment of mediation entrusted to art, not in its sublime and "superior" capacity, but in the more strictly artisanal terms by which it had been understood for centuries (including the artisanal moment inherent even in the so-called great artistic practices).

Within a century, then, we witness a progression that could be schematized as follows:

aesthetics → art → the beaux arts

But our contemporary age has seen the enactment of a series of even more rapid mutations. Almost immediately we find an inverted historical vector, which leads to a rejection of the beaux arts in favor of generic technique, manual or mechanical labor (this was also because we had to reconcile aesthetic values with the forms of industrial production that was slowly but surely imposing its mark). Finally, we rediscovered the vast continent of aesthetics as an exercise of merely sensory practices, not directed toward the production of objects, thus setting the stage for a possible return to Baumgarten.

Aesthetics: Knowledge or Experience?

As we have already suggested, not all the concepts that enter into Baumgarten's definition of aesthetics are still acceptable in our own times (and this is entirely to be expected). Today, in fact, we can no longer agree with the notion that "sensitivity" (or the sensory) belongs to the sphere of a *cognitio*, even if our reasons for refusing to adhere to such a "cognitive" function do not correspond with those given earlier by Croce. Baumgarten was still moving in the field of a philosophy dominated by theoretical, speculative, and cognitive principles. A century later, however, we have come to recognize the fundamentally pragmatic character of our basic operations: living, acting, moving in the world means exercising a praxis, even if it is correct and indispensable to recognize and preserve moments of knowledge themselves, that is, those activities not directed toward immediately practical ends. Even in this case, it is clearly a question of deferred praxis, temporarily suspended but not completely abrogated. In other words, the disinterestedness of scientific research is merely temporary. Praxis is the beginning and end of any process (even if the intermediate phases of a cognitive or scientific order intervene in such a way that the final praxis ends up with more efficient instruments; the very term efficiency, as suggested by its root, is saturated with practicality).

If this more or less immediately pragmatic character is always inherent in every operation (and it is significant that today we so frequently use such a word, itself implicated in action), it adheres even more obviously to those acts of a sensory nature that evidently require the full intervention of the body with all of its physical abilities. Smell and sight imply the movement of organs and nerves, the contraction of muscles on some level, no matter how subtle. But there must be a nucleus of action, even if minimized and contracted, in any sensory act. It has become increasingly improper and misleading to assign these acts to a field of pure knowledge. In such a case, it is necessary to employ a more capacious term-concept that emphasizes the operative character of the relation without, however, forcing it into a merely physical mold. We are not suggesting a dichotomy between the practical and the cognitive that would separate them into two contrasting but equal camps; the practical sphere is actually much larger and includes the other in itself as part of a whole. Therefore, we need a term that does not exclude the possibility of a configuration that would be, at times, strictly cognitive, but that could also be expanded and made more general.

Some scholars of aesthetics that we will examine later have proposed the terms "useful" and "efficacious" to just such an end. John Dewey, in his general philosophical writings, speaks of "experience." During the 1930s, the Czech Jan Mukařovský spoke of "function," but beginning from quite a different set of theoretical premises. We could also cite the English term "attitude" as one that has been successful in this context. As we see, the list includes rather vast terms that encompass human beings as totalities possessing body and soul, intellect and affects, practical and cognitive life. In fact, these terms presuppose a fundamentally bipolar conception in which a subjective moment (the human being) enters into contact with an objective one (the world, nature, exteriority, the environment, or any other term we might use).

Common, Scientific, and Aesthetic Experience

Given their very generality, such terms not only concern the properly aesthetic phase, they actually precede it, characterizing above all that which we might call common experience, the basis of everyday life, or, to adopt Mukařovský's terminology, the elementary, degree-zero functionality that links us to the world. We can also distinguish two functions or experiences that are more specific and rigorous, the aesthetic and the scientific or, in the strictest, most proper sense of the word, the cognitive.

Turning our attention for a moment to common experience, we must begin by rejecting the suspicion that it is a field of physicality or sensation, lacking any sign of intelligence. On the contrary, the most valid contemporary philosophers (such as Dewey, for example) avoid this fracture between the two spheres and demonstrate how nature and culture, the senses and the intellect, are always reciprocally implicated. In particular, common experience avails itself of that form of practical, synthetic intelligence, which is capable of reducing and encapsulating the multiplicity of single events: in short, habit. At the very foundation of common sense we reveal ourselves as fundamentally habitual animals. This certainly does not mean we are beasts, merely that the intelligence inherent in habit is rehearsed passively, according to tradition, and corresponds to an unconscious mechanism that guides our acts as we move skillfully and assuredly through an insidious world. We might think of the casual attitude with which we maneuver through various traffic jams, mechanically making the gestures necessary to change gears, brake, accelerate, and so on. The hands and feet move from the clutch to the accelerator with marvelous assurance, without any reflection on our part. Indeed, we would be embarrassed if asked to describe with any precision the operations we perform so rapidly and fluently. In the most elemental sense we are all prisoners of routine. This is a beneficial force because it allows us to economize our energies and to dominate circumstances, to reach a healthy equilibrium within a given situation. It is also a negative and sterile force because it "flattens" or "levels" emergencies, it reduces the diverse and the various to sameness, to repetition, it leads us to repeat behaviors ad infinitum.

At times, however, habits are not enough to dominate events that quickly turn into emergencies or fracture our equilibrium: our affective energies, no longer adequately channeled in any usual way, urge us to a state of freedom, "derailing" us from our tracks. Finally, we express emotions; our shock can only be quieted when we overcome that particular situation of confusion by submitting it to an investigation that leads us to step outside of ourselves and to alter the instruments of reaction.

At that moment the need to overcome routine or repetitive mechanicity is born. We must seek out "new" forms of behavior. It is also at this moment that the most selective and conscious phases of aesthetics and the cognitive sciences enter the picture. Novelty is thus an initial feature shared by both fields. Without some anxiety to renew and modify our relations with the world, there would be no passage from one phase to the next. Beyond this common prerequisite, however, aesthetics and the cognitive sciences diverge. Scientific experience (or function) is of an eminently instrumental nature: it decomposes and analyzes a situation in order to discover what is wrong within it and then seeks to remove or overcome a given obstacle. Its task is one of limited mediation. Scientific experience extinguishes itself in order to make room for common, practical experience, which once again settles serenely into habits that have been reconstituted on more efficient foundations in the meantime.

Aesthetic experience, on the contrary, is essentially "final"; its end resides in a reconsideration of the situation of departure in the largest, richest, and most intense sense, beyond the mechanicity of mere routine or habit. Its scope seems to be that of introducing onto the face of the earth a paradisiacal state in which one can see the various aspects of the world with the greatest intensity, without having to worry about economizing one's energies. Aesthetics might also include a renewal of the earthly paradise experienced in the earliest moments of infancy, when the drive for sensory pleasure meets no repression or censors that might oblige one to reckon with practical or social exigencies.

With the aid of this essential differentiation between the two types of experience or function, we might begin to trace two series of distinctive characteristics that appear as simultaneously comparable and contrasting. We will note that these characteristics, in turn, are ordered into three different groups (which might correspond with what would be termed "categories" in a more rigid theoretical language). The number three results from a practical need, from the internal economics of the situation, and not from any particular logical necessity. Nothing would prohibit the groups from being raised in number to four or five for the sake of a more efficient economy. Moreover, in the course of outlining the nomenclature used here, the classifying task that directs us will become more apparent: it is not simply a case of inventing altogether new terms, concepts, and categories, but of economizing with what has already been put forth by other contemporary thinkers, connecting various propositions that have remained rather disparate until now, and bringing them into communicating relationships, regardless of the lexical differences that seem to separate them.

We have already suggested that the first characteristic or category, novelty, is common to both science and aesthetics. This fact indicates that both diverge from the same initially shared experience, and are thus contemporaneous and do not succeed one another chronologically. But we will return later to this argument concerning the reciprocal relations between the two fields in the global scheme of activity.

Scientific Experience	*Aesthetic Experience*
1. novel	novel
2. transitive	intransitive
transparent	opaque
discursive	presentational
extrinsic	intrinsic (autotheistic) (self-sustaining)
univocal	plurivocal (ambiguous)
homogeneous	heterogeneous, varied
specific	global, totalized
3. linear	articulated
sequential	rhythmic
progressive	dramatic

If the positing of novelty among the various prerequisites peculiar to aesthetic experience seems rather obvious, perhaps it will seem less so when we attribute it to the area of scientific research. Yet even in this case we encounter the fundamental rule that it is not worthwhile to repeat experiments, calculations, or investigations that have already been undertaken by another, at least if the results obtained seem correct, and if they furnish us with a practical power of prediction and dominance over the external phenomena surveyed. If, however, a given approach proves inefficient, then it is important to reopen the case and search out other means of proof.

The split between the two types of experience is more significant in the second and third groups of characteristics (but, as we shall see, this split is far from definitive or irreversible). Here, the essential difference between an instrumental and a final task is at stake. For scientific experience, what counts is the final result. The intermediary stages are purely functional; they are transitional points that can be erased from all memory (or from the page, the blackboard, the computer) as soon as the process of investigation has passed a certain crucial point and has incorporated the partial results obtained until then. It is enough to recall the classroom technique of the development of an equation on the blackboard that permits, precisely, a cancellation of all intermediary stages if they are no longer significant except to the extent that they brought us toward the final solution. Moreover, once we have arrived at the solution, it is accepted as unequivocally valid regardless of how it was obtained. This experience also suggests that the temporal element enters a scientific experiment only incidentally, precisely when it does not act as an obstacle. Given the instrumentality of the task, it is better to work toward a conclusion as quickly as possible (as long as the result obtained is correct). In the extreme case, the almost instantaneous velocity of a computer seems preferable to the dullness of the human mind. But within the cognitive limits of experience itself, based, that is, on the measure of its "truth" or effectiveness, time is an external incidental. Scientific experimentation seems substantially a-chronic.

The exact opposite is true in aesthetic experience. It appears to be suspended between two extremes: the beginning and the end. Whatever happens in the middle enters constitutionally to form it, so that nothing can be left out. Returning to the example of the equation written out on the blackboard, if an essentially similar experience aspires to be considered within aesthetics (we will see that this is not only possible, but legitimate), it is essential that we do not skip any intermediary steps, and that each calculation should be made to coexist and interact with all the others presented simultaneously to the individual undergoing this experience. In such a case, no single phase can be passed over or allowed to fall into oblivion. If, from this rather casual and certainly low-level example of a possible aesthetics figured in the development of an equation on the blackboard, we now pass to the more consistently applied one of a true and proper work of visual art, we find that even here our visual perception can traverse from one part of a painting to another, but this transitive state will never be definitive. Eventually, the eye must pull back and gain perspective so that all of the various zones in the painting are linked for the sake of aesthetic fruition. Playing with the Greek roots, we say that in the field of spatial perception aesthetic experience demands syn-chory (*choron* = space), just as in the temporal field it demands syn-chrony. This latter need is especially valid for any aesthetic experiences of an acoustic nature that do not permit coexistence or material synchrony (sounds inevitably occur in time); but in such a case the intervention of memory is essential. In order to evaluate a novel, a poem, a film, or a musical work, it is essential that we somehow retain all of the passages in our minds and that they interact with the final "sound," even when it moves away from the actuality of execution to the virtuality of that which has already happened. If we forget the beginning or the middle of any work of a temporal nature, we find ourselves in trouble. We are unable to bring to fruition the aesthetic experience. We might consider, for example, the case of detective novels that are always constituted on the basis of a final resolution. They are transformed from intransitive to transitive works: that is, one rushes to arrive at the end. Time flies, and once we realize "how it is all going to end," in general, it is no

longer worthwhile to reread the beginning or to indulge the process of de-
nouement. The various intermediary passages now seem mechanical and
worthless unless the writer possesses a particularly refined ability or has
managed to insert such intricacy into the plot so that we might find the
narrative per se gratifying and rewarding.

Given that syn-chrony belongs to the phenomena of a temporal order,
the passage to sym-phony, that other, equally appropriate term-concept, is
rather brief. According to its common connotation, symphony also implies
a sense of equilibrium, of internal compensation of all elements. Moreover,
since space and time are strictly linked, synchory never appears without
being accompanied by either synchrony or symphony.

This intransitive peculiarity, in turn, leads to a valorization of all the
materials that enter into aesthetic experience in their self-contained state,
through their own intrinsic consistency. So, in the two distinct series we
have traced, an important part is played by the oppositions between, on the
one hand, the opaque, the dense, the intrinsic, and so on, which should
be recognized precisely as the components of aesthetic experience, and, on
the other hand, the transparent or the interchangeable, which are intrinsic
to scientific research. What counts is that these open the way to successive
steps. Once this has been accomplished, the individual elements responsible for the transition can be discarded, as happens with the various stages
of a rocket in flight. Naturally, we must specify, from time to time, the level
of the materials that are effectively relevant from an aesthetic point of view,
and that thus enjoy the privileges of the intrinsic. Quite often an aesthetic
experience may be constructed from transitive and purely utilitarian materials. We might invoke all literary texts, whether printed or in manuscript
form, and even musical works after they have been scored. Contrary to what
we said earlier, even these texts might seem to be manifestations of a
graphic order and thus primarily visual-spatial, where, however, such a
space, that is, the sequence of pages marked with characters and the notations, might appear extrinsic and thus interchangeable, replaceable, in
comparison with a true and proper aesthetic experience. But here it is precisely a question of aesthetic experiences that come to be realized at the
moment of their execution (even if this takes place as a silent reading that,
nevertheless, contains a kind of minimal, interior sonority). They thus recover the characteristics of synchrony or symphony. In addition, the un-
doubted substitutability in the field of graphic notations or "writing" has,
as a prerequisite, the attainment of an equal degree of symphony: all translations, substitutions, and variations of the graphic characters and of every

other external property are acceptable as long as the *performance* (executed out loud or even mentally, by the reader) yields an equivalent result.

Homogeneity and Heterogeneity

Continuing with the characteristics listed in our second group, we notice yet another subdivision. Up to now we have insisted on binary opposites such as the transitive (scientific)/the intransitive (aesthetic). These distinctions are based on formal conditions, that is, on conditions limited to the examination of the materials that enter into the respective experiences, and into their chronological relations or reciprocal implications. We have not bothered with questions of content that are more precisely concerned with the external world. Such problems emerge when we pass onto another couple that we have nevertheless found to be appropriately placed in the same group, namely the opposition between the substantially homogeneous character of the scientific experiment and the expressly heterogenous character of the aesthetic experience. This desire to make distinctions concerning the types of materials within an experience by deciding whether or not they exhibit internal homogeneity implies a reference to a basic experience that is also the experience of the outside world (or more simply the world). In turn, the very notion of a common or everyday experience is radically heterogeneous: we need only think of what happens each day from the moment we begin our drive (or walk or bus ride) to work. The "lived" experience is also mixed with memories of past events (whether happy or sad), expectations, and apprehensions about the work that awaits us, objects that enter our visual field along the way, weather conditions, and encounters we may have with others. This entire experience is a confused and intricate collage in which many different "types" of experiences (physiological, psychological, meteorological, sociological, and so on) are grounded. Naturally, the desire to place them into such precise disciplinary categories is obviously pedantic, given that these moments appear and disappear rapidly, like so many apparitions. Moreover, within the field of common experience, we are subject to the rigid rule of habit. This serves to flatten the whole varied panorama of phenomena and obliges us to ignore many things or to perceive them only "out of the corners of our eyes."

Let us suppose that, alas, there is some glitch in our car's motor (or the bus is late or takes an unexpected detour). Now we have to deal with a disturbing factor that shakes us and forces us to open a new phase of research of an embryonically scientific character. We must first of all focus on the situation [*fare mente locale*], reducing it to homogenous terms. We must live it, that is, *sub specie mechanicae.* Our daydreams (pleasing or otherwise) have to be placed on hold, our plans for the future, our distracted glances toward the countryside and fellow travelers, deferred. Or rather, the energy devoted to each one of these aspects must now be diverted to the mechanical problem that we are immediately facing. For this reason we will only select those memories taken from other analogous situations that might offer us some key for resolving the present case. The glances over the countryside, the experiences brought on by the weather conditions will also be utilized. (Are we by any chance near a gas station? And how is the weather: too humid, too cold? Could this be at all held responsible for the motor problems? Are there people around who might help us?) This elementary case serves as a good example of that which we understand when we talk of "homogenization," or the reduction of a situation to elements that are univocal, of the same "type," species, or family. Once this unification of the various components has been effected, other mechanisms of an internal or formal character such as we have outlined begin to function. All of these unified ingredients will be dispensed in the proper sequence, all will be directed toward the goal of solving the enigma (why has the motor stopped working?) and toward removing the obstacle. But as soon as the motor begins to whir and we are back on the road to our place of work we will quickly forget all the intermediary passages and dive back into the placid automatism of common experience.

This very unexpected stop (or any other similar, minor incident) may give rise to a different sort of sequence, one oriented toward the aesthetic pole, one that obliges us to lend a more acutely focused attention to the various ingredients of our experience: for example, to finally "see" a certain strip of landscape (houses, trees) at which, up until that moment, we had merely glanced; to have a more precise awareness of the environmental conditions ("Say, what a beautiful day! The sun is out, and that reminds me of another time"; or else, "There is something new under the sun," or rather, something quite old, as Pascoli would have said, with no offense to Proust). As we will see, in such a case all of the various types of materials of experience are present, or rather, they all reinforce their multiple presence. In the case of common experience some terms were negated by others, but here all shine with equal intensity, all are orchestrated under expert direction, coming to the aid of one another according to those internal, formal properties we saw earlier, that is, with the aim of synchorous, synchronous, or symphonic effects. Heterogeneity is no longer simply an incidental fact, imposed by external criteria as happens in everyday experience, but on the contrary it has become something we have willed, programmed, and administered. An aesthetic experience is born and developed. It will be all the more lively, happy, and intense depending on the variety of types brought into a relation of reciprocal tension, with an objective that thus seems the polar opposite of the one posited for scientific experience. This latter field is all the more rigorous when it effectively reduces the various materials to a high degree of homogeneity. At best, we may introduce to it symbolic elements that are, in contrast to the indicators of type or content of aesthetics, completely abstract and neutral: the arithmetic or algebraic signs, and perhaps even the letters of formal logic. Aesthetic experience, on the contrary, seeks the unification of diverse materials, friction, the clash of disparate types, such that they must then enter into a relationship by maintaining and reinforcing their respective peculiarities.

Finally, any aesthetic experience must tend toward a totalization in itself of various multiple types of activity and interests. But evidently that is valid as a tendency or an aspiration and not necessarily as an effective result. It may be seen as a push toward qualitative rather than quantitative order. In fact, it would be materially impossible to concentrate the infinite multitude of types and aspects through which we articulate our lived relations with reality into the space-time delimitation of an aesthetic experience. It is enough that whoever organizes the aesthetic sequence should allow it to be constituted by materials that are sufficiently varied in such a way that they indicate, even if only in a symbolic sense and through a compendium of samples, a similar need for totalization. This implies that it will be important to obtain a loose-knit, extremely porous totality, and that this result will be reached especially when confronted with the reduction of unity that is proper to scientific experience. Within this description, we also find another group of characteristics to be placed following those we have already seen as constitutive of the totalized. These contrary characteristics have come to be termed "ambiguity," connotation, and plurivalency of meaning. We use these precisely in order to indicate, even if only tendentiously, a similar drive toward heterogeneity. It is essential that every ingredient or element brought into "symphony" belong at the same time to different types: physical and mental, high and low, cognitive and emotive. And we must continue to keep in mind that all of this "ambiguity" is controlled, or at least favored, by the register of aesthetic experience and not simply tolerated, as happens, rather, in the course of everyday life.

In any case, this dialectical divarication, this double face that appears in the aesthetic properties of the second group of characteristics is most important. As we have seen, several of these properties are valid in terms of their internal faces, others for the external faces that look out on the world and contents (when later we introduce elementary semiotic terminology, we will be able to speak about the respective faces of signifiers and signifieds):

intransitive	totalized
self-sustaining	connotative
presentational	ambiguous

Many of the misunderstandings surrounding the debates that have lacerated the field of aesthetics throughout history, and especially in recent years, derive precisely from a lack of sufficient reflection on these strictly linked categories. We must accept them as faces of the same page (recto and verso), as a sort of Janus, or, if we prefer an algebraic analogy, as equations of two variables that can only be solved if we consider the two terms together. Otherwise, we will have uncontrollable swings from one extreme to the other, without any possibility for understanding. In fact, if we play solely with the properties of the first column, we will find that aesthetics sanctifies a certain absolute void or formal purity. It would then be necessary for every glance to be internalized, focused on the sequentiality of materials, on their reciprocal order, without any concern for external order, as if the world had suddenly ceased to exist. If, however, we play with the second column, we are in the presence of a "fullness," of an absolute density, a supercontent in which all the possible contents meet and are held in equilibrium or reciprocal suspension. But it is precisely that "fullness" (at least in a tangential sense) that best defeats the pretensions to supremacy advanced by various types of content to the detriment of others: there are no hierarchies or extrinsic finalities, and so we are returned to an internal, formal order according to which the various contents are then assembled.

Drama

We have now reached the moment for introducing the distinctive characteristics of the third group. In fact, these are precisely the characteristics that best justify the passage from the total void of the absolute, formal self-sustaining element to the total "fullness" of hypercontent, the totalized nature of every type of experience. This third group tells us, in fact, that in an aesthetic experience the various elements do not follow one another in a linear mode. In contrast with scientific experience they do not march in single file, moving in an orderly manner toward a conclusion. Rather, these elements are ordered in a "dramatic" mode, according to a staging that must know how to dispense healthy doses of variety. In short, this mode must be capable of producing moments of peak tension, followed by moments of relaxation and limpness: plots and denouements, rapid and slow developments, punch lines. All of this is expressed quite well by the need for articulation and rhythm. The internal timing of the aesthetic experience must be of a qualitative and not a quantitative order. It is synchronized, not with the regularity of the clock, but with the pleasing variety and intensity of a drama that "captures" us, sending a charge through all of our faculties and avoiding any dead time. Now, if we were to begin with a need of pure formality, how would materials that are all equally internal succeed in reassuring such a variety of impacts? Here it is indispensable to invoke the heterogeneity of these materials and thus to pass from total void to total fullness. Aesthetic experience becomes like a microcosm, both qualitative and symbolic, in which all possible experiences essential to the chaotic macrocosm of everyday experience are articulated within a carefully studied order. Yet beginning from the "other pole," that is, from the fullness of the more disparate types, how can these avoid choking one another or becoming a huge undigested mass? The solution seems to be that we must organize a formal distribution of them, according to a calculated rhythm of appearances, of entrances and exits from the stage, of summonses. Articulation and rhythm appear as fundamentally dialectical or double-faced properties, capable of embracing and converting the formal face into that which we have termed the content-based face of aesthetic experience.

All of this brings us back to the characteristics of synchrony and symphony, of experience in which time enters constitutionally, as a quality and not as a quantity, not reduced, that is, to a succession of stations, as happens, conversely, in the scientific field. And so in this case the notion of progress, of marching forward in a unidirectional mode is not valid. A successful aesthetic experience must, rather, balance digressions as well as steps backward and sideways. In this sense, aesthetics corresponds to the Bergsonian notion of "duration," even if this famous construct remains ambiguous from our point of view: in fact, it is difficult to know whether duration belongs to the field of everyday experience or to that of an experience privileged because of intensity and qualitative richness, as might be the case with aesthetics. In reality, things become distinctly clearer when we recall that the Bergsonian "duration" would be the originary experience of humankind if the mechanical schemes and habits of everyday life had not interfered with it, nor had those rigorous schemes controlled by the intellect in the scientific phase. Moreover, both of these schemes seem to merge in the name of a cooperative economic need. The world of aesthetics would thus be that which assigns itself the task of retrieving such an originary mythical experience. All of this can be transcribed in terms of Freudian doctrine: in fact, "duration" corresponds to the liberated life inspired by the pleasure principle against which the forces of the reality principle intervene. In effect, even for Freud, art (or aesthetics in general) must retrieve repressed energies and thus recover qualitative time.

Galvano Della Volpe

In composing this compendium of labels and definitions proposed by the most authoritative scholars of our time, we have not utilized the nomenclature or the conceptual framework of the Italian author who has contributed most consistently to this field, namely Galvano Della Volpe. This lack of attention is certainly not meant as a sign of disrespect toward the particular importance of his contributions, but rather our intention has been to grant him his own space, given the notable perspicuity of his definitions (which in turn owe a great deal to "Anglo-Saxon" aesthetic thought, already outlined in our synoptic picture, and so the circle closes on itself).

Della Volpe begins with a clear, three-way division of functions or types of experience, just as we have done here. The difference is that he assumes the term "discourse" as the common denominator, whereas we feel that it may be incorrect to privilege the field of verbal phenomena by positing it as a foundation; still, we must not forget that until this moment we have been moving in an aesthetic field based on general sensorial behavior, without distinguishing among visual, tactile, motor, or auditory senses. This is explained, in part, by the fact that there is a vast degree of synergy among these (symphony, synchrony, and so on). Perhaps Della Volpe's term "text" may be considered more ample, and thus more acceptable. "Text," understood in its most literal sense, is a network obtained by linking together various threads, that is, by combining and coordinating diverse materials of experience. Now, such a text can be constructed in a variety of ways by weaving various threads together in a haphazard manner. This is what happens in the field of everyday experience, which will thus be termed "omnitextual" in the sense that everything becomes a text, without measure or reason, and because there is no beginning or end to this text, but a continual and indefinite evolution. Returning to the discursive-verbal field, and recalling that it avails itself of sounds and "voices," Della Volpe speaks of a place of the "equivocal," that is, a place where various voices are equalized and become largely interchangeable, imprecise, and suggested by immediate needs. This gives rise to meaning essentially derived from the confusion or imprecision of those terms and phrases utilized in a given situation.

Scientific discourse, like poetic discourse (the term used by Della Volpe to indicate the general aesthetic field, given that at the verbal level, it corresponds precisely to *poiein*), seeks to provide us with a "context," that is, the threads are interwoven according to reason, implicated in one another so that their order is not a matter of indifference. But there is one well-known distinction: the scientific context is inorganic in the sense that the threads woven into it can be replaced by any others of equal value, parallel with the ends of whatever needs are being addressed in a given situation. In fact, scientific discourse is easily translated from one language to another, given that it is possible to establish an exact correspondent for any given term. In other words, science is directed toward univocality, toward the elimination of every margin of ambiguity or dissonance. Exactly the opposite can be said for poetic discourse, whose contextuality will be organic, that is, the various elements engaged will turn out to be linked to a particular and definitive context. Moreover, they are directed toward plurivocality since they seek to "connote" various types (various semantic areas and fields of interest) simultaneously. So we note that in the terminology borrowed from Della Volpe, the binary faces we mentioned do in fact play a significant role. Poetic discourse or context (aesthetics) is simultaneously termed organic, "self-sustaining" (referring to internal, formal properties), and plurivocal, which implies a certain richness of voices, references, and meanings. One type of property recalls the other, and reciprocally they form an integral system.

The Interference of Functions

Now that we have addressed, if only summarily, the various distinctive characteristics of the three types of experience or functions (attitudes, discourses, texts, and so on), it is worthwhile to reexamine a potentially rather serious objection, namely that we may have been proceeding to "define" each of these characteristics in order to pigeonhole them into static, restrictive categories that cannot possibly lead to their respective separation, exactly what we criticized so vehemently in Crocean aesthetics.

We can demonstrate how, according to the model that we intend to follow, the two phases of conscious experience, aesthetics and science, are able to manage a kind of reciprocal convertability without ever falling into separate and impermeable substances. In this sense, the graph of bifurcation in which each one is separated from the block of everyday experience acts positively. This indicates that science and aesthetics face one other, positioned in a relation of mutual coexistence:

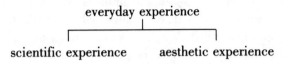

everyday experience

scientific experience   aesthetic experience

The graph that corresponds to the Crocean conception, however, must indicate a relation of succession, of a series of links (that which we have proposed is more of a family tree). As we already indicated in the Introduction, Croce demonstrates himself to be a rightful inheritor of the scale of values, of the diachronic measurement system born in the eighteenth century with Vico but reconfirmed by so many others, including Baumgarten, for whom aesthetics and logic (the category that, in the Crocean system, properly embraces space as a spurious element that others would rather assign to science) alternate:

Aesthetics
↓
Logic

Naturally, in the later Crocean model (the culmination of an idealist-romantic aesthetics) the succession is no longer conceived in chronological terms, but only as a logical ideal. Moreover, it assures the self-nourishment of the system by a cyclical passage through the positions that have already been covered. And every hierarchical-valuative connotation concerning "first" and "then" disappears (rather, we know how highly Croce valued the two mundane or primary sciences: aesthetics and economics). Nevertheless, this does not negate the fact that they must "die" in order to yield to successive phases.

According to the conception of a "family tree" linkage, however, aesthetics and science remain continually in one another's presence, assuming the functions of a bipolar couple, such that they generate a "field" in which every point finds itself subject to both of the forces, although with varying degrees of intensity. The obvious analogy is that of gravitational magnetism with its relative poles, North and South, that exercise a simultaneous attraction in every area of the earth's surface, with greater or lesser force depending on the distance of the area in question from each of these poles. This is also the case with our two polarities.

In practice, this means that every experience can be seen through each of the polarizing filters (just as a landscape may be viewed through different lenses that filter it, precisely, according to various criteria, but the superimposition is totally reciprocal). Thus there is never any separation or exclusion, only a variety of approaches or attitudes. The materials, the ingredients of a certain experience do not change, only the modalities according to which we experience that change. If we were to adopt the categories of our scientific order (the transitive, the progressive, and so on), these give rise to a scientific type of sequence. If, however, we make them the object of an intrinsic and globalizing consideration, then we return to the field of aesthetics. We mentioned earlier the example of the development of an equation on the blackboard as typical of a logico-scientific process; but suppose that, rather than being obsessed with reaching a final result or attempting to beat the clock, we were to halt our actions and take a global view of the various calculations, considering them in their very synchronicity and so also evaluating the intrinsic consistency of the signs that we are drawing, in terms of their graphic beauty? At that moment, the algebraic occasion would provide us enjoyment of a purely aesthetic sort (as demonstrated by many examples of "conceptual" art that at first do not seem to differ substantially from a page of mathematical calculations, except for the contextual intention that defines them). Moreover, let us also recall the fundamental example with which we began this discussion, that of the banal situation of a mechanical breakdown that obliges us to reflect, to undertake rational and conscious investigations. That moment may also give rise either to the progressive and linear time of an embryonically scientific experiment directed toward removing the obstacle or to the qualitative and cumulative time belonging to aesthetics. Between the two there is a certain degree of copenetration and interchangeability of facts, even if, in an ideal sense, each one responds to the attraction of its own pole.

It is also worthwhile to reflect for a moment on the advantage of having recourse to such a broad notion of the scientific, that it goes into effect almost immediately within everyday experience, right in the middle of the most banal and quotidian situations; as long as such cases usually remain polarized along the axis of transitiveness, filtered by homogenization, and so on. In this way we manage to avoid the *querelles*, no matter how legitimate they may be, that have opposed and continue to oppose various types of science—whether methodologically inductive or deductive, analytic or experimental, formalized or descriptive. The "polar" criteria proposed are larger than each of these more specific determinations and manage to contain them or intersect their coordinates. In particular, these criteria internally comprehend the most relevant *querelle* to which all the others are reducible, that is, the opposition between the physical-mathematical sciences and the human sciences (with the adjunct suspicion that this latter group, in general dependent upon rhetorical-evaluation methodologies addressed to complex, qualitative data, is closer to the terrain of aesthetics). To put it another way, this refers to the traditional subdivision between the sciences of knowledge and morality. But our version, following Dewey, demands a radical elimination of the relevance, at least at a macroscopic level, of such a contrast; we must recall that even the so-called cognitive phases always refer back to the practical sphere, even though they may enjoy a temporary suspension; and even moral situations, when applied beyond the quotidian situation of the exercise of preestablished, involuntary moral habits require a cognitive investigation (that is, sequential, progressive, and so on) not primarily different from that which was valid in the most typically cognitive (or, to use the proper term, epistemological) sectors.

CHAPTER 2

From Aesthetics to Art

Two Examples of Aesthetic Experience

In an effort to summarize the results obtained by our investigation into the properties of the aesthetic experience, we might now take two extremely common, everyday examples into consideration: the act of breathing and the act of eating a meal. In the first case we find ourselves at the limit of all biological-physical acts. Breathing belongs to the sphere of nature rather than that of culture and would seem to have nothing to do with the field of aesthetics or with any other field in cultural studies. The second case constitutes a typical circumstance within everyday experience. And yet, if the conditions we examined previously are in effect, both of these actions, despite their extreme banality, could become aesthetic experiences. What is interesting is precisely how this comes to be, with, so to speak, "a minimal investment," that is, without the introduction of mechanisms, processes, or materials of any particular sophistication. We need only follow these two experiences according to the modalities we outlined earlier in order to be able to distinguish them from the thousand other, similar acts in which the aesthetic objective is lost. This amounts to an assumption that the doors of the aesthetic are flung open to anyone, at will, as long as a given individual knows how to proceed toward a particular goal.

The act of breathing takes place for the most part on a completely unconscious level: we can do it without being aware of it. Breathing is like a conditioned reflex as long as the act is not threatened by any obstacle, whether internal or external. And perhaps we need precisely such an impediment in order to set off that innovative process inevitable in any aesthetic experience and that allows it to be considered aesthetic. That is, we need some difficulty that obliges us to pay attention to an otherwise mechanical and instinctive action. Imagine that you have gone running (performed some athletic activity), or else that the air has become thinner, but purer (as in the mountains). Suddenly you become aware of your breathing, and you retake possession or control of the muscular contractions in your thoracic cavity: you attempt to increase their force, you seek to prolong your breath, or perhaps to suspend it at the point of greatest tension, and you even follow the process of letting out air. Nor is that action localized or entrusted to a few organs; it is accompanied by acts of the entire body. That is to say, we do not simply breathe with our mouth or lungs, but also with our arms, following inhalation with sweeping gestures, toward full capacity (think of aerobic exercises that always begin with a renewed attention to the cardiovascular system). Even the border between the body and the environment disappears. Here, more than in any other case, the word environment should be taken in its etymological sense, as that which is around us and encircles us. If breathing must become an aesthetic experience, it is no longer a matter of indifference *where* we breathe; it has become essential that we breathe in some stimulating setting, spurred on by the beauty of a landscape. We must present, finally, that "holistic," contextual, totalizing connotation that we earlier identified as intrinsic to any truly aesthetic experience. And then we must introduce the third characteristic (or category, to use the more difficult term), rhythm or articulation. If instinctual and unconscious breathing is accomplished in two separate periods, which succeed one another in a brief cycle, regular and equalized as if timed by a metronome, this is not the case when that same process is directed toward a level of aesthetic dignity where, as we have already noted, either inhalation or expiration must be protracted, almost held in suspense, brought to bear on various other apparently marginal circumstances. It must be as if we had consumed an entire landscape, returning it piece by piece to its place. Even an outside observer must be gratified, as if in the presence of a performance by a true and proper actor.

It is clearly easier to demonstrate that a meal can become an aesthetic experience. First, eating is generally a longer and more consistent process in which not only "nude" behaviors of the body but also manufactured ones are brought to bear, that is, essentially "artistic" actions are carried out with technical precision. Obviously, even in this case, the difference between the meager fare we allow ourselves in the middle of a workday, on the run, with the excuse of saving time, and, say, the state dinner, elevated to the distinction of aesthetic dignity, lies in the introduction of the familiar three categories: novelty, totalization, rhythm. It is important that the various dishes surprise us somehow. We cannot entertain a mundane plate of spaghetti with the usual tomato sauce (or worse yet, with some dietetic butter or oil dressing). Instead, our fare must be characterized by some degree of the extraordinary, in the type of pasta chosen or the sauce garnishing the dish. As for the contextual character, that one experience must include the greatest number of disparate elements. This can be considered a factor even within the routine functioning of dietary habits. We look down on a monotonous meal, and we demand that it include a calculated balance of proteins, carbohydrates, vitamins. This prescription is of a medical order, and so belongs to the field of scientific experience or, inasmuch as it expresses prudence, to common sense. But if we wished that same meal to assume aesthetic connotations, we would have to accentuate some totalizing characteristic and so play with contrasts, with innovative couplings: meat-fish, raw-cooked, bitter-sweet, and so on. In a certain sense, the wider the gamut of alternatives and contrasts, the more certain the attainment of the aesthetic in a given meal, even if, at the same time, the interjection of critical criteria is essential. We must make certain that these symphonic couplings do not clash in a way that would degrade the symphony into cacophony. There must also be a limit to the material quantity of the various ingredients that have been introduced in the various dishes. But it is precisely in such choices that we bring to bear our critical judgment with its typical categories: like the typical aesthetic experience or work of art, a meal can be made to conform to the tenets of classical or baroque, simple and rural or sophisticated and decadent, and so on.

And just as in the act of breathing, so in eating it is not only the material ingredients of the food that comprise the symphony or totalizing context but also many other elements that are more or less external. The quality of the furniture, the table, the settings, the room, even the individuals partaking of the meal count, as well as the air one breathes and the emotions that are evoked. It is much more fruitful to apply the third column of properties to the experience, those linked to articulation, or to the dramatic character (if such a formulation does not seem excessive) that these elements then reflect in every aesthetic experience. In fact, in the most banal and commonplace meal, the sequence of courses is also somewhat mechanical and largely predictable: in Italy, pasta or soup, a meat dish and a vegetable on the side, followed by dessert. Each of these elements is articulated, in turn, according to a limited number of variations. Yet in the meal as an intense aesthetic experience one dish must succeed another in a carefully conceived order, interrupted by pauses, moments of relaxation, and intermissions just sufficient to whet the appetite further.

The Passage to Art

Both breathing and eating definitely belong to the continent of aesthetics inasmuch as, in order to experience them, the human protagonist is limited to "acting," living, and behaving, although within certain conscious and guarded modes that allow the passage from the commonsense dimension to an aesthetic one. But in these cases, our standard subject is not called on to produce or confect a work either by hand or with the aid of some instrument. These actions do not then properly belong to the sphere of "art" or "technique." We must now confront this vast continent that forms such an important part of any treatise on aesthetics, even if, as we noted in chapter 1, no trace of "technique" remains in the etymology of "aesthetics" itself. As we have suggested, this is related to the paradox that aesthetics was born as a science of the senses but turned decisively toward the study of the artistic, as if it were ashamed of its "inferior" and insignificant origins. Our own objective, in line with our present needs, is to attempt to connect both aspects, the "aesthetic" and the "artistic." Just as it was proper to begin the discussion with aesthetics, we can no longer delay our investigation of the artistic, which carries equally significant weight.

But here we immediately find ourselves at a fork in the road that can cause many theoretical difficulties. In aesthetic experience only behaviors or acts exist. Our only recourse is to discover whether they are lived or undertaken according to characteristics that are, precisely, aesthetic, or according to characteristics that are either banal/common or scientific, without excluding the possibility of intersections in or the coexistence of such diverse points of view. In the case of artistic experience we must immediately contend with physical objects (paintings, books, verbal or sung performances that take place in halls specifically set aside for these purposes) that may or may not be accompanied by or invested with aesthetic value (or, by the usual characteristics we have already examined that allow for the possibility of aesthetic experience). Who will establish whether or not such an accompaniment exists? How can we define a particular relation of adherence? Of the two compositions, the physical and the virtual (mental? ideal?), which is stronger or more characteristic? Is the relation between the object and its ancillary one of extrinsic cohabitation, posited according to convention between the parts, or one of immediate proximity?

Here is a group of insidious problems that have been raised in several central dilemmas of philosophical reflection since the beginning of time.

Several well-known tendencies in the history of thought lead to the cancellation of these dilemmas, by following various unilateral, even if antithetical, paths, but even here there are tremendous difficulties. On the one hand, the idealism born in Germany during the early nineteenth century and powerfully revived in our own century with particular relevance for aesthetics by Benedetto Croce declares the philosophical impossibility of all that which is defined as possessing a physical or natural consistency. There are no objects that are not also products of the spirit, the only reality that philosophical reflection must take into account. For this reason, aesthetic experience posits itself entirely at the level of pure acts of consciousness. In comparison, material objects or so-called works of art play the role of proto-memory, of extrinsic, utilitarian notations, as precarious resting points that are by definition superfluous. This declaration represents a most convenient solution, for it clears the field of the tiring presence of material "things" and of the obligation to furnish some theory of how they coexist with the mental or spiritual aspects that "inhabit" them. But it is too convenient, given the inevitable question of why we go to the trouble of fabricating such an enormous repertory of works of art, of patiently building a career, of acquiring any technical ability directed to these ends, if their role is simply to furnish useful notes or practical references.

On the other hand, there has been a radical attempt to deny the existence of a "mental" or spiritual dimension in art. For some thinkers, there are only physical objects and the equally physical movements that put them in motion. This position, born and developed particularly in the United States beginning with Charles Morris, is known as "behaviorism." Objects and behaviors refer only to each other, never to any external field. Such a mode of thinking allies itself immediately with a theory of signs. It is accompanied by semiotics, but even this is rigorously one-dimensional in that each physical object can "stand for" another, it can act as a sign, but only in reference to another object of the same nature, that is, one that is equally physical. This position also represents an easy solution because it eliminates in its own way the divergence between various planes of experience; but it is equally untenable, given that it precludes the passage to culture, to that which renders us human.

We could prove this clearly with our argument concerning the work of art. Let us take one of the simplest and most common examples, a painting, with its pigment and oil layered on a surface of canvas that is, in turn, stretched across a frame, and hung on a wall. A being outside the human condition—an animal, that is—would completely "miss" the aesthetic dimension of such a work and perceive only its physical aspects, in an effort to determine whether the work might serve some useful purpose in the areas of nourishment, shelter, or sexual activity. It is also possible that this object might function as a sign capable of sending the animal on the trail of another object. Basically, then, all of animal existence is a continuous interpretation of various objective opportunities, signs to be followed toward other, more fruitful opportunities or actions. Nothing prohibits human beings from enjoying a work of art at this elementary, literal level, taking it solely in its physical dimension. Without a doubt, the first stages of human evolution, whether in terms of *phylogenesis* (history of social groups, of collectivities) or *ontogenesis* (development of individuals), came to know perceptual conditions that were quite close to those of the animal. Humans were arrested, that is, at a highly elementary semiotic stage, provided by a single flat and linear relation of the "one to one" (one thing corresponds to another, absolutely homogenous, one), which might best be designated by the term "denotation."

The Symbolic Dimension

Let us admit, then, that the sign is not enough, in itself, to "make" our humanity. Moreover, the most rigorous semioticians, including Thomas Sebeok, one of the founding fathers of the discipline, have never pretended to discriminate between humans and the animal or vegetable world to the point of making a kind of Kantian transcendental condition of experience. Rather, Sebeok has attempted to formulate a large and wholly comprehensive *zoosemiotics*. The human being is not an *animal segnicum*, or at least this condition is not sufficient to constitute humanity. Rather, a more appropriate definition, following Ernst Cassirer, would be *animal symbolicum*.

It is not that the notion of the symbol clears or resolves on its own the problematic node, the difficult coexistence between a physical dimension and one that is "other." Rather, if we return to the etymological significance of the symbol, we are not terribly far from the semiotic-denotative function. Originally, the word symbol was employed in reference to two pieces of the same strip of material that were broken up and distributed to different individuals who, as a sign of recognition, had to recompose them (*syn-bállein*), a custom continued in our own times by gangsters (or characters in detective fiction) who carry torn cards or halves of paper money as a sign of identification. Very quickly, the term symbol came to designate a bridge-operation in which something provided with a physical consistency was linked somehow (by convention? by affinity?) not with another "thing" (for this would keep us within the field of denotation), but rather with some formation that was not physically present, no longer graspable by the five senses, an entity that could not be seen, touched, heard, or smelled. This explains why animals are completely unaware of the symbol. But does it represent the phantasm of mentalism or idealism, which the behaviorists, exercising both courage and rigor, attempted to shun forever? And are the idealists correct? It does seem, on the one hand, that humanity discovers a need for this "other" dimension, distinct from the merely physical, the merely sign-oriented, flattened to nothingness. On the other hand, we are dealing with an "alterity" based purely on position, collocation, or functionalism, rather than on some intrinsic quality. Finally, the empiricists, the old and new physicalists, are right in their assertion that concerning the present, or what is verifiable with the senses, there is only effectiveness of behavior, corporeal process, or experience, to return to a phrase we have already used. Even those present-absent signifiers, held in reserve at the level of a potential power, have to be activated sooner or later, and will thus have to take on a body and concrete form. It is important, however, even fundamental, that we have access to a sort of virtual gymnasium in which we try out various consequences or opportunities that have not yet materialized or come into our path, in order to prepare ourselves to confront them. This space is like a situation room in which we predict future moves, imagine obstacles in order to remove them, evoking them with a minimum of effort thanks to the immaterial character of symbolic signifiers. Moreover, it is rather useless to ask how such a symbolic, mental, or ideal atmosphere is born; at least this is an inquiry better left to specific studies of genetics, neurology, and psychology. The fact is that it *does* exist, that it *is* knowable, at least at a functional level, and irrevocable, if we are to give a complete and reliable account of how that primarily human element known as culture acts.

So are the "mentalists" correct in saying that there exists some force corresponding to "mind" or "spirit," endowed with its own autonomous reality? Let us not forget that the very notion of a symbol demands an encounter between two parts, one of which must retain its physical, objective character, and which, moreover, belongs to the modes by which we correctly understand cultural anthropology (it could also be defined as culturology *tout court*). It finds its foundation not in postulating that humans possess a "mental" capability, but, at least as pertains to the initial act, in recognizing the human capacity to furnish our own arts, our own natural organs, with bodies taken from the outside: our first postulate is that we are capable of providing ourselves with extraorganic extensions that, by the way, should not be assigned a nature any different from that enjoyed by the very physical organs belonging to humans according to the pattern of any other animal. Our second postulate recognizes that these extraorganic prostheses, in turn, can be changed over the course of time. And our final postulate is that something called technological innovation does exist. We do not limit ourselves to a sickle; we also provide a handle for it, and so we replace it with an object resulting from the heated fusion of several minerals. And then again, we wield such an object not only through the expenditure of muscular energy, but through recourse to electromechanical charges, and so on, along an inexhaustible series of quantitative and qualitative mutations.

Now, this innovative capacity can exist precisely because human beings are able to suspend the immediate blow that the tool must bring to the external elements of the environment, and, in a potential dimension requiring reflection or abstract examination, consider other modalities of intervention. This and only this is the dimension of the symbolic, or the evocation of a level of "signifiers" that, for the moment, do not correspond to concrete, physically present occurrences. Even if these occurrences can be said to exist, they are only physical in exemplary terms and certainly do not exhaust the virtual potentiality of the symbol itself.

As we see, both of these components must enter in equal proportion and with equal weight into the functioning of the symbol; the physical component prolongs and even extends into this field the benefits that humanity receives, in general, from the typically cultural ability to provide itself with extraorganic prostheses that are more consistent and more durable than those provided by Mother Nature. Finally, we might observe that we normally entrust the meaning of our acts of verbal expression to a sound system every time we make use of a spoken language; in this sense we do not differ greatly, except in the grade of articulational capacity, from other animals that are also capable of emitting sounds toward some semiotic goal. Perhaps the final symbolic dimension (that is, the act of signifying over long distances, in absentia, and without a physical correspondent) is born precisely from the fact that humans have been able to extricate their signifiers, or the physical parts of the symbolic function. We have been able to elaborate them exactly as if they were formed from material objects, choosing with care their forms and possibilities for conservation and transmission, requiring them to demonstrate their own economy, to be inexpensive on the physical end, but rich in terms of signifiers, of absent entities summoned. Certainly, if it were not for that material anchoring on precious external supports, on the symbols in their concrete consistency, the entire edifice of connotations, of "mental" implications, would have collapsed after enjoying a brief existence of little importance.

This is why, along with Cassirer, it is essential to declare the human being an *animal symbolicum*, but without confusing this label with "mentalism," and without abandoning the healthy materialism that seeks to recover from experience the alpha and omega of all our activity: as long as the concept of experience is clearly understood and investigated, and as long as it demonstrates its articulation at the most functional levels, as the very concept of culture itself demands when it inevitably requires the development of the dimension of virtual-potential intervention. Even this is a gift that nature has chosen to concede to a particular (human) animal, not to a being that might imagine itself blessed and close itself up in a superior and uncontaminated atmosphere. Our beginning and our end is to give way to transactions (as Dewey would say) or to functions (as Mukařovský would say) that see to the creation of a single system including both us and the environment such that we transform it, bend it according to our specific needs, and even improve it in the name of "quality of life." An essential difference is that in order to achieve such material and concrete changes, we have one extra weapon in our arsenal (not granted to other animals): the ability to take our time, to try out different scenarios, to "imagine." But then this suspended activity must also result in a choice, in the putting into action of the hypotheses we have agreed upon, even if only to prove them correct once and for all.

Linguistic Symbolism

Nevertheless, all of this makes our life truly unfold in a forest of symbols, not in any particular, emphatic sense implied by Baudelaire's use of this phrase, but in a rather more banal and quotidian one. Practically all artificial objects produced by humanity are symbols, along with the more or less directly functional character of the utensils that serve in the process of production. Specifically, the various forms of writing, whether alphabetical and numerical, graphic and diagrammatic or sign-oriented, all constitute symbol systems. But the symbol system corresponding to one's native tongue, spoken by a community that is contained within specific geographical and political boundaries, stands out above all, whether it be Italian, French, English, or any other. In fact, in the case of linguistic activity, the *double face* use of the symbol as such, with reference to its etymological significance, reaches an optimal grade of economy inasmuch as the intervention of physical elements is held to a minimum. We might think of the minimal expense required to produce graphic traces on a piece of paper (writing "by hand"), to hit the keys of a typewriter, or to procure the necessary elements for an industrial printing press in order to produce a book or newspaper. We should also recall that typography or printing in movable type once signaled the triumphant entrance of Western humanity into the industrial system of machine-based manufacturing. This had as its object "mass" production, the copious flow of merchandise in the marketplace, with a resulting decrease in prices.

In comparison with such purely economic references, we might cite various other effects achieved with extraordinary richness. In fact, through the convenient use of words, we can state our "intentions," we have access to every object, circumstance, and creature in the universe, past, present, future, or even nonexistent (the hippogryph, for example), as a result of purely "mental" editing operations. This implies a recognition that, along with the denotative or semiotic capacity through which the written or spoken occurrence of a word leads us to seek a nearby, corresponding "thing," the enormous, the even more ample and capacious, sphere of connotation opens up. Moreover, in keeping with the symbolic linguistic system, until now we have reasoned in rather rough and ingenuous terms, as if the virtues of such a system merely resided in the "richness," that is, in the single concretizations of sound and graphics, in individual words, with their relative correspondence to other blocks of physical reality, to objects, to "things" or persons, according to a relation that we term "one on one." But language can also link sound sequences and graphic traces. It can form syntagmas by utilizing voids or certain elements that in and of themselves are not immediately convertible into corresponding externals without denotative power. In fact, the exercise of the linguistic instrument guides, orients, prescribes, and leads us to imagine not necessarily a forest of objects evoked individually but a series of actions, bridges, and links between one thing and another. In the extreme case, they *disappear* as such, apprehended in the flow of lateral and sequential processes.

We have not yet examined what is perhaps the most surprising economic virtue of language that we encounter if we turn back toward the material, namely, the signifier. In fact, earlier we discussed a simple task requiring little expense that leads us to speak or write, if, as we suggested, speaking and writing are understood as operations dedicated to linking together various words, perhaps with the help of "empty" particles. But it is well known that individual words—essentially the elements found in a dictionary—result from the combination of even simpler elements, that is, "letters," or phonemes and graphemes, in more correct and sophisticated terms. This observation is valid as long as we remain within the field of so-called alphabetic writing, or more generally, phonetics, where it is precisely symbols, whether written or spoken, that correspond to these elementary emissions of sound, as if to the pieces of a marvelous mechanism. Thanks to successive joints of increasing complexity, this mechanism creates the entire edifice of language. The property called double articulation (one relative to the minimal components, the "letters," the other to the components that constitute words in a finished sense) has accounted for all the power of the linguistic symbol system throughout the centuries, placing it at the center of Western culture and bringing all the other symbol systems, in spite of their intrinsic excellence, to bear on it in a subordinate or ancillary role. There has even been an attempt on the part of structuralist linguists and semioticians in recent years to seek the very same presence of two levels of analysis and decomposition in symbol systems other than the linguistic. This led to the temptation to impose such a structure even where it did not appear to exist. In other words, we faced a risk that double articulation would become a normative model, or at least a heuristic instrument, and that a vast amount of energy would be spent in order to equip symbolic forms other than linguistic ones with it, beginning from the presupposition that only the presence, whether real or potential, of a similar grid of analysis would allow any scientific formulation to emerge. This is how Roland Barthes proceeded, to give one example, in confronting the "fashion system," during those years when he believed that it would be possible to extend a semiotics based on highly structured criteria to every possible field, precisely because such criteria were calibrated to the peculiar characteristics of language.

Equivocal, Univocal, Plurivocal

Earlier attempts to conjoin arbitrarily various symbolic systems in the Procrustean bed of the double articulation of linguistics have been largely discredited. Yet we not only continue to recognize the centrality of language, we use it as a basis for examining various properties of the symbolic universe that our own investigation has now entered. The advantages of linguistic activity also lie in the fact that it is found in each of the larger fields we have traced previously, namely in the essential functions, types of experience, or behavior from which human action emerges: common, aesthetic, and scientific experience. Essentially, we must now redo a scheme that had served us when we needed to establish the boundaries between these families of activity by intervening directly with behavior. Now, however, the level of objects, of signifiers from which the sphere of the symbolic arises, remains central, but nothing allows us to reexamine and review all of this material better than linguistic practice itself. In fact, this is one use of language that may be called common, as distinct from the other uses that will be termed aesthetic (artistic, literary) or scientific, but with all the intersection and contamination that we so carefully outlined in chapter 1, and that we will certainly attempt to maintain even within the field of symbol systems.

Basically, we have already posited a tripartite division, following the perspicuous clues furnished by Galvano Della Volpe. Perhaps we used these clues imprecisely, or without proper reverence, in our attempts to individuate the characteristics of the three fundamental principles at the level of general experience. In fact, Della Volpe has always maintained a link with the linguistic dimension as evidenced by the terms he employs, "discourse" in particular, which itself is termed either equivocal, univocal, or plurivocal, depending on the context. It should be clearly understood that even *vox*, or the word, is at the center of every specific linguistic reflection, even if the fullness of individual *voces* can never be separated from the functional efficacy of the mute particles entrusted with the precious task of binding. Still, given the supremacy of linguistic forms, the terms born in their wake can be easily extended to other sectors in a more or less metaphoric sense. Thus there is no term more vague or generic than that of discourse, which sees its own precisely linguistic peculiarities restricted to the point that it becomes synonymous with every attempt at rational organization in a given sector of investigation.

We now know that according to Della Volpe's terminology common speech would be the locus of equivocation, scientific speech that of univocality, and literary speech, plurivocality. It is precisely the field of verbal expression that offers the greatest possibility for illustrating this theory. In fact, if we pronounce the word "dog" in the context of common speech or everyday life, we find ourselves facing an entirely open and indecisive format (although various other factors will come to bear on intentionality or semantic range, such as the tone, gesture, or circumstances under which the word was uttered). At this level we do not yet know whether the person uttering the word is exercising a sign-function or a symbolic one. In other words, is the referent of that phonic act, that quadrupedal animal capable of barking and biting, present in the immediate vicinity, ready to jump on us? Does the utterance of the term "dog" serve to function as a warning against danger or, even as a mere demonstration, perhaps as a preparation for a warm reception by a member of the canine race, as might be the case when we address a child, assuming a didactic stance? Until now, we have made no discrimination in terms of the behavior of the animal, which is itself certainly not capable of achieving similar articulated or well-controlled phonic acts (animals do not "speak"). But if the dog takes the words precisely as signs, it can react to them, linking them to the presence of food, say, or danger.

Certainly at the level of common speech human beings are better equipped for the symbolic use of words; and so, if the word "dog," used here as an example, is uttered, we do not respond with a set of conditioned reflexes, instantly moving our eyes to locate a corresponding physical occurrence. Instead, we make use of our cognitive apparatus to retrieve a repertory of signifiers from our memory banks. These signifiers, however, belong to various disciplinary fields and planes of interest, hence the "equivocal" character of any generic connotation. We cannot exclude, for example, the possibility that the speaker is referring to an unattractive individual ("dog" in a pejorative sense) or to the metaphoric dog well represented in the constellation Sirius, and so on.

It becomes easy, by contrast, to define the "univocal" field of scientific discourse, which has as its primary task the elimination of numerous ambiguities that are permissible, or at least inevitable in the field of common speech. Here it makes sense to recall Della Volpe's insistence on context; as we already know, common speech is created by somehow weaving together thousands of threads, or, to move beyond this metaphor, thousands of verbal symbols, with the panoply of connotations that each of these carries. Within the scientific realm, however, the open work (both horizontally and vertically) must find closure in a context in which all the threads become homogeneous and share the same nature. In other words, we must first specify the disciplinary field, and then, if it is narrowed, say, to zoology, the "dog" in question will clearly be understood as the quadrupedal animal; in astronomy, the utterance may be understood as an homage to the whole tradition of the Dog Star. To return to the first case, the direct and literal use of the connotation, even zoological science will not be content with such rough definitions as those we have been able to furnish in the field of common sense; that quadrupedal animal must be traced to much more pertinent data, still apparently marginal in comparison with the usual mode of description, so that any possibility of confusion with other animal species can be excluded. Consider the care taken by science to regularize certain units of measure. Basically, at the level of common sense, there is nothing more diffused or familiar than the meter as a unit of length. But now we are learning that in order to arrive at a truly univocal definition, one not subject to variations and errors in calculation, this unit has to be reduced to an infinitesimal fraction of the distance covered by a ray of light in one second.

Moreover, we know that quite often since antiquity scientific practice has instituted symbolic or artificial languages in an attempt to arrive at increasingly univocal and universal definitions. Mathematics, practically since its origins, has developed more or less effective and economical systems of numeration. Little by little the natural sciences have followed, at least to the degree that they also maintain the pretense that they are based on axioms as exact and rigorous as those of mathematics. Such is the case with physics, and also with chemistry: the ninety elements of Mendeleyev's table have all been conveniently linked to the letters of the alphabet, and opportune conventions for indicating the number of atoms that compose their molecules have even been added. In turn, the atoms correspond to the products born from various "syntheses." This procedure basically constitutes an example of double articulation similar to that on which the supremacy of linguistic expression is grounded; however, these linguistic expressions survive, in spite of everything, in numerous areas of the natural sciences. Their total translation into the naked terms of a sort of *mathesis universalis* has not yet been completed, and we can affirm with sufficient authority that it *never* will be. The field of scientific research, finally, must continue to utilize linguistic description within many different terrains. In order for this usage to be truly effective it must resemble the characteristics of common or literary speech, at least to the degree that it allows passages and continuous interpenetrations between one field and the other. Naturally, still following Della Volpe's useful nomenclature, poetic discourse or, more generally, the work of art is the typical locus of the plurivocal; we might also invoke such synonyms as "plurisignification" or "polysemia." At one time it was essential to employ the term "ambiguity" closer to our current lexicon (among the classics of literary criticism in our century is the famous essay of William Empson, *Seven Types of Ambiguity*), but then it was discovered through a play on words that ambiguity is itself "ambiguous," and so was relegated to the field of equivocation. Ultimately, this is correct inasmuch as any rigorous discourse, even when addressed to questions of aesthetics and art, belongs to the territory of science.

For example, the word "dog" that served us earlier can be said to be inherently ambiguous, and so it constitutes one of those typical moments when common speech fails to administer adequately the various meanings it arouses. If we like, this is also the proof of the fertile richness, of the vital abundance, conveyed within common speech. The tendency toward plurivocality, and thus the passage to poetic discourse (or, more generally, to art), comes into play when the coexistence of various "voices" is desired and controlled by the author of a text, or at least when these voices are declared permissible. (In fact, in our own times, characterized by the influence of psychoanalysis, it is difficult to establish what an author truly "desires," and what part of a text is produced by the unconscious, that which, from Plato up until Freud, was reserved for "inspiration" or the "mania" provoked by the demon inhabiting the poet's spirit.) The various meanings recalled here for the word "dog" can all come into play, provided that the word appears in a literary context, or that it arises somehow unexpectedly, for example, in a text that is actually entrusted to the univocality of scientific discourse. This is the totalizing characteristic that we have already recognized as one of the most distinct categories in the field of aesthetic experience, and that, moreover, can be articulated in so many other synonymous terms: organic contextuality, self-sustenance, intransitivity.

Signifier-Signified

Once again we have neglected to mention what is perhaps the most characteristic property of the process of signification within the work of art, and which also accounts for its irrevocable centrality: the fact that in art the "voices" or signifiers, the symbolic referents, or however one wishes to define them, adhere to some physical support. The signifiers are so intrinsic to this physicality that we would be at great pains to separate them from it. Essentially, this is one property that already exists in the field of common sense and that corresponds to the very economy of symbols: a material cluster (phonic, graphic, or gestural) that in itself amounts to very little but sets ideational processes of extraordinary complexity into motion. This also means that interferences and supplantation will become inevitable. In other words, a single signifier serves as the basis for multiple signifieds, or rather, somehow, signifiers, especially linguistic ones, share certain similarities because of their simplicity and elementariness, and this produces a forest of encounters or interventions. In practice, it is as if numerous signifiers were compelled to coexist in a single body; and not only this, but simple modifications in the structure (one letter in place of another) are sufficient for the introduction of quite distinct signifieds. The slightest shift can send the mind reeling after these phantasms called up by a given situation (or from the unconscious itself?).

But normally, whereas common speech submits passively to such an outmoded fecundity, acting with pleasure or suffering numerous inconveniences, poetic-literary discourse systematically exploits it, or rather, poetry knowingly increases the very output of ambiguity. This can clearly happen even when all the possible differences of poetic style are taken into account. Every maker of texts, every school or tendency creates its own rules, with an eye toward the exploitation of such plurivocal gifts in more or less generous ways. We know very well that a poetics, generically grouped under the rubric of classicism, will advise us to proceed with care and moderation, whereas those whose tastes are more baroque will attempt to add flames to the fire of the analogical demon (to exercise, as Baumgarten said, the *analogon rationis*, the art of *pulcre cogitare*). This demon, particularly in the case of poetic texts understood in the most restricted sense of the term, will also come to know the permissible instrument of meter. To return to our poor, abused "dog," we will be able to make it rhyme with "fog," "log," "pawed," and so on: a brief segment of homophony provided by the final consonant and the preceding vowel allows us to associate various dictionary "entries" that are semantically quite diverse and not linked by any logic. Moreover, meter, although certainly an illustrious institution, is clearly not eternal, either in its moment of origin or in terms of its developments. Unknown to its classical antecedents, it enters the Romance and Germanic languages only to be severely contested, especially in the nineteenth century, when it made only rare appearances, normally as a fortuitous episode, expressly retrieved from a small repertory of lyric forms. It is not for this reason that the muse of homophony saw the end of her days. Rather, she can be considered ingrained in the family of works of art that avail themselves of linguistic material. Throughout history, whenever there are no external rhymes or something close to them, then we find a vast recourse to internal rhymes and to so many other forms of partial consonance or echo (alliteration, insistent returns to certain dominant phonic sounds such as labial or liquid sounds). The field of poetry properly understood (as the production of a linguistic work particularly grounded in the exploitation of the potential of verbal material) is then that which best exemplifies, almost by definition, the characteristic of intrinsic meaning belonging to art in general. It is the property that leads a thinker such as Langer to define the symbol of the artistic field as "presentational" in contrast with that of scientific discourse, which remains fundamentally "referential" in that the tangible level of signifiers can have no thickness. The scientific symbol must neutralize itself in order to allow an easier, more rapid transition to that which stands on the other side, whereas the artistic symbol, or rather the organic system of symbols that constitutes a work of art, presents, incorporates into itself, or nourishes the broader series of signifieds summoned in the process. This series is ample and varied precisely because it is forced to lift itself up from a body that is ultimately narrow and constraining. This is as if to say that the characteristic of systematic organicism (totalization) of art is articulated on two faces inherent in any process of signification, which are nevertheless strictly implicated one in the other. They summon one another at close range, and there is polysemy because the signifying body is reduced, concentrated, "economical." This is acceptable; it is all right to avail oneself of this forced coexistence at the level of signification, because the artistic symbol has the precise task of selecting an ample spectrum of signifieds.

This characteristic of adherence, of the "presence" of signifieds for signifiers in the case of the work of art, constitutes the best argument against the "spiritualist" or idealist theses of those who maintain that it is possible to do away with the material-tangible level in confronting the problems of art, or to limit oneself to a consideration of art as useful proto-memory. We discover, however, that the incidence of the processes of homophony in the field of literary-poetic discourse is both necessary and irrevocable, and that in every case, should we wish to follow the idealistic thesis to its logical conclusion, it would be necessary to proceed to a troubling duplicity. Let us imagine a spiritual level at which the material components of a work of art would be faithfully reflected, or an equally spiritual level relative to the signifieds or symbolic implications. The entire work would then have to establish itself on a dyarchic, bipolar axis, so impeding the attainment of that one-dimensional unification so eagerly sought by monistic philosophical currents such as idealism itself.

Again, the "presentational" nature of the artistic symbol raises well-known problems concerning the material level of symbols. To what degree can they be substituted, modified, translated?

These problems do not seem to pose a particular threat in the case of scientific discourse, given that it is engaged in an attempt to reduce as much as possible the margins of ambiguity introduced by signifiers. In such an atmosphere, it is decisively the signifieds, that is, the ideal elements to which the symbol refers, that lead the selection of their own physical points of reference (once it is established that even these cannot be eliminated). If we pass from one language to another, we will attempt to seek out in the lexicon of the second the closest semantic term to that of the first, regardless of how greatly the two terms diverge phonetically. At best, in the scientific fields, we will have as our objective the attainment of a single language for all researchers. Latin served this purpose for centuries; now this role is being assumed by English. Beyond natural languages, the scientific field (particularly the physical-mathematical disciplines) foresees the institution of artificial languages whose signifiers (numbers, letters, the most reductive and precise symbols possible) will replace long, uneconomical verbal expressions, which are especially subject to error in translation from one language to another.

The Acoustic Symbols of Literature

Perhaps it is necessary to pose a preliminary question concerning the location of the symbols that characterize this substitution at close range before we confront this problem of the eventual substitution and translation of the physical dimension of symbolic forms. Given that our discussion for some time now has privileged discursive, linguistic symbols, let us address the question in these terms. First, we must exclude the pertinence of the graphic dimension. In other words, the physical level that "presents" or incorporates the signifieds of literature (poetry, novel) is not the same as that of "letters" and writing, whether these are formed by hand or, as has become increasingly the case for centuries, by means of a press. We should not forget that the exercise of the word is above all an acoustic experience; the use of language, as even the founder of contemporary linguistics, Ferdinand de Saussure, recalled, corresponds to the emission of an uninterrupted flow of sound, even if, in the name of conservation and transmission, humanity has been quick to avail itself of a translation into graphic terms, at least until recent times when technological progress has assured direct forms of conservation thanks to various electronic applications (the record, the tape recorder). In practice, for centuries we had grown accustomed to consume linguistic expressions (whether literary or scientific) through the silent reading of those acts of transcription that correspond to the press using movable type, invented by Gutenberg. And yet such an exterior dressing must not distract us from the fact that the primary nature of linguistic communication remains both acoustic and temporal. The obvious consequence is that it is perfectly acceptable to alter the typographical, or at least the graphic, signifiers of a product of literary art. We can read any poem, lyric sequence, or novel with a certain indifference to the format of the book, the body, the typeface chosen by an editor. Certainly the material conditions of legibility (a more or less comfortable and rapid reading) can influence our enjoyment, but this really brings us into a sphere of extrinsic, utilitarian considerations of convenience. If the physical significance of literature consisted in this, then idealists such as Croce would be correct in sustaining the thesis of its marginality. Of course we might wish to defend the opposite position, affirming that even these physical components enter into our determination of the aesthetic weight of the entire operation, and that thus we cannot ignore them: many movements of the contemporary avant-garde, those that have given life to different phenomena of visual or concrete poetry and of "new writing," would be quick to affirm this notion. But all in all, it is true that for several centuries under the impact of the Gutenberg Galaxy, Western culture has retained the capacity to neutralize such aspects, accepting that the poetic or literary message in general is spread through the impartial and neutral channel of typography.

This does not negate the fact that, at a more internal level, verbal expression has always relied on the acoustic, on the phonic values of that flow of sounds discussed by Saussure. In the context of scientific discourse those phonic values are endured almost as though they constituted an inevitable evil by those seeking to protect the univocality of their signifieds as much as possible from the caprices and idiocies inherent in individual natural languages. Yet these values are fully exasperated in the case of literary discourse or, more precisely, in the case of the so-called poetic or lyric genres in which homophony, as we saw, functions as a factor of primary importance in weaving together, in managing with abundance, with controlled excess, the threads of plurivocality. Hence the enormous difficulty in translating poetry, because with poetry one must find in the new language certain significant bodies that reproduce the allusion, double meaning, assonance, alliteration, and even meter of the original. These tasks are most difficult and affirm that in reality, through translation, a new work of art is born, itself directed toward "presenting" coexistent evocative references no matter how different they may seem from initial verbal material. We also should not exclude the possibility that often the translated poetry is more sublime, for the very richness with which it proposes such "ambiguities," than the original.

But already in prose literary works, that is, in the various narrative genres, the "presentational" character or adherence at the level of signifiers is weakened. In many cases a good narrative passage from a novel or short story may share largely the same prerequisites as scientific discourse, making use of rich descriptions of landscape, the environment, of states of mind that may well contain a certain univocality of reference; that evidently facilitates the retrieval of corresponding signifiers in the target language, precisely because they are charged with ruling, in turn, a unique signifier, or an array of signifiers that are relatively close to one another semantically. Does this mean the demise of the category of plurivocality that we determined was intrinsic to art? No, it means that we must seek this plurivocality at other levels, on a grander, more macroscopic scale; these various and rather internally univocal descriptive processes will have the task of designating individuals or situations that may, in turn, be defined as "open" or ambiguous, still keeping within the field of global activity. Even in this case, the literary work will not cease to present, to "stage," to dramatize the problematic and uncertain character that emerges precisely from our "lived" experience; but it will do so with broad strokes, in a large and capacious context constituted by entire blocks of prose. Internally, this context may not exhibit many differences in comparison with the development of a proper scientific description, if this is at least relevant to disciplines that are not excessively formalized. This gives rise to the very concrete possibility that narrative may interfere with and confuse its contributions with those of psychology, sociology, or psychoanalysis.

Yet in other cases a prose writer (of novels, short stories) can deepen the phonic level of his or her context, by introducing, for example, dialectical forms, or better yet, by permitting idiolects and speech that are direct creations of single characters, or that are of an extremely reduced comprehensibility. This is to say nothing of the difficulties encountered in the translation of poetry. We might refer to the stories or unfinished novels of Gadda, which clearly pose enormous problems not faced by the translators of Svevo, Pirandello, Moravia, or Calvino, for example. And certainly we should consider the producers of texts who, for explicit poetic reasons, refuse any distinction between the lyric, disposed as it may be to playing on homophones, and narrative, more frequently disposed to neutralize the acoustic dimension. We may evoke James Joyce's extreme attempts at experimentalism in *Finnegans Wake*, in which each word intersects diverse lexical forms by condensing these forms in neologisms. It is not for nothing that this "poem" of the Irish writer has up to now seen only partial or fragmentary translations. Indeed, it remains to be established if these are truly translations or simply autonomous recreations.

Musical Symbols

Now let us turn to an examination of this same problem concerning the adherence of signifiers to signifieds in other fields of artistic endeavor. If we take music into consideration, it might at first seem as if we had discovered numerous correspondences with the field of literature, or with the symbol systems that avail themselves of the linguistic instrument. In fact, even for music, the physical level is linked in a dimension of sound, compared with the graphic transcription, which rests on the various systems of notation and plays a decisively extrinsic role. It is not certain, then, in this latter field, that we must seek some characteristic of adherence, and thus of indispensability. Musical scores can be drawn by hand, for example, by the composer in the process of composing. They can also be printed, and thus varied in terms of their formats, stylization, the *design* of the various symbols, without this process implying some appreciable influence on the signifiers that really count, the sounds. In this sense, musical symbolism behaves much like linguistic symbolism. We may even go so far as to ascribe to it the first articulation, inasmuch as it contains the graphemes that can be associated, in a conventional or constrictive mode, with sounds. This system of conventional graphic notation actually presents the enormous advantage, in comparison with verbal languages, of not differentiating itself in the various national languages. It is the same for all users, as long as they share the same conception of music, and thus does not pose the difficult problems of translation.

Along with the advantages, however, there are also disadvantages, or at least peculiarities that decisively differentiate music or any artistic endeavor in the field of sound from literature and the use of linguistic symbolism. Musical symbols, including their graphic notations, seem to be of little utility in the fields of common speech or scientific discourse, and this serves to limit substantially their diffusion, their apprehension, and so also our capacity for writing and reading them. To put it more simply, only a small number of individuals have a sufficient technical capacity to "write" music (in the literal meaning of this term), or to interpret it, that is, to reverse the action performed earlier by the composer, deriving the proper sounds from the graphic traces. Consequently, the musical arts in general must be performed. To be precise, this is also true for literature; the normal form of silent reading flattens and strongly reduces the acoustic dimension of sounds, of the immanent musicality inherent in literary forms, especially when we think of the lyric genres (of poetry in a strict sense). But in our culture, at least since the age of movable type, we have become accustomed to avail ourselves of this reading in the privacy of a room, perhaps in bed before we fall asleep, even if a psychologically controlled investigation might demonstrate that this apparently mute syllabication we perform is actually accompanied by some elementary act in which we sketch out the processes of phonation. Ultimately, even in the case of silent reading, there is an execution, but maintained *in nuce*, at an embryonic level. Moreover, it is essential to recall that we have now left behind the Gutenberg Galaxy, thanks especially to the various electronic instruments capable of recording and faithfully replaying sounds, so also in literature the values of orality are in a clear phase of growth; readings of poetry or brief literary texts are becoming ever more frequent, whereas for long texts (novels) silent reading still means a certain economy (although it is increasingly battling the insidious competition of audiovisual media such as cinema and television).

But let us return to the musical field. The fact that these systems of notation serve only a specific artistic purpose, and have no further practical or scientific uses, implies a necessarily lower grade of literacy. Hence the importance of bringing a mediator-executor to bear on the process, whether this mediator is of an instrumental or vocal nature, such as a soloist or orchestra, or even a "conductor" in the case of a performance undertaken by a larger complex of musicians. Apropos of this phase of the evocation of the physical level of sounds, it is also important to recall an important shift that has occurred since we entered the electronic age of tape recorders and other sophisticated systems. Earlier, the tangible dimension of musical performance was volatile in nature, like the corresponding level of verbal signifiers (*verba volant*, as they were known). Even the most accurate and valid *performance* was destined to disperse into the air, and all that remained was the weaving of graphic signifiers (the score), until some subsequent performance. Today all the various executions of a musical piece, however well performed, possess an equal capacity for permanence, for preservation, even if this is enacted through processes other than that of graphic notation. This latter method is fast becoming superfluous, and it might almost be dispensable, unless some gigantic catastrophe were to occur, some explosion capable of erasing all our electronic recordings.

The musical arts differ from the literary arts in another, perhaps more significant respect. If we can attribute a primary articulation to music, analogous with linguistic symbolism, it does not seem equally possible to recognize a second articulation. As we may recall, in the linguistic exercise this is the process by which various phonemes and graphemes are composed and give rise to words, to symbols whose network of signifieds, however ample and open, is nevertheless also recorded, and shared again, either by common speech or scientific discourse. This process occurs, even though, with respect to the differences we have already outlined, in a common field as in a literary field, the signifieds must be multiple and summoned at will. Yet this does not negate the fact that we are dealing, precisely, with signifieds. The universe of linguistic communication is ample and "open," but, so to speak, discontinuous and composed of discrete entities. Vocabulary exists, and it can serve as a subsidy, a deposit of lexemes (whereas grammar, in turn, furnishes morphemes that are not less linked, or else concerns itself with participles and verbal conjugation, that is, with elements that do not signify directly). Naturally, we will have to confirm that the linguistic-literary use of language must attempt to penetrate the regions of a vanishing, intersected, subtly shaded meaning, but it will still be possible to follow it through these complex zones, to apprehend them at close range, even if only in imprecise ways, with the help of paraphrase or transpositions in terms of common or scientific discourse. Finally, the fullness of meaning of a literary text is only grasped with a maximum of adherence to it in the context of its symbols (and so that context is truly organic, as Della Volpe would say). Any attempt to offer an equivalent description of it gives rise to what a proponent of American New Criticism, Cleanth Brooks, correctly termed "the heresy of paraphrase." This does not negate the fact that the area of meaning commanded by linguistic symbols, to which the various literary genres have recourse, might be closely followed, controlled, and mediated by confrontations with adjacent fields of a common or scientific nature, all responsible for some interwoven meaning.

But, as we have seen, musical symbolism is too underdeveloped in the areas of practical or scientific use to be able to protect us from the arbitrariness of meanings evoked in its general sphere. There is no direct equivalent to the paraphrase in the case of music, or rather, this must be entrusted to the extrinsic instrument of linguistic description. So we have a profile of this so-called abstract rather than semantic property, typical of the musical arts, which lack the power to refer to physical or conceptual objects. These must be designated by other means, they must maintain a certain level of subsistence outside the context of sound, to which they are organic and in which they find their existence and location.

Must we then conclude that in terms of musical arts the level of adherence of the value of meanings to the physicality of the symbol is total, and that, in fact, the symbol might even lose its binary, dyarchic nature? There would be no more meanings, that is to say, referenced objects, except according to those modalities of assent and generality that we termed typical of the symbol. Instead, there would be a total identification of the two faces, or rather, the signifiers would be the signifieds of themselves, positioned precisely in a relation of absolute immanence.

It is not necessary to leap to such radical conclusions. Instead, we should insist on maintaining, even in the musical field, the dyarchic character of the symbolic function, and thus confirm that even the level of the acoustic employed in music enters into the nature of the symbol inasmuch as it does not fail to refer, to evoke general conditions of experience that each of us has known or is capable of knowing: states of tension, relaxation, waiting, falling or ecstasy, drunkenness, soaring, plummeting. The gamut of our psychophysical behavior is magnificently symbolized through acoustic signifiers. In fact, it is indispensable to refer to these signifiers because only in this way can such a field of signifieds be grasped. We would not be able to reach it with only linguistic symbols at our disposal. Humanity has availed itself of the exercise of the musical arts (as well as the graphic and plastic arts, which we will examine later) precisely because without them so many areas of experience would defy suspended symbolic (that is, virtual) elaboration. Susanne Langer is perfectly correct when she insists on defining even music as a symbolic form, capable of articulating, putting into evidence, valorizing our lived experience, that intricate network of perceptions, emotions, volitions in which each one of us is submerged during every hour of every day, even if the articulation in music follows different paths from those of linguistic articulation, entrusted to the lexical. Finally, it is true, in a certain sense, that musical meanings are ineffable; in the literal definition of the term, they cannot be "said" in words. At the very least, in such a case the "heresy of the paraphrase" would be excessive, unnatural, but that does not negate the fact that even musical meanings possess the characteristic of mental objects, of general modalities of experience shared by the larger public.

Graphic Symbols

Now we will consider those works of art committed to graphic-plastic materials (painting, sculpture, architecture), still keeping to the problem of the relative adherence of signifieds to signifiers. In the meantime, we defer to chapter 3 any questions that concern the criteria according to which we can proceed to a classification of the various arts. In the present field we quickly confront a rather consistent difference with respect to both the literary and musical arts. In these two areas previously discussed, the conveying sensory dimension is of an acoustic nature, which is supported in a utilitarian manner by graphic transcription. In the graphic and plastic arts, however, the fundamental dimension is visual (it is not mere chance that the entire territory can be termed the visual arts), so even the basic material must be immediately graspable through vision, although, obviously, it is difficult in general, and in the fulfillment of the aesthetic function in particular, to isolate a single sensory channel from the others. Almost by definition aesthetic inventions are also synaesthetic, so the visual quality of painting and related genres puts into motion sensations that are tactile and kinesthetic, as well as acoustic.

In any case, the first consequence resulting from the primarily visual nature of the signifiers in such a field is that the graphic (or plastic, or chromatic) elements composing these become irreplaceable and play a fundamental role. In the visual arts we find a maximum level of adherence between the two faces of the symbol. To trace lines, to prime surfaces, to model plastic substances, the visual artist performs an essential act that cannot be delegated to another individual, and that does not permit substitutional processes, as in the translation of a literary text from one language to another. An exception is made when the artist is the one who seeks a multiplied image, as in the case of printed works (engraving, lithography). Even in these instances, however, the artist personally oversees the preparation of a template from which the copies will be made, and so is responsible for transferring to these copies the very property of a basic signifier to which the relative signifieds must adhere.

This graphic-plastic dimension is intrinsic to every work of visual art. Not only does it differentiate these from works of a literary-musical origin (hence its absolute necessity), it also makes no use of the articulating characters we noticed in the other two fields. In the case of the visual arts there is no precise correspondence with the articulation of linguistic phonemes, and certainly none with words themselves in a complete sense. Finally, the symbolism of the plastic-visual field is of a continuous nature, knowing no discrete entities, except through primarily arbitrary acts. This explains the difficulty encountered by semiotics in its attempt to take over even this field, and its failure to institute a supposed iconic sign that might have some representational link with the world of external experience, while also participating in the characteristics of discretion and conventionality that should belong, in general, to signs, according to the model of successive composition inherent in linguistic expressions.

The fact is that the visual artist does not, at the beginning of any undertaking, make use of a system of preestablished and codified graphemes. These are not linked to the future product so as to leave open a liberal margin of error only in the interstices, in the ligaments between one nucleus, one entirely predetermined segment and another. Rather, the artist's "hand" is free to trace, to prime, to model, even if the artist eventually intends to follow preestablished models. In this sense artistic intervention is similar to that exercised by a writer who writes by hand, adopting a quite personal graphic system. It is not by chance that when an interest in the level of verbal signifiers has been aroused in recent times, there has been talk of a "new writing," and the products of this genre have been circulated especially in art galleries, for they are the precise equivalent of visual works.

But, then, is the visual artist totally free? Evidently no, for even the artist is forced to observe general modalities with reference to what is banally termed reality, to the world of experience, whether physical or "internal," made up, that is, of imagined ("mental") objects. Two general systems instruct us how to attain this reality by choosing only certain aspects of it and resolving a basic problem, reducing its tridimensionality on surfaces that will most often emerge as flat for reasons of economy. If we speak about plastic blocks ("sculptures"), even these, while maintaining a certain volume, will appear simplified compared with the bodies that move about in the world, if for no other reason than the fact that they are immobile and primarily made of a single homogenous material, sometimes even lacking any color (a long, classical tradition demands that marble or bronze sculpture should renounce that painterly mantle of real things). These are the properties that characterize symbols wherever they are employed, that demand they be of a reduced, economical nature. But in the visual field more than ever it is improper to speak of individual symbols. What counts above all are the criteria by which an entire symbol system is organized and that this organization obey certain precepts or procedural rules followed by every single practitioner, within generous margins. An example is linear perspective, instituted in the first decades of the fifteenth century by the *homines novi* of Italian art. In their honor this became known as Renaissance perspective in order to distinguish it from other forms of perspective developed both before and afterward.

We can clearly state that these symbolic forms, indispensable in the visual field, are nothing other than the different perspectival systems that have been instituted, little by little, in the various historical periods in order to assure the criteria for obtaining images that would somehow correspond to external reality. Perspectival choices range from the simplest to the most complex systems; we find archaic forms in which distant bodies are indicated through a juxtaposition with close bodies, or more sophisticated forms in which depth is indicated by oblique lines that, nevertheless, do not meet in a single vanishing point as they do in Renaissance perspective. We find perspectival forms that consist only of parallel lines, as in the graphic manifestations of the Far East. Then, when Renaissance perspective enters a phase of crisis, contemporary art will offer various solutions. All of these systems must nevertheless indicate the general modalities needed to animate a flat surface and so give rise to the illusion of movement, depth, and volume, yet with rather different criteria than those dear to the long historical period that stretches from the Renaissance to impressionism.

But we must recall that, as with linguistic manifestations, graphic-plastic symbolism is shared by common and scientific experience (as opposed to what we determined for the field of music). Although lacking both the first and second articulations, the visual arts share with music the possibility of giving rise to spheres of "abstract," nonfigurative, nonobjective, or "concrete," autonomous meaning strictly incorporated in the conveying elements. In fact, the developments of contemporary arts have rendered these terms extremely familiar.

The general modalities of relation between the experience of the world and its "representation," which substantially correspond to the various forms of perspective, are not unique to the artistic field, given that (the observation is obvious) even in common sense, for the practical needs of life, and clearly in science, there is a need to use schematic renderings, diagrams, and relatively faithful or conformist representations. The same phenomena occur in language, the common vehicle for the three types of discourse, but with a substantial difference. As we have already seen, although language is decomposable and made up of discrete entities, the symbolic forms used by the continent of visual representation are not, even though they seem to be entrusted to prescriptive systems, to "codes," if we wish. We refer here to codes in the sense of a Napoleonic Code, for example, and not of Morse code, which is, on the contrary, a perfect example of an artificial language, discrete and conventional.

These symbolic forms of representation of the world, of the most basic experiences that emerge from every historical period, and that, on a certain general level, are shared by the three types of experience, constitute the object of study of the history of culture more than that of art, even in those cases when scholars are particularly interested in general mechanisms. On the whole, the various perspectives, the various representational codes, are like the "languages" that actually predate the intervention of a given artist and that can be limited to executing, retracing the functional rules that we have already encountered in terms of the executions of a musical score. This is, again, a case of exercising so many free speech acts that even when they repeat the rules codified in common speech, vary common speech by introducing margins of error or by anticipating the results of different languages. Meanwhile, the execution itself already begins at the level of graphic traces, allowing the artist to give weight to the gifts of an individual "hand," draft, or the ability required for the composition of the context of a given work.

Our previous observations will allow us to note that the work of visual art, however, walks a line parallel to the linguistic-literary sphere by permitting meanings that are also graspable by other means. This then corresponds to the acknowledgment that those meanings can be termed figurative, iconic. But they may prefer to skirt those properties that we already encountered in the territory of music, and thus point decisively toward the nonfigurative. We encounter the first case when operators in the visual arts adopt codes or symbolic forms that share some affinity with those pursued even in the seat of common sense and of scientific research, fields that in general require us to obtain images conforming with reality, endowed with some degree of recognizability. Thus even the "figures" that appear in paintings or sculpture are rather similar to those that in the very same cultural phase would be graspable in the other two seats more closely linked with practical ends. It is as though even here, in the visual field, there is something similar to a "paraphrase," to tension in the most accessible and publicly verifiable symbolic terms. In such a case the artist will have to seek out his or her own margins of specificity because of the fact that graphic figures are actually entrusted to an irreplaceable manual factor, just as, at the level of signifieds, they are wrapped up in a shroud of plurivocality. Here we are referring to open figures that evoke notions and circumstances of another order of experience by playing on heterogeneity and on expressive density.

But in other historical periods the visual artist could decide to separate his or her responsibilities from those of common sense or the descriptive sciences, or else to avail him- or herself of the possibilities recognized even by these latter two fields, using codes that were not directed toward representing, or more particularly, toward representing psychological states and microscopic levels of nature. In this case the mediation of recognizable "figures," comparable somehow with what are termed words or lexemes in linguistics, no longer exerts a particular influence, and expressive meaning seems to be totally dependent on graphic or chromatic traces, exactly as in the musical field. Yet even here, that is, in that which is called abstract art, or better, concrete art (inasmuch as it is founded on apparently autonomous sensory concretizations), the symbol does not cease to fulfill its bipolar function; the material elements are "disposed to" movement, tension, and bursts that make up lived experience, as Langer would say. This holds true, even if it is not possible to translate or paraphrase these rather sui generis aspects of our behavior in terms of clearly legible "figures," things, or persons.

Innovation and Drama

It is now time to speak about the other two properties (categories) that, in chapter 1, we assigned to aesthetic experience, and that thus continue to adhere to it when it is rooted in a layer of physical elements or gives rise to a work of art. These properties are the search for the new and "drama" (internal articulation, rhythm), but we can deal with them quickly because we can often exploit the most accurate investigations in order to shed light on what is perhaps the most central and difficult category of the group, that of the "presentational," of adherence that links the two faces of the symbol, in the case of the work of art.

The push toward novelty, let us recall, is not particular to the aesthetic-artistic field, but is also found in scientific research. This means, then, that the symbol systems employed in both cases must be submitted to careful regulation, unlike what happens in the case of common sense. The felicitous terminology of Della Volpe has helped us in this endeavor by emphasizing the distinction between the equivocal, the plurivocal, and the univocal. Obviously, the search for the new, shared by both art and science, is not an absolute prerequisite. On the contrary, it must respect the peculiarities of the physical-material layer of symbols employed. This means that when art is in fact entrusted to linguistic material, its author must generally respect the two articulations, and so cannot be permitted to introduce personal or capricious variations in the individual "letters," or in terms of the lexicon or morphology. Even if there is no absolutely valid prescription, there may be experiments that attempt to innovate, even in literal terms, by bringing themselves, for example, to a subsegmental level, refusing the unity and conventionality of single phonemes or graphemes, and instead breaking them apart into the most minute fragments. This yields what is called "new writing," as mentioned earlier; however, this experiment is hardly considered in literary circles, except in those that encompass the visual arts (if such a project is conducted, that is, through graphic modes), or in those of performance, that is, a minimalist spectacle including an acoustic dimension, with its inevitable gestural accompaniment.

Innovation at a semantic level is clearly much easier, forcing the meanings provided by a particular word and retrieving other, more archaic ones, seeking to impose new meanings by analogy. And we have not taken into account that, even here, one may dare to use neologisms, fusing together several verbal roots. We may have the so-called *mots-valise*, invented by Lewis Carroll and employed later in vast measure by Joyce in *Finnegans Wake*, not to mention certain recent experimental writers. Finally, even at the grammatical and syntactical levels it is possible to force codified usages. At a certain point, far from the present context, we leave behind the territorial waters of the lexical or grammatical and enter in those that the scholastic manuals would attribute to style or to rhetoric. Here we confront choices between, let us say, a rhythm given over to asyndeton or polysyndeton (phrases linked without conjunctions, in a rapid-fire sequence, or else linked traditionally), to coordination and subordination, to the abundance of phrases dependent on and contained within each other like Chinese boxes. Ultimately, we can observe that all innovative intentions, if exercised in a linguistic-literary field, are held to respect the discrete, discontinuous character that this field demands. This means that the writer has limited powers to intervene into the full nuclei, whether these are material or graphic, while having considerable powers at the points of articulation.

On the contrary, the material layers of the visual field (graphic sketches, color drawings) allow for the possibility of continuous, limitless intervention. The artist is called to "execute" something with his or her hands, aided by the intermediary filter of relatively tractable and flexible instruments. The artist has neither graphemes nor words or figures that preexist his or her intervention, yet the so-called figurative artist—one faithful to the more traditional canons—is called upon to develop figuration with a direct and free intervention. If anything, restrictive prescriptions belong to the past; they reside in the codes, in the institutions that dictate how one is to translate three-dimensional, mobile bodies of reality into the symbolic fiction of the surface. Codes, instructions that can be rather forceful, cogent, and long-lasting. Renaissance perspective enjoyed a vigorous life for not less than four centuries, from the third or fourth decade of the fifteenth century through the final years of the nineteenth, when innovators such as Cézanne, Seurat, and Gauguin came to decisively abolish it by substituting other short-lived perspectival systems that admitted a conspicuous margin of personal variation.

But let us not insist too much on an analysis of this type, given that we will be compelled to confront the problem of the multiplicity of the arts, which will be discussed in the next chapter. For the moment, it is enough to recall the survival of the search for the new in the territory that can generically be termed artistic, with the added property that such research must move within the parameters of many peculiarities intrinsic to the basic material.

We will not linger on the third and final of those categories that we have already determined as necessary and sufficient conditions for an aesthetic experience, namely, drama (with all of its relevant synonyms), because we wish to avoid finding ourselves forced into a precise investigation of the various arts. Nevertheless, it is evident that the field of art, that is, the presence of objects, of manufactured goods, of elaborations provided with spatial and temporal dimensions, tangibility, weight, and volume, greatly favors the inclusion of this final category. Drama seemed all the more dubious, almost imposed by theoretical necessity in order to balance the accounts, in the minimal case of aesthetic experience taken in a pure state. Let us recall the example employed at the beginning of this chapter, the respiratory act: it is certainly difficult, but not impossible, to furnish the act of breathing with a particularly dramatic character, with an orchestrated periodicity of alternating rhythms of tension, slowing, swelling. On the other hand, it is much easier to locate these diverse phases within a literary, musical, visual, or dramatic text. In such cases, the third category and the second one (totalization or organic plurivocality) take turns resting upon one another. The totalizing breath can easily entrust itself to the times and spaces of a rhythm that is not played out quickly, and that thus facilitates even the phenomena of retention and the intransitive. Symbolism of a scientific nature seeks to run as quickly as possible toward the end of the investigation, ideally canceling out the various stages that are first embraced and then abandoned. Meanwhile, artistic symbolism organizes an echo, a permanence of the network of signifieds from beginning to end. The consistency of the physical object is there in order to guarantee a similarly dense space, folded in on itself and acting as a container to impede any escape or dispersion.

CHAPTER 3

The Multiplicity of the Arts

The Senses, Space, Time

As we saw in the previous chapter, there can be no art unless a physical object intervenes, some work elaborated with relatively specialized technical criteria and leading to a recognized professionalism. But the possibilities for technical intervention are multiple and exhibit a remarkable diversity, and this in turn leads to the phenomenon of the multiplicity of the arts, which assumes a constitutive character in such a perspective. There can be no art except through theoretical abstraction. In fact, we find ourselves in the presence of a rather diversified panorama of arts unless we refuse to accept the idealist declaration according to which the technical component of the artistic fact has the value of mere accommodation, of an exterior proto-memory; but this is a hypothesis that today is widely discredited. At best it should be considered an eventuality that does not merit serious consideration.

And not only does the technical fact enter in a constitutive measure, becoming intrinsic to every reflection on art, but along with the diversity of formations, of material consistency, it is necessary to immediately take into account an inevitable diversification in time. Techniques themselves are not necessarily stable throughout the course of history. They come and go as they are instituted during certain cultural phases, only to lose their relevance and be replaced by more efficient procedures. No one can pretend to establish a fixed map of the various arts once and for all. In the brief space of one century we have seen the birth of new techniques for the production of images, including, for example, photography, followed by cinematography, and then television. In general, our age, characterized by accelerated technological development, has provoked changes consistent with every productive sector and, consequently, enormous disturbances in the map of the arts. In the present volume, however, we can only hope to indicate certain orientational criteria that might serve as a prolegomenon to an effective classification of the arts, taking care to leave ourselves open to possible variations.

Naturally, the root of this project lies in the territory of "est," that is, in the field of aesthetics, or the sensory. The traditional five senses are the doors to external data, the channels through which our interaction with the world takes place. Yet, in the realm of aesthetic experience examined in the first chapter, it is not by chance that we did not encounter the problem of differentiation between the various possible types of such an experience, because at that level the validity of an aesthetic order (according to a rich and intensive definition of that term) is realized only when the "five senses" renounce their claims to separateness and intermingle among themselves. Every aesthetic experience is thus fundamentally synaesthetic and has as its primary objective the cooperation between the various sensory channels that give rise to an undifferentiated "continuum."

Moreover, keeping within this level, there does not yet exist a problem of recording or conserving the sensory data: aesthetic experiences are consumed as they are lived, from the inside, so there is no difference between producer and consumer. But as soon as we pass into the territory of "art" and seek to entrust the wealth of aesthetic experiences to some material base, thus undertaking a symbolic operation, we realize almost immediately that the various sensory orders do not necessarily behave in any unified manner with such a result in sight. This is the origin of the millennial privilege enjoyed by the "noble" senses, sight and hearing, which resulted in an imbalance in favor of the visual, a priority not placed in question until electronic society has allowed us to record sound. For millennia, however, humanity has enjoyed access to graphic traces (writing, design, painting, and so on) as the only possibilities for fixing and handing down our own symbols. Sound also furnished an optimal symbolic instrument—we need only think of the oral use of language—but it was invalidated by the impossibility of preservation (the previously mentioned *verba volant*). And although the possibility of crossing over into the aesthetic has not been denied to the fruits of the other senses (smell, taste, touch), it has been diminished, again because of the difficulty in preservation. The experience recounted by Proust in his *Recherche*, the pleasure aroused by bringing a pastry immersed in an infusion of lime tea to the mouth, is one of the greatest and most intense open to the senses. Certainly when the author himself experienced this, it was one of the strongest imaginable aesthetic experiences, and each one of us can experience something analogous. But what has reached us is actually only an "artistic" transcription through the linguistic instrument, which is, in turn, dependent upon typographical characters. It is possible that one day technology, whether of an electronic character or not, will be so advanced that it will be able to reproduce the bombardment of particles, the sensory stimulation that gives rise to the pleasures of taste and smell, and then repeat them at our command.

Today, in any case, we cannot preserve the impressions of the senses other than sight and hearing, which means these other senses can be present only by proxy. It is not arbitrary to speak of olfactory, tactile, or taste values aroused in us by some visual or auditory work of art. Rather, this happens through a synaesthetic, sympathetic reaction, not through some direct mode. We thus see two great areas of intervention for the continent of "art"—vision and hearing—with the respective technical resources that allow for their manipulation. But it is not enough to conduct a reflection based simply on sensory data—or, at least, this would no longer be acceptable in our present cultural phase. In fact, contemporary culture has its origins in, among others, Kant, who put into effect the famous Copernican revolution, suggesting that humans no longer appear as the tabula rasa dear to the empiricists of the early eighteenth century. The subject is active, which means that we accompany the exercise of the sensory with the imposition of formative processes. To feel is also to organize, to put into form, or, to use Kantian terms, to apply a priori aesthetic forms. There is no visual sensation that does not intrinsically convey a spatial organization, just as acoustic sensations implicate temporality. Along this route we find the most noted and classic of all the classifications of the arts, that proposed by Lessing, dependent precisely on the distinction between the spatial (painting, sculpture, architecture) and the temporal (literature, music) arts. Such an elementary and commonsense criterion still rules, and can be employed or even extended according to the same model. In fact, those arts that might be termed arts of movement (dance, spectacle) remain excluded from such a classification. But movement, in turn, is nothing other than the result of space and time; even in physical terms it is defined as a function independent from the other two. Movement, however, is a sensory event: it can be grasped or verified. It is much less volatile in this sense than taste and smell, and, especially since we have entered the technetronic age, movement, like the acoustic, has broken free of its dependence on graphic description, to which both were condemned for centuries.

The Arts of Time: Literature

Now let us address the arts of time according to Lessing's criterion, which may be old but not altogether out of service, perhaps because its generic status allows for so many additions and corrections. Among the primary arts of time stands literature, and in this case we will not bother to repeat what was stated in chapter 2 when we were defining the physical state of which this "art" avails itself, or rather, the material face of its symbol system. We had to recall all the ambiguity of an art born as an exercise of acoustic meanings, but which then, at least since the existence of writing, seems to have transferred itself to a radically different field. Yet it is only an appearance, and the best confirmation of this lies in the fact that the graphic layer through which literary products are manifested is not the conveyor of any adherent values. We can modify or neglect it without any damage to the layers that truly count and that "make up" the work's artistic consistency.

So we are in the presence of a literary text, or rather, context, and this term is already quite familiar, given that it was precisely around this term that we conducted the first approaches to both "est" and "art," following Della Volpe, a philosopher who is most amply informed about literature, and thus in an excellent position to translate his general nomenclature for the entire map of artistic phenomena into the specific terms of literature. The character of an organic context or plurivocal discourse, to use Della Volpe's terms, is ultimately ascertainable within the boundaries of a literary work more than anywhere else.

But, as opportune as this may be—almost cut to measure—the term "text" seems to us rather general to cover the vast continent of literary production. At the very least we must immediately admit the existence of texts of many different lengths, destined for a variety of purposes, fates, and receptions. Such a diversity, here as in every other case, can be verified or measured either in synchronic terms, that is, in its existence here and now, framed by a particular civilization, or in diachronic terms, that is, in its variation through historical changes. We note the necessity to confront a final classification as soon as we have defined a field of artistic products as literary: that which concerns the classical and traditional "genres," which themselves emerge as constitutive, as intrinsic to artistic production of a literary sort. It is not enough to assert that this is addressed to the completion of "texts." We must also examine the criteria that preside over the diversification of such texts, from the brief and intense pieces of the lyric genres to the longer works of the narrative genres.

From Rhetorical Discourse to the Lyric Genre

In order to confront this material adequately, we must take a step backward, returning to the general classification of the three types of experience or discourse with which we began, including that discourse we termed scientific. However inarticulate this definition is, it now merits a more refined precision. There exists a well-known subdivision between the so-called physical-mathematical sciences (physics, chemistry, biology, and so on) and the human sciences, which are concerned with investigations of the animal capable of culture, but not simply as one more animal to be placed among the most developed mammals. This disciplinary distinction is undoubtedly open to scrutiny and exhibits highly fluid confines, yet gains credibility from the fact that the disciplines of the first group have recourse to inductive-experimental or logico-deductive methodologies that are valid, especially because they can be approached and studied through mathematics. Of course, these sciences may be termed analytic inasmuch as they find their primary and most illustrative foundation in Aristotle's *Analytics*. Here, an examination is made to determine how we might deduce certain consequences from premises given as acquired (the problem of whether this character of certainty derives from natural or conventional causes, or from other sources of legitimation). If these same premises are placed in doubt and constitute an object of debate and if, again, such a debate is conducted by only a few experts, in a refined and specialist environment, what we have is dialectics, also examined by Aristotle, in the *Topics*. Finally, if the debate takes place in a public forum and is addressed to a general, non-specialized public, we have rhetorical discourse. Yet almost all of the disciplines we might term humanist involve forms of logic that insert themselves between dialectic and rhetoric, inasmuch as it is quite difficult to begin with widely accepted premises, or, at the very least, it is difficult to arrive at definite assertions. Their very definition becomes one of the principal tasks of the debate. Those materials concerned with a type of dialectical-rhetorical discourse, according to a long tradition arising during the Greco-Roman period, are relevant for all occasions of a public nature: politics, law, ethics, aesthetics, and the field of the judgment of values, founded on qualitative rather than quantitative criteria.

Charles Perelman, who has made a significant contribution to the increase of interest in rhetoric in our own times, has accustomed us to distinguish between "convincing," proper to logical-analytic discourse, and "persuading," which characterizes rhetorical discourse. In the first case, the end is demonstration; in the second, argumentation, which may seek to be more or less probing and persuasive, but does not convince us in any decisive way. We have a series of consistent differences between the two types of discourse, even if both can be said to be endowed with a certain logical dignity serving as a sort of reinforcement or through-line for all scientific discourse. Analytic logic avails itself of *docere* alone, and proposes to elaborate and transmit information, ideas, or relatively vast amounts of "knowledge." The more cut-and-dried the transmission, the better it serves this function (here we return to the characteristic we defined as "transitive"). But rhetorical logic, which is not backed by the inconceivable force of initial certainties or procedural constrictions, seeks to increase its own credibility by other means while refusing to renounce its duty to teach; but it must intensify the *docere* through its recourse to *delectare*, for example, with variations on the themes and terms, with insistence, with abundant eloquence, or better yet, with the help of exemplars, an optimal rhetorical tool (replaced by the experimental proof in physical-mathematical discourse). Finally, humanistic materials cannot be treated separately from a certain level of emotional depth, whether because this is called into play by the very themes confronted, or because it is inevitably aroused in the audience.

We see that a form, whether belonging to scientific or rhetorical discourse, comes to assume consistent aesthetic characteristics, almost to the point of bridging an intermediary gap between the two spheres and of confirming the utility of maintaining a bridge over the caesura that seems to separate them, but ends up considering them as two poles whose effects may intersect and interpenetrate. The fact remains that the gap between the practice of rhetorical discourse and that of certain poetic genres or brief texts exhibiting a lyric flavor is rather small. We have already recalled that certain of the typical occasions for rhetoric lie in debate and judgment. We may now add a third, vast "genre" to this list, namely, praise. Even lyric poetry, in the most disparate historical moments, has been concerned with debate, judgment, and praise as they are transposed into a field of play or diversion, or often invested with an emotional depth. We have to admit that the components of lyric can be considered as brief debates in which the poet, or the individual put in place of the poet, argues in favor of his own virtues in an attempt to persuade a female love object to accord him certain favors; or he denounces and accuses the woman's cruelty using subtle logic, which permits him to remain insensitive to any amorous advances; or again, he celebrates the woman's virtues and merits, or, if he has been rejected, her defects, both physical and mental. This schematization refers primarily to the love lyric, but the epideictic genres may also be viewed within the model of rhetorical debate, that is, those works that praise or blame famous personages, celebrating their virtues or denouncing their vices. The object of praise (or denigration) may be a collective person instead of a physical person. We can hurl invectives against a country or a faction, or declaim incitements to arouse the soul of an entire community.

These are the characteristics that concern internal conformity, the logico-persuasive status of the lyric genres; but it is worthwhile to reconsider the external circuit, the social occasions that have motivated writing throughout the centuries and have determined the resurgence of specific professional competencies, finally creating the "letterato," a furnisher of products to meet a precise demand, at least in determined, official circumstances. A study of literary genres that attends to these external perimeters, and that dabbles in sociology, may end up with a minutely detailed set of functional rules; we will have epithalamia, or the lyrics written "for the marriage of," encomia for official celebrations, elegies and funerary laments, poems written "on the death of," and so on. The list may grow and become more specialized, but what will emerge is an affinity with those occasions liable to be treated through recourse to rhetorical discourse.

Naturally, these various external, sociological occasions, as they are born in response to the needs, expectations, and habits of various cultures, are destined to fade, to be replaced by more stringent occasions and modalities; but they tend to be maintained out of respect for the old traditions. They are treated as ideal spaces for the exercise of poetic-literary work in the most restricted sense so that they may respond to the essential categories that this book intends to problematize. For example, our own society no longer knows of epithalamia, encomia, royal entrances, or poetic complaints, and even the amorous song has lost most of its useful social traits. Similarly, the professional role of "letterato" has all but disappeared, that is to say, as a composer of texts ready to exercise his or her abilities in the service of a powerful sector desirous of ritualistic forms of praise. A "poet" of our times knows full well that, because there is no more social need for this sort of skill, he or she will have to live by other means. The contemporary poet may perhaps attempt to remain closely linked to the field of "letters," choosing a profession such as teaching, or work in the culture industry (publishing, editorial), inserting him- or herself in some sector of culture that amounts to an adaptation, in contemporary terms, of the old epideictic genres so typical of rhetoric or advertising. In fact, many poets today lend their skills to advertising agencies or public relations departments for the task of furnishing highly persuasive rhetorical texts concerning the virtues of the products sponsored by their respective "houses."

This means that lyric texts, today, are finally free to pull their own weight, to pursue various combinations of the larger categories that serve as the source for poetic (artistic, aesthetic) discourse at the level of pure craft. Today poets engaged in the creation of "lyric" works will respect the occasions that gave birth to the various forms; they will write love lyrics or poetry "in memoriam," commemorating weddings, or denouncing, as in the case of invectives, and so on. They will also attain effects of novelty to the greatest extent possible, to say nothing of plurivocal contextuality, and they see to it that their lexicon engages the largest possible number of semantic references. In addition, they will study balanced movements, rhythmic alternations between components, various games of equilibrium and disequilibrium. The "knowledge" of their era will also be present, but dressed in pleasing garb, consisting of the same plurivocal fullness as their references or permissible associations. We may also notice a mastic of emotions, tamed and controlled, used as the adhesive binding together the various materials that enter into the operation. Naturally, we must limit ourselves to general observations, given that, beyond this threshold permitted to scientific-theoretical discourse, we find ourselves at the opening of the space belonging to a historical-critical evaluation of individual experiences. This means that we would have to examine the various groups and schools of contemporary lyric poetry, each one characterized precisely by its relative accentuation of these three parameters. Certain schools will suggest a parasitical use of metrical or lexical novelty, even up to the point of imposing the use of neologisms; other groups will be directed toward a crazed and frenetic associationalism; and still others will preach a return to more placid and neotraditionalist meters. But here we begin to enter the vast continent of critical evaluation, which we will discuss in the next chapter, always, however, remaining at the level of theoretical generality.

Narratology

Leaving behind those brief texts of a lyrical nature, we next encounter a plurisecular tradition that presents us with longer texts. These may also properly be termed "poetic," whether according to etymology or in a historical sense. In fact, as we saw in the first chapter, the Greek root "poie," from which we derive poetry, poem, and poetic, signifies a "making," but in a fuller sense than what is indicated by that other root of vast importance, "techn." This latter root, and its Latin equivalent, "art," both refer to an act of producing with ability and intelligence and through the aid of various instruments; but "poièn" designates construction par excellence, and is thus connected with the privilege traditionally granted to verbal material (whether auditory or graphic). The making of poetry is thus identified with material of a linguistic-literary sort: a making that in archaic cultures was primarily entrusted to orality (there was no writing in Homeric times, during the composition of the *Iliad* and the *Odyssey*), accompanied in turn by sonority and musicality. This is why the "poem," in the sense understood by Aristotle in his *Poetics* (the original title of *Poetica* being a feminine, adjectival noun that also embraced the more general term of technique) included both the "epic," recited by a single *eidos* with musical accompaniment (in this we discover the predecessor of our contemporary narrative genres), as well as the theatrical version, recited and staged (tragedy and comedy). Certainly, notions of length and labor were then added, in the sense that the poem, whether narrated or recited, was in any case considered a composition, a fabrication of notable complexity, so that the institution of a specific study, or at least a body of precepts elaborated for these purposes, was called for. The briefest components of the lyric genre, however, although also fruits of poetic production, were left to the study of rhetoric.

But as in the field of the "brief" genres where we have had to refer to a large matrix, an amalgam of the fundamental models of experience and discourse, so also for long poems we must shed light on a broader, murkier terrain. It is difficult to ascertain if we are in the field of common experience, aesthetics, or science. A central problem is to determine the presence of "mythos," or of the *fabula* (the Latin equivalent of the Greek word, invested with the same depth and ambiguity of meaning). We could also speak, more generally, of a tendency to create fables that forms an essential component of human nature: a bridge between "common" needs and the more sophisticated exigencies belonging to aesthetics and science, and so subject to greater control. Even in the creation of a fable, the *docere*, which is a very basic set of notions or concepts, is presented as strictly cemented to pleasure, no longer entrusted to the abundance of words and images, but to the narrative sequence of the "fable," with an added dose of emotions excited by the fable itself and so also aroused in the reader. Obviously, this essential and primary sequence that constitutes the fable or myth posits itself at the level of symbolic discourse, and so deviates from the level of existing, raw, and immediate facts. It does not belong to the dimension of the "true," but to that of the "probable"; not to history, understood in the literal sense, as a certainty, documentation, testimony of that which we see with our eyes, but to philosophy, that is, to a reconstruction and imaginative projection. With these intentionally rough and generic terms, we offer a paraphrase of the observational notes that open Aristotle's *Poetics*, recognizing the centrality, for this and for all that concerns it, of the notion of "myth"; in the beginning was myth, as we might gloss it, that is, a principally human capacity for extrapolating from history, from events, from invented but prepatterned sequences in which humanity itself, following the patterns of what usually happens, imagines, invents, and hypothesizes various scenarios or abstract successions.

It is worthwhile to recall that until now this need for mythical, fabled sequences has been immanent in all the fields of human endeavor, or, to put it another way, has appeared primarily in the area of common sense. The same holds true for rhetorical discourse, which, as we have seen, "resides in the middle ground," between science, aesthetics, and the everyday exigencies of humanity. Hence this compelling need to consume mythical products gives rise to primary and primordial acts such as the narration of fables. But later we develop a need for ever-longer, richer, more articulated "poems." All societies and cultures have manifested needs of this type, satisfying them with different products adapted to individual situations. A zone of professionalism and precise competencies becomes delineated. This might include technicians or artisans who have had to furnish this type of product throughout the various phases of culture and in various social orders.

Developing such reflections was important in order to clarify the fact that the vast continent of "mythopoetic" productions, directed, that is, toward furnishing the public with narrative texts of various lengths, cannot be entrusted entirely to the field of art and its concerns. Throughout the course of time, hundreds of honest professionals have existed who saw fit to respond to similar needs in rash or facile ways, satisfying these needs for the most part, but missing certain objectives in the work of art itself, either because such objectives were not even addressed while preference was given to some activity of honest entertainment, or because the objectives were pursued, but too many compromises with the most popular and obvious schemes were accepted along the way. We might recall the Greek *eidos* who endlessly repeated various "places" of the so-called formulaic style characteristic of oral cultures, when, in order to enhance memory, it is necessary to avail oneself precisely of sequences of prefabricated phrases. Or we recall literati, who in the later eras of classical antiquity and in the Italian Renaissance returned to the models of the epic poets, or "popular" writers seeking success through recourse to well-worn dramatic situations. Even in our times, we might consider how many professionals dedicate themselves, often with positive results, to the formulas of the mystery novel, detective fiction, science fiction, or the "romance" genre. This preliminary list does not even include our contemporary "mythographers," specializing in tailoring these narrative sequences for the new possibilities offered by technological developments, including cinema and television.

Although it would be inopportune and unproductive to give over all of this vast strip of detail to the continent of art and its strict and rigorous needs, we must also consider the impossibility of totally ignoring art; we cannot immediately exclude the possibility that some narrator by profession, even without renouncing the objectives of a positive impact on his or her public or the objective of a wide reception, will achieve valid "artistic," literary results, almost in spite of intentions. That is, the narrator in question may offer us texts that interest literary critics or, in any case, a sector of sophisticated readers. Throughout many centuries the dominant societies have certainly not allowed their writers to pursue purely literary ends, and so works that seem positive from our point of view were achieved almost in an unintentional way, as a surplus benefit to which we, as posterity, are particularly sensitive. But above all, with the arrival of our own period, when finally the conditions of a mature society, developed in every sector, allow us to delineate the figure of a writer who is largely authorized to pursue ends of a notable purity and rigor, even this "superior" author cannot avoid taking the opinion of the general population and consumerism into account. At most, we will be able to permit ourselves not to dismiss these factors easily, but to insert innovative ticks into the work itself. This describes the circumstance under which many writers of our times seem to imitate the detective genre, but without appropriating every aspect of it. For example, in *Quer pasticciaccio brutto de via Merulana*, Gadda includes a detective-style episode, complete with assassin and police investigator, but then he decides not to conclude the affair, leaving the guilty verdict to the reader, preferring instead to lose himself in a sea of concomitant circumstances and red herrings. Even Umberto Eco's *Name of the Rose* follows a typical mystery plot derived from the *Ten Little Indians* of Agatha Christie, but he intercuts it with elements taken from other genres, thereby enormously increasing its intertextual character, that is, the richness of references that must be present in any artistic-literary product.

The *Poetics* of Aristotle

All of this is to say that we can redeem the bounty, the fixity of the three
fundamental categories we proposed for the territories of "est" and "art"
(innovation, organic contextuality, rhythm), but we must agree to weave
them, in the case of the production of longer, narrative texts, with the body
of traditions and specific needs of that sector. In our attempt to single out
these needs and traditions, the classic Aristotelian treatment in the *Poetics*
emerges as enormously useful. This text dedicates itself to an analysis of
the ideal poem, distinguishing in its verbal component at least four parts,
and still others are brought in for the theatrical staging. In the first place
we find *mythos*, the fable or nucleus that is also the rather mysterious *quid*,
not subject to decomposition into those simpler elements with which we
began in our attempt to arrange that whole area of artistic production, declaring it an ambiguous collection, just one of so many different functions
of human action. In the second place is *ethos*, the component that concerns
the moral-psychological depth of human actions. Then also *dianoia*, the
complex of ideas and beliefs nourished by the society that gives birth to a
certain poem and that also contributes to its destruction. Finally, we have
lexis, the type of language or rhetoric put into the mouths of figures, of
"characters," of those who, while they promote myth, also outline the various ethical depths put into play by the work.

We could take up each of these constitutive parts in rash, conformist
ways, and then we would have the pure products that interest economic,
social, and even market-based considerations. Or perhaps we could take a
bold approach, applying the categories we previously recalled, but we
might risk inhibiting an immediate popular consumption in our desire to
"open" a good literary work. For example, myth can be simple or predictable, and the same goes for the modality according to which it is enacted
(Aristotle uses the term "diegesis" to describe this). But already at the level
of popular consumption it does not hurt to add elements of variety and of
the unforeseen, and so the same author of the *Poetics*, here following the
model of classical texts that preexisted him, advises poets to complicate
diegetic development by anticipating certain facts and retrieving previous
events thanks to a retrospective recounting (the technique that today is universally designated with the English term "flashback"). The great Homeric
poems are constructed around this savvy stratagem; for example, Odysseus
recounts a substantial portion of his prior peregrinations after he has already reached the final leg of his journey home, at the court of King
Alcinous. It is true that later a similar diegetic variation becomes a mere

expedient, faithfully repeated by Homer's followers beginning with Virgil in the *Aeneid*, setting up the challenge for poets to add their own innovations to this model. In any case, we see that the push toward innovation can also take possession of the mythical component. Every instance of this, moreover, plays with the characteristic of calculated rhythm that must be part of any successful work of art. As for the *ethos*, even here we can find elementary and obvious results (the staging of predictable character types) or quite refined and penetrating ones, whether in the field of individual psychology or in that of the great social forces. Even *dianoia* within a certain narrative work will be able to move easily between the two extremes of univocality or plurivocality, augmenting its literary value in this latter case. As for *lexis*, this is obviously the point of greatest tangentiality between the long genres of the mythopoetic tradition and those brief genres associated with the lyric. In both cases it is acceptable for the "poet," as opposed to the rhetorician or the scientist (of psychology or sociology) to refer to intense verbal expressions, relevant even in an autonomous degree. Yet, at best, *lexis* in a poem or a long literary text must be more controlled or tailored to the general ends of the work and its large mass, than in the limited context of a laudatory composition. In general that which we could call a narrative "passage" exists; however, as soon as we announce such a principle, we immediately discover the possibilities for transgressing beyond it, finally enlarging it to include the prerequisites of any work of art at all. For example, in the case of Gadda mentioned earlier, the author does his best to render his own *lexis* dense and opaque. James Joyce also comes naturally to mind, especially his final work, *Finnegans Wake*, an uninterrupted series of neologisms created according to a clear plan through the interweaving and contamination of various lexical roots and morphological cognates. Today, in effect, we are living in an era of enormous contextualization compared to the prerequisites traditionally assigned to the individual genres.

In any case, whoever confronts this disproportionate continent of mythopoetic products faces the need to conjoin two radically contrasting aspects. On the one hand, we have the impression that "there is nothing new under the sun." The classical and canonical indications offered by Aristotle's *Poetics* are still in existence, very much present in critical language. Their validity has not been diminished in the wake of the many and wise innovations in method and terminology introduced by current work in narratology. But at the same time such indications offer a plot made precisely in order to be submitted to contestation, fracturing, suppressions. This plot is useful, finally, because various parts can be negated and canceled, but with the consolation prize that we periodically see a reflowering of that which in a previous phase seemed to have been made utterly obsolete.

Naturally, it is not the task of the present work to offer a faithful, or even minimally exhaustive, retracing of the thousands of transformations undergone in the course of history by the map of narrative genres. We propose simply to furnish a synchronic account of the principal problems and of the possible responses, limiting ourselves to the unravelings, the bifurcations, the openings that lead to various possibilities, without, however, going down any of these lateral paths. Let us be clear that these paths do not merely open up through the intervention of innovations dependent on artistic-literary work; this work interferes continually with every other aspect of culture belonging to a certain arc of time. In turn, this culture is articulated at various levels and in various sectors (basic technology, scientific research, common sense sayings, and so on). For example, the treatment given literature in Aristotle's *Poetics*, a work embedded in a culture that was largely capable of writing, pays tribute to an earlier, oral phase of poetry. This explains the juxtaposition of examinations of the genres dedicated to reading alone (the epic) and the genres destined for the stage (tragedy and comedy). Because the subsequent centuries, at least within Western culture, saw the persistent predominance of writing until its unequaled growth in the modern age thanks to the Gutenberg revolution, we are accustomed to a split between the two fields of narrative and performative-dramatic literature. Even the present treatment depends on such an attitude, as it reflects a fact of culture and not any intrinsic nature of the genres. We will speak of tragedy and comedy when we arrive at our examination of the *performance* arts, of drama, in the next section, and this discussion is merited, even if the existence of today's electronic media has reopened the possibility that such a rigid separation might no longer be acceptable. We could then proceed to a classification of the arts that might include the various threads of mythopoesis, adding even those that today are entrusted to the media of film and television.

We also know that the epic poem, appointed to preeminence by Aristotle according to the model of the customs of his time, lost its primacy over the course of the centuries. *Mythos*, which Aristotle delegated to a somber use in order to privilege the epic (and the proverbial connections of the unity of time, place, and, especially, action), has known periods of wild proliferation, as it is particularly favorable to primordial and popular storytelling. The Middle Ages saw an inordinate interest in the courtly cycles, or rereadings of the ancient cycles, but with the obsessive multiplication of peripatetic moments, even within the confines of such forms; and because the epic sui generis was continued primarily in the nascent Romance languages, it was linked to the concept of *romanzo* (romance, novel) and destined to see monumental developments. Yet historically and in current usage, the term "novel" signifies the fantastic proliferation of the elements of plot, perhaps with a connected diegetic intrigue. Even *ethos* underwent a process of augmentation during such historical phases, but in a direction primarily opposed to that of the *romanzo*, such that in any case it was brought out from the tempered equilibrium of Aristotelian poetics. Perhaps as early as Boccaccio, at the border between the Middle Ages and the modern age, Western culture, on the verge of instituting a so-called bourgeois economy founded on the systematic exploitation of commercial and productive activities soon to be entrusted to machines, inaugurated a notable capacity for the analysis of individual and collective behavior. From that moment on, in a long tradition culminating in nineteenth-century realism, the *ethos*, that is, the examination of the psychosocial depth of characters, accompanied by large descriptive passages dedicated to the natural and social environment, decisively takes up a primary position in the general economy of narrative. These descriptive passages seem to have been a response to the needs of modern bourgeois culture to comprehend the scenes in which it wages its own battles for the conquest of power. Perhaps this rich component of introspective analyses and environmental descriptions is exactly where "myth" and diegesis come to be linked in an instrumental role so that they can furnish the occasions to develop their relative interests. In other words, this "poem" best corresponds with the dominant definition of *romanzo*, at least in the areas of Romance languages. The Anglo-Saxon domains, however, remain faithful to the etymological distinction, and so by "romance" these languages continue to designate products rich with mythical and diegetic invention, while for other types they prefer the term "novel." Returning, then, to the Romance languages, we find that the word "novella" is closer to the etymological root. It has come to mean a fact so "new," bizarre, and eccentric that it merits some "historical" recognition, even here in the etymological definition of this term, the equivalent of an ocular testimony: a fact or circumstance so narrow that it cannot be furnished with the typical features of a true and proper poem, scarcely creditable, then, either by "myth" or by characters in the round.

But certainly the term "narrative" contributes to a unification of these various genres, even giving rise to a discipline that is specifically directed to such a study, that is, narratology, as we mentioned earlier. Even in the Anglo-Saxon world a unifying term—*fiction*—appears in library catalogs or in the classifications of publishers. This term is also derived from Latin, *fingere*, with which we designate the symbolic dimension we have called essential to "myth" itself, an image of the development, of the intersection of the facts of life, but precisely an image, redone in a suspended space, reflecting on lived experience although not immediately confluent with it. This is also the concept that Aristotle groups under the rubric of mimesis.

Our present age has experienced a grave disturbance in the map of the narrative genres, produced by various factors, including technology, which sees the destruction of the primacy of writing and, consequently, of silent reading. Today the fruits of mythopoesis are reaped, for the most part, through the vehicles of mass media, at least in the sense that these are concerned with "public" means destined for some collective enjoyment (cinema, television). This has clearly led to a reevaluation of the "mythical," interweaving components brought out from the half-hidden oral-popular-folkloric tradition to which they had been relegated by the "modern" centuries, dominated by the primacy of literacy (although already in the nineteenth century there was an imposing phenomenon of the *feuilleton*, of the so-called appendix novel that sought to reconcile a background of luxuriant popular imagination with a system of distribution characterized by the industrial modes of the printing press). We could also mention the evident crisis of the wise "ethical" and descriptive analyses that had characterized the modern novel from Boccaccio through Manzoni and Balzac. In other words, contemporary culture must confront an ethics and a psychology (that is largely psychoanalysis), and so also a *dianoia*, all of which appear as essentially different from such manifestations in the previous century. And so we find contemporary narrative attempts disquieting; every aspect of them is charged with some crisis of plot or psychic depth. The behavior of characters may be "opened," little by little, as they discover the presence of the unconscious in themselves. Descriptive techniques must adjust to these changed needs, and so they strive toward forms of perplexed inquiry, or a faithful recording of a similarly fluid set of techniques (interior monologue, stream of consciousness, dream sequences, and so on). Or we may begin to ask if it might not be better to reduce, to flatten the depth of the characters in order to make room, as in the archaic and medieval periods, for an inordinate complexity of plot, even making use of multiple techniques. What we find then is the triumph of the *romance*, but in a sophisticated new key, conducted as if in a laboratory. Finally, we ask whether the narrative genre of the novel still has validity, if it should not be channeled into a more vast production of literary texts, canceling the distinctive traits that, in other times, existed among the lyric and mythopoetic components, especially considering that these latter appear by now largely as features of cinema and television, meaning that the producer of literary texts must specialize in sophisticated operations. The same could be said for the visual artist (as we will see), who by now has left the faithful mimicry of reality to the photographer and the cinematographer, and instead turns toward boldly autonomous elaborations.

Music

The other significant field of artistic production related to sounds and immersed in the dimension of time, is that of music. In chapter 2 we already initiated a comparison and contrasting of music and literature. Literature has consistently moved away from its initial origins in the flow of sound. The capacity, the right and responsibility, to revive acoustic values already established and calculated by an author is left up to the reader, who, in general, prefers to undertake a silent reading. Two categories of factors determine this procedure. First, the impact of the forms of writing, of graphic notation, becomes both enormous and oppressive during the "modern" centuries since the revolution of the Gutenberg Galaxy. At the extreme, we have seen almost a genetic mutation of literary expressions, which seem to assume the nature of facts of a visual order such that these expressions are consumed in the silence of one's own room. A similar mutation has influenced, above all, the long, mythopoetic genres in which, as we just mentioned, the values of the *lexis* appear less decisive. In the lyric genres, however, signifiers preserve a greater weight, and so it remains true that the best means of exploiting signifiers is presented by a performance, an oral recitation, perhaps ensured by the professional competence of an actor so that, finally, the ancient oral matrix of the work remains present and active. Even in the case of the long, narrative genres, recent technological innovations that have seen storytelling possibilities increasingly entrusted to various means of tremendous richness, including those of the "spoken," have undergone a significant disturbance even to the point of placing the very survival of such genres in jeopardy. Silent reading, although it persists in the case of long poems, is increasingly threatened by strong competition from oral and performatory forms.

The other factor that influences silent reading concerns the very diffusion of the linguistic means, the communicative channel, which, as we know, is valid not only for artistic ends, but also, and in even greater measure, for scientific ends or for daily communication in the field we have designated as common sense. This factor constitutes a widely diffused instrument, which has even provoked its differentiation from national languages and, gradually, from dialects and local idioms. It is an instrument of an eminently practical nature, and each community has attempted to shape it according to its own desires and capabilities. This has also led to the profitability of literacy, although even this is rather limited, especially in other periods of time, and, in any case, is linked to social assets (literacy has always come easier to the leisure classes than to the lower classes in general) as well as to technological factors (the press has substantially increased the possibility of learning to read and write). To sum up, we find that vast social strata, from our own times but also in a more or less recent past, have been in a position to avail themselves of silent reading, thus facilitating the assignment of literary works to the medium of printed books (until the current impact of the technetronic age has placed all of this in question again).

Even musicians have been quick to embrace the possibility of entrusting their compositions to graphic symbolism in order to increase the potential for their survival and preservation, and we have witnessed the opening of the vast chapter of "musical notation." In many respects, this is not much different from the kind of notation made by the literary writer; musical notation particularly resembles phonetic writing in that a graphic symbol corresponds to a clearly ascertained sound, determined by precise scientific prerequisites such that the symbol binds every process (whether vocal or instrumental) directed toward reviving it. Even in musical notation, the individual graphic symbols (commonly called "notes") are only abstractions, as they must be considered in the context of various connections, of the syntagmas according to which they are ordered and carried out. But here all similarities end because the graphic systems of musical notation, unlike phonetic writing, only serve an expressive, artistic field, despite their usual extension to a vast artistic quality, indistinguishable from the areas reserved for entertainment, for pleasurable and gratifying consumerism. These systems of notation do not, however, serve either the broader aims of practical communication or those specialized and rigorous aims of scientific communication. They are preserved, then, from the phenomenon of diversification into natural languages. In this sense, they have the status of conventional languages, established by a community of professionals who recognize themselves as existing above and beyond possible ethnic, geographical, or linguistic confines. The troubling phenomenon of linguistic diversity with its related obligation of translations is not opened in this way, but this specialist status of notation does favor a sort of laziness, or at least renders the labor of learning scarcely remunerative. To put it plainly, only a small number of individuals, even among those who are provided with a good dose of general cultural preparation, can make use of the capacities to "read" music, and so this mental operation, effected in silence and privately, is rather rare. Moreover, such an activity also appears unproductive or ungratifying because musical expression decisively aims toward aesthetic areas, and so also aims to live again in the fullness of sensory values, in the reconstruction of elapsed time. Even the literary work (whether brief or long) has its own internal time, its context in which the sequence of motifs of waiting or relaxation, of tension and release, emerges as carefully calculated by the author and linked through the reader, who must reconstitute the sequence during the individual reading experience. But we can easily concede that this ideal time is entrusted to a free reconstruction. No one reads an entire novel in one sitting. More frequently, we take up a book, time and time again, over a period of hours, days, months, or sometimes even years, but always with the obligation to reconstruct in our memory the proper sequence, the internal time, that must be present in its totality when we arrive at the moment of forming a judgment about the entire work.

In the case of the musical composition, we cannot concede so easily this faculty for private execution and reconstruction. Only professionals in the field possess the necessary technical capacity, but even they, if they were to undertake a private and imaginary execution, would lose something along the way. From an individual reconstruction there springs a sort of duplication that influences the musical work much more than the parallel case of the literary work. It is almost necessary that the existence of a composition, conceived by the author and entrusted by this same individual to some system of graphic notation (which can then intersect with various phenomena of reproduction, printing, and multiplication that are themselves rather irrelevant), be supported by the fact that here and there, in space and in time, there will be executions or performances, whether instrumental or vocal, of which the primary responsible actor could be the very author. In the history of music, composers quite frequently and practically inevitably are also executors, not only of their own pieces but of those composed by others. The professional identification of the two roles is valid for music even more than for literature.

Yet for centuries, even for millennia, this "double" interpretive-executive role of musical compositions could not be preserved, except in the memory of the artists' contemporaries and in their chronicles or historical testimonies—but, once again, translated into writing. This lack of preservation persisted until the technetronic age furnished us with the record player and other forms of tape recording so that the dimension of sound was able to "remain" and actually add itself to an existing body of graphic notation. The two souls of the musical product came to obtain a parity of status, and then, at this point, one could witness the obsolescence of the graphic version of notation. Without a doubt notation becomes the less pertinent of the two musical "forms," it seems to respond to an inept attempt at genetic metamorphosis from the acoustic nature of musical experience to a visual one. The visual enters into a useful relation with certain characters of acoustic experimentation of our own times, directed toward sampling the recourse to sounds of physical properties that are not easily certifiable and repeatable, linked to a single production, here and now, which greatly diminishes the possibility of recourse to graphic symbols. In the extreme case, the musical-acoustic experience lives only in the moment of its actuation and in the recordings yielded by the high-fidelity reproductions of current technology. The graphic score becomes superfluous or, more precisely, impossible, in the attempt to follow the new "noise" frontiers opened by contemporary work in the field.

Before the mental openness of our times, legitimately supported by the extraordinary means of recording, allowed us to enjoy these more ample and free adventures in sound (or better, in "noise," as it has been known since the futurists), for centuries musical composition preferred to work with pure sounds, according to physical prerequisites well defined by convention, so that the sounds were made to correspond with equally well defined graphic symbols and could be reproduced through instruments, also furnished with preestablished characteristics.

The Visual Arts

After the arts of sound with their adjunct dimension of time, we should now concentrate on those relevant to sight, whose constitutive dimension (the a priori synthetic form, to use the Kantian term) is space. In this case the fundamental technical modality brought to bear resides in a graphic or chromatic trace on some supporting material or canvas. Here we also have the first technical possibility for recording and preserving offered to humans or, better, of the first symbol system in which the enormously economic material intervention of some minuscule entity allows us to question concepts, circumstances, and general modalities of action. At the same time, in order to facilitate the task of recording ideas and facts, humans have always employed symbols, which, in turn, fit perfectly into the area of cultural objects (that is, of those prostheses, those extraorganic additions not connected with organic equipment). Throughout the history of humanity, the symbols of a graphic order, among these prostheses, among these discharges of external cognitive material, were the symbols most quickly introduced. These symbols essentially consist of certain physical acts directed toward engraving or scraping away at external supports (tree trunks, cave walls, the surfaces of stones). For many centuries, symbolism of a graphic nature, and so necessarily of a visual nature (the eyes are the inevitable intermediary, the door to our faculties of understanding), has assumed the burden of recording and preserving the artistic facts of the acoustic, literary, and musical fields, at least until the electronic revolution furnished us with instruments capable of recording even sounds (the spoken word, or musical values). Both writing and musical notation constitute systems of a graphic-visual nature unto themselves. If we then introduce the idea that, originally, the earliest forms of writing were ideographs, and these have remained in the language of many cultures (including the most developed, such as those of the Far East), we find that truly, in a primordial sense, there existed one, undifferentiated channel in which the graphic symbol collected ideas and images linked in a single node. But then phonetic writing developed, and following this, "letters" took on an increasingly specialized function in the connotative processes directed toward the meaning of signifieds, abstract notions, without any further need for visual mediation except for the minimal amount relative to the decoding of the individual letters themselves. For the signifieds of meaning, the intrinsic modalities according to which the letters are traced seem unimportant, and, in fact, it is better to neutralize them even if a certain level of beauty persists in how writing is laid down, at least if this happens through a manual act (chirography). But generally the visual arts, or else certain recent tendencies directed toward retrieving the totality of the aesthetic-artistic act by overcoming the division between the various arts, may take on those immanent values of *ductus*.

Let us resolutely begin down the path of ideographic symbols, so to speak, leaving phonetic writing to the universe of letters. This path finds itself fundamentally obliged to confront the disparity between objects, the circumstances to which it means to refer, the real occasions of existence, expanded for the most part in the three dimensions of space and almost always provided with movements, kinetic effects. We must confront the necessity that signifiers or graphic traces always be infinitely simplified and reduced, conforming to the essential prerequisite of economy. In fact, the symbol only exists if the signifier, the physical entity of which it makes use, appears to be easy to make, if it presents properties that are equally satisfying with regard to preservation and transportation. To sum up, it must be a portable, comfortable, manageable tool. In general, such prerequisites are assured by a two-dimensional support, while in light of these general ends of economy, recourse to some plastic, three-dimensional object already appears less valid. Certainly, this would impose fewer sacrifices, inasmuch as three-dimensionality might reproduce the volume of persons and things under examination, but it requires a more exhaustive elaboration and presents notable problems for its own preservation. In any case, a natural bifurcation appears here between the two-dimensional work of art (painting, design) on the one hand and, on the other hand, three-dimensional objects (sculpture), with the possibility of numerous intermediary and mixed genres (low relief, and even collages, *assemblages*, "environments").

Both the two-dimensional supports and the materials for the realization of plastic works have varied ad infinitum throughout the course of history, and they certainly will continue to do so. This variation will also give rise, as we have just suggested, to a rich spectrum of reciprocal hybridizations. The factors involved in this variation should be sought in the general conditions of culture over time, including broadly available technological possibilities.

As for the two-dimensional supports, we are in murky waters in the case of graffiti or so-called prehistoric painting, until the light surface offered by an adequately prepared canvas mounted on a frame, which has come to constitute the privileged means of support for a great part of the history of Western painting in its modern phase, that is, from the seventeenth through the nineteenth centuries, with a notable capacity for survival even into our own century. This privilege is increasingly threatened and questioned within the forms of painting itself. Nevertheless, until recently, the canvas had been sufficient to excite the temptation to identify the use of this sort of support, familiarly called a "square" (*quadro* means "square," but also "painting," in Italian), with the general characteristics of a visual work of art. Even today, many would be ready to swear that "painting" is essentially identified with *quadri* or paintings on canvas, but this amounts to a totally discounted and improper simplification. Usually, we have no difficulty in identifying the technological factor that has contributed to the imposition of the privileging of "painting," that is, of the image painted on a canvas of a rectangular format, perhaps riveted in a frame, ready to be exposed on a wall and to be "read" with a gaze that travels in a perpendicular line. Such an apparatus of elaboration and use is perfectly homologous with the page of a printed book. A convincing parallel can be made between the birth and the diffusion of the Gutenberg Galaxy and the fortune of painting itself, that is, a picture in oils on a canvas for the presentation of illusory and naturalistic images. With the collapse of the supremacy of printing in movable type, we witness a parallel shift toward visual art intent on exploiting different supports and techniques.

It is well known that all symbols are two-faced. After a reference to the problems that concern the face of signifiers or, rather, the material supports, now let us turn to the face that presents more complexities, at least in terms of the theoretical questions that are raised, relating to signifieds. In other words, how do we reduce, how do we represent three-dimensional reality on the two-dimensional surfaces of the graphic-pictorial plane, or on the plastic elements of sculpture, which are themselves simplified and economical? Even this is primarily a cultural problem of a general sort, rather than one specifically concerning the arts, given that, as we have already said, graphic symbols share with the acoustic symbols of language the property of introducing a single channel for practical-common functions as well as scientific and artistic ones. But the symbolic, acoustic systems of which music avails itself avoid any enormous assumption of responsibility that might be attributable to widespread usage. The utility value of representing real facts on a "comfortable" support and on a reduced scale by recourse to the opportune tricks assuring a certain degree of responsiveness (analogy, conformity, isomorphism, and so on) between that which is represented (existing in all its immensity and complexity) and graphic signifiers (or even chromatic and plastic ones) presents itself in numerous areas of human action. Many opportunities in practical, everyday life lead us to make sketches or maps, or form shapes without much concern for the modality engaged or for any internal coherence. We can easily locate Della Volpe's notion of an equivocal discourse (or text) in such cases. Or rather, there are scientific (geographical, topographical, planimetric, architectural, urban, cadastral) needs in which the recourse to representation must avail itself of univocal criteria that are both clearly established and equal for all users. Finally, we should address artistic representation where organic contextual factors may intervene even without belying the adhesion to representative systems inherent in the culture and shared by both the artist and the public, and where signifiers themselves acquire value by begging to enter into the overall judgment. Establishing how the graphic lines and connected chromatic elements are traced is thus also important.

We might say that a certain modality of perspective nearly always enters into play in the recourse to symbolic, two-dimensional visual systems. The word "perspective" derives from the Latin *perspicere*, to see through, to see from a distance, and thus it is the first necessity on which our very act of perception rests (which is itself, according to its etymology, a *capere*, a grasping, in spite of distance, to make present here, within reach, whatever in terms of real existence stands there, without betraying this interval of separation). Naturally, there have been many different forms of perspective throughout history, and in fact each cultural phase produces its own. Each culture institutes forms, or records the coexistence of waxing and waning systems, in step with the latest developments of technology. Already the first intervention of a graphic trace or a chromatic blot on a surface may be said to generate a system of perspective, however rudimentary, at least for the human eye whose physiological response protracts itself into perception and knowledge. And so we find ourselves, once again, at the border between generic sign function and symbolic function: the animal, when facing a graffito inscribed on a rock, does not "read," its eye does not "execute" the rhythmic games, the alternating movements that lead to distinguishing that which is enclosed within the outlines from that which is not. The human eye, however, grasps the symbol from the first moment, that is, it distinguishes the shape of a bull and a deer, for example, from the surrounding background. Already this is a form of perspective, dependent on the capacity of our perception to form graphisms and to complete them in a dynamic sense, helping them to close and to open, to delimit planes, and then to graduate them according to a back-and-forth rhythm, as the psychology of perception will prove when it becomes a science.

In chapter 2 we refuted the claim that iconicity, that is, the correspondence between signifier and signified at a visual level, in the image, is something categorically inherent in the signifier itself, like that which, in language, links the grapheme with the phoneme, the written letter with the spoken sound. There is nothing analogous in a visual field; the various historical perspectives we can name are closer to codes, something like the Napoleonic Code, prescriptive in the sense of law. The only valid point is the possibility of an adequate (linguistic) description directed toward codifying exactly a certain praxis to which we have recourse in a determinate cultural situation in order to confront and resolve the "mystery" of the more or less conformist and faithful reduction of that which lies in a body of graphic-chromatic or plastic interventions. Obviously, after having been exemplified in the dominant practices, this descriptive code in turn assumes the character of a binding prescription for all the members of that culture (similar in this way to the language discussed by Ferdinand de Saussure, provided with a strong institutional value and prescriptive in terms of the speaking subject).

Only at this point does the space for the specificity of the artistic intervention open up. The artist (sculptor, painter) is one who accepts the perspective of his or her time and actually contributes to its imposition, or institutes limits to it and becomes dedicated to invalidating it, attempting to constitute new perspectival possibilities. Finally, what really matters are the "manual" modalities by which the general code is "executed," making it relevant, endowing it with a sensory incarnation.

Representation and Expression

Perhaps at this point it would be a good idea to interweave the idea of representation with that of expression, even if only to accentuate the apparent opposition between the two. Representation, it has been said, is the task of making present in a reduced and comfortable format the vastness of the real; expression, according to its etymology, literally signifies to press, to crush something in order to extract the juice or essence from it, as in the low-vernacular word "to squeeze." There is a false or improper belief that some act of self-squeezing is enacted by the artist, and from this it follows that the field of the expressive corresponds to the dimension of subjective interiority, as opposed to the exteriority of the real world from which "impressions" come. According to this formulation, we really have two movements: expression, deriving from the internal toward the external, and impression, the reverse of this process. But on closer inspection, the two movements are inseparable; they do yield without some consequence to the opposite sign, or, to put it another way, they also have a bipolar nature, like so many of the phenomena we have encountered. Let us even admit that graphic symbolism, rather than moving from an intention to "represent" the external world by signing a declaration of dependence with it, moves boldly to extricate emotions, affects, internal drives; but in the very act of extrication, in the placing of black on white, form on form, it cannot avoid offering itself to spectators who are endowed with "impressions" coming from the external world and so are motivated to identify certain equivalents of everyday phenomena from the public sphere in those apparently autonomous expressions. In addition, because it is quite difficult to separate the internal from the external, our "inside" incessantly feeds on the "outside," chewing it up and then spitting it out, exactly as in the act of breathing where the air that now is in my lungs had, a moment earlier, rested in those of the surrounding public.

In particular, as far as visual artistic experience goes, representation and expression cannot help but intersect, inasmuch as even the painter, like every other artist, in order to be recognized as such in the fullest sense of the word, must engage in some totalizing (contextual, organic) activity containing *motion*, *teaching*, and *delectation* in equal proportions. The artist exploits the descriptive-perspectival code offered in a given historical period in order to "express," that is, to trace outlines or shapes through the filter of his or her own emotions, and by making evident or accentuating, while avoiding the kind of univocal, depersonalized impassivity characteristic of the graphic-scientific. Borders, diagrams, shapes, and so on will be proposed in "ambiguous" ways, alluding to various experiences. This also means that the objects and circumstances of everyday experience will be "squeezed" to yield a dense and polymorphous juice.

These considerations will serve to accentuate the contrast that otherwise might arise between so-called figurative artistic tendencies and other nonfigurative ones—what are also called, more crudely, abstract, or, more precisely, nonobjective or "concrete" tendencies. The two sides of the opposition should rather be seen as the terminal points of a continuous scale that allows many intermediary positions, and that in any case contemplates the coexistence and prerogative of both types in both solutions. Thus figurative styles cannot lack abstraction as long as the term "abstraction" is taken in its etymological sense, signifying extraction, placing into evidence, choosing. We began with the admission that, given the split between existing objects and symbolic representations, each one of these cannot help but base itself on the selection of traits. This selection, in turn, is conducted according to the descriptive codes assumed by the historical era from which a given work of art arises. Even so-called realist works rely heavily on conventions and symbolism, and we know that animals placed in front of images obtained through specular mimetic systems (images reflected in a mirror or reproduced with photochemical processes or artistic techniques indebted to these systems of "high fidelity") remain utterly indifferent. The image fails to give off any perceivable properties for the animal. Thus there is no difference in substance or nature between the largely schematic styles that we find in archaic cultures, prior to the rise of "modernity," and those that we define as realist or naturalist, which belong to the later, classical eras. The difference resides in cultural organization within the general parameters around which the entire social cycle is based.

The archaic phases of humanity preferred stylization, as we know, and they represented depth, in general, by superimposing nearer bodies on farther ones. Later the convention of oblique lines was introduced in order to suggest a sense of depth. Yet until the dawn of the modern age, during the first decades of the fifteenth century, artists were unaware of the expedient of making lines that would in reality be parallel, but would, on the canvas, then converge in what would be called a vanishing point. Classical, Greco-Roman antiquity did not practice such a linkage; it is thus primarily an invention of modernity, and does not appear at all natural. It depends on particular optical conditions that are highly artificial, the first of them being the single, stationary vantage point. This type of perspective works as if we were looking at the external world not through two eyes and two retinas, two reflecting spheroid and rather extended bodies, but through a single entry hole for visual rays. It is as though no psychic correction intervened with what are purely optical responses. The fact is that knowledge acquired earlier, or, more simply put, the a priori forms of visibility, mold our retinal reflexes. So-called Renaissance perspective, instituted by Italian and Flemish artists during the first decades of the fifteenth century, is thus a rather arbitrary and partial construction—in fact, it was unknown until that historical moment, although from time to time antiquity had raised questions about the recourse to oblique convergence toward the background or the foreground.

The modern age can also be called the age of the machine, because it ushered in that powerful machine used to transmit information, the movable-type printing press (Gutenberg typography). Analogously, the same age saw the invention of perspective, that is, the ideal machine for representing three-dimensional reality with the greatest degree of rigor and conformity in a way that anticipates the photographic camera, which would arrive on the scene approximately four centuries later. We are talking here about the long lapse of time during which Western culture rose to power, and then adapted itself to its own schemes, until it mistook that which was invented by its own protagonists for the natural result of organic perceptual faculties. Therefore, one among the many symbolic forms introduced gradually by humanity, that is, the perspective of Masaccio and Leon Battista Alberti and Dürer, became "the" system of perspective par excellence, taken as the correct, natural system for representing nature.

But then the contemporary age, in which we still live, deinstitutionalized similar dogmatic certainties. In great measure this can be attributed to a student of Cassirer and his philosophy of symbolic forms, namely the art historian Erwin Panofsky, who in a lucid essay in 1927 demonstrated how Renaissance perspective was only one among various possible systems. This assertion came at a time when contemporary art had already been experimenting with other representational systems for at least half a century, retrieving older modalities dear to the various archaic eras, which had inaugurated nonrepresentational modes, that is, "concrete," nonobjective ones. These changes resonated with the large technological changes of this time—the gradual replacement of the civilization of machines driven by thermal energy with the derivations of electromagnetism and electricity—and the changes coming about in the field of scientific research.

Expressive, nonmimetic styles had not been lacking in the past; abstract-geometrical solutions, or those constituted by graphic or chromatic "concretizations" with no clear relation to external bodies, were accompanied for centuries or even millennia by various more or less stylized or abstract forms of naturalism. But in the median area of the scale, the respective systems became confused, and the result included works of such a stylized naturalism that they yielded a certain "concreteness," or total plastic autonomy, a pure *fabula de lineis et figuris*. Yet even works given over to this criterion did not avoid the suggestion in a given beholder of the general structures of experience. We might think of one of the most extreme and heroic examples of concrete art in the early twentieth century, the pure surfaces created by the Dutchman Piet Mondrian, constructed according to horizontal-vertical schemes of few areas, painted in "primary" colors (red, yellow, blue). Someone once observed that such a reduced and essential grid is the representation of space as experienced particularly by the Dutch, in a low-lying landscape composed of flatland and sea, where, thus, the horizontal dimension remains dominant, interrupted only by a few vertical lines of trees and man-made structures (towers and windmills, which served as a basis from which Mondrian was then able to "abstract" his pure rhythms, only to propose them again later as decisively self-founded concretizations).

One could also say (along with Panofsky) that there is a substantial difference between figurative art and concrete or nonobjective art, inasmuch as the former permits two levels of reading and the latter only one. In fact, figurative works contain some illustrative content that is also shared by scientific systems of representation peculiar to a determinate era. ("Illustration" was also the term used by Bernard Berenson in opposition to "decoration" with regard to the autonomous and intrinsic aspects of art.) It is thus possible to describe in rather objective terms which figures and actions are narrated in a work, and then to draw a conclusion from this with public parameters corresponding to the knowledge of the period in question. Such a study of images, of the "icon" as such, gives rise to iconography and iconology, the disciplines in which Panofsky distinguished himself after an early phase in which he was closely linked to Cassirer and to the problems of space understood as a particular symbolic form belonging to an entire culture. So we open a field of interdisciplinary interests in which historians of art are asked to collaborate with historians of ideas, of scientific, religious, mythical, astronomical thought, and so on, in a fascinating intersection of expertise. But certainly we are talking specifically about art when we turn to technical questions of "how" figures are produced, even within the parameters common to the general knowledge of an era; hence the resurfacing of expression, of the interventions of the "hand" according to which the artist has accentuated or brought into relief profiles, shapes, thicknesses of things and persons, and senses of distance, heaviness, and lightness. And so we return to the sphere of organic contextual values proper to each work of art. But at such a level of analysis, there is no longer any difference between a "figurative" product and one, perhaps in the same historical period, that renounces the plane of icons and entrusts itself only to aspects of concrete composition. According to Berenson, we should say that in such a case the artist renounces "illustration" in favor of "decoration." For this reason, conversely, even where the self-sustained aspects of decoration seem to triumph, as happens in so many "concrete" styles of our own age, there is still a collusion with the opposing criterion of illustration, given that even in cases of this type the expressive systems adopted by a given artist have many traits in common with the conceptions developed contemporaneously by science. The various manifestations of concrete art of the twentieth century are incomprehensible without reference to the diagrams and schemes used to visualize the movements of the atom, electronic orbits, wave phenomena, or, in another direction, without those marvels of the "slide," the biological cultures brought to light thanks to the electronic microscope. Today we could also add to this list the applications of wave and particle theories, prolific producers of magnificent phosphorescence.

Reproduction and Multiplication

In the visual arts the prerequisite organic relation between the two faces of the symbol—the physical one of signifiers and the ideal one of signifieds—is even more important than in the artistic fields already examined (literature and music). As we have seen, the other two arts make use of symbolic devices that are for the most part heterogeneous in terms of their primary consistency, that is, their acoustic nature. For this reason, the graphic transcriptions of these symbols truly enjoy an economic-utilitarian weight, whereas in the visual arts the relationship is one of homogeneity, suggesting movements, effects, and affects of a spatial and visual nature, truly dependent upon means that can, in turn, be called spatial-visual. Only with great difficulty can the painter and sculptor entrust to others the tasks of recording or technical expression of their work. They must personally choose colors and materials, tools, and the supports on which the work will be mounted. All of this implies the learning of an exact craft that remains complex and difficult even today, when the aids furnished by the external technical-industrial system are significantly greater than in past centuries.

Yet we live in what Walter Benjamin called the "age of mechanical reproduction" of images, even at the cost of dissolving the very intimate relation between the physical and virtual levels that would give rise to what the German thinker calls an "aura," a sacred sense of "holistic" presence, of the uniqueness of a work of art. Upon closer examination, however, this disappearance of the aura, of uniqueness, takes place in two entirely different ways, one truly attributable to technological factors, the other, persisting *ab antiquo* and only intensified by the new possibilities offered by our age. This means that it is worthwhile to distinguish between the reproduction of the work and its multiplication in models, according to a process that is more or less directly controlled by the "author."

The first, the reproduction of the work, is extrinsic to the work itself, and in relation to the work it is a utilitarian and didactic, even if highly relevant, aid. It consists of photographic reproduction (and later also cinematic and electronic reproduction, and even reproduction by the hybrid procedure of photolithography, where the continuity of the image is "read" and decomposed according to a retina that oversees the constitution of a typographical matrix). Such a procedure can represent a solid technical understanding of the work and be conducted with a high degree of accuracy and still manage to betray the original expression, that "synolon" (substance) elaborated, conceived, and conducted by the artist. In fact, the support (whether canvas, paper, and so on) disappears. In general, even the format is reduced, and so the single effects of a particular hand are flattened and diminished. If we must lament the disappearance of the original, of the work "in flesh and blood," strengthened by the pigments or the materials directly treated by the artist, the loss would be grave and incalculable. It would be grave, even though we must admit that the general information concerning the corpus of artistic masterpieces preserved in the world's museums today is, for the most part, entrusted to that crowd of surrogates furnished by textbooks, journals, monographs, or films, and now even videocassettes, even if we must recognize the strong impact that this presence of reproductive systems is making on creativity itself as exercised by individual artists. One finds more and more frequently that these systems inspire a "secondary" level of images entrusted to the retina of the photolithograph, or the "electronic mosaic" of luminous impulses, of the "pixels" that come to constitute electronic reproductions. We could cite here the work of the American artist Roy Lichtenstein, who makes novel use of the usual *pattern* discounted by the retina, bringing it to macroscopic proportions and so making of it a defensive weapon against the propagation of visual stereotypes.

When the multiplication of works is planned by the author, the result is altogether different. In fact, this procedure has existed for millennia and actually constitutes the rule in the materially costly and difficult realm of sculpture, where, above all, the physical level of the symbol must endure insidious climatic assaults if the manufactured article is situated outdoors, exposed to inclement weather. This accounts for the choice of durable materials (marble, metallic links), a practice already prominent in antiquity and then confirmed through the Middle Ages, the modern age, and even today. Confronted with the particularly complex and difficult technological exigencies of fusing parts or of sculpting large marble statuary, the artist concedes him- or herself the luxury of working on a model of reduced size, with full and direct exercise of manual labor, and leaves to competent work- ers, more or less under the artist's control, the procedures of enlarging and fusing, and even, at times, of working the marble on the required scale. Today we add the alternative possibilities furnished by synthetic materials (polystyrene, polyurethane, Plexiglas), which above all allow for over- coming the austerely monochrome character of the earlier "classical" media and permit the artist to imitate the painted surfaces of objects (to include even the "more real than reality" effects such as those offered by the Amer- ican hyperrealists Dwane Hanson and D'Andrea). Now it is even possible for the artist to exploit true and proper industrial procedures, but this dis- cussion will be better saved until later, when we confront the problem of industrial design.

Techniques for multiplying images have existed for centuries even for two-dimensional objects, thanks to printing. The ability of the artist resides in the adequate elaboration of the matrix, and in following, as closely as possible, the very acts of "printing," that is, the acts of pressing paper or other supports onto various templates: acts that, however, can be carried out in the absence of the matrix and even postmortem. As for the matrices themselves, these can be obtained in relief on woodblocks (woodcuts), the oldest printing technique, serving as the basis from which Guten- berg derived his "printing in movable type," destined to revolutionize the whole field of writing and information. In the Renaissance, metallic ma- trices (copper plates) were corroded by acid in areas where the designer's "tip" scratched away a protective layer of wax to allow little furrows to form in which the ink would later be deposited (engraving, chalcographic technique).

At the beginning of the nineteenth century, lithography made its appearance. This technique, the only one that can be clearly identified with a known inventor (Senenfelder), consists in rendering areas of a stone matrix sensitive to ink. Before the invention of photography, these various methods replaced, for the most part, the task of faithful reproduction, and therefore their status remained a step below that of the true and proper work of art. Engravers were minor artists who placed their skill in the service of the formal inventions of a renowned painter in order to popularize masterpieces. But certainly these "reproducers" had ample margins within which to work and were often allowed to "abstract" from the painting they were translating according to rather personal choices. If the techniques used were woodcuts or engraving, the reproducers had to strain their ingenuity in order to find equivalent chromatic, tonal, or chiaroscuro values through almost purely linear elements; lithography, however, allowed them to render pictorial values more adequately. With photographic reproduction came the possibility to create numerous images of a given masterpiece, and so the techniques of printing assumed an autonomous status, that is, they became an artistic medium equal to design and painting, even if on a mercenary level we cannot ignore the fact that the existence of numerous exemplars ("circulation") lowered the price of each in comparison with the price of the unique piece executed by the hand of the artist.

Photography was the earliest, and perhaps the most sensational, of the new technological means brought to bear in modernity, and these oblige us to augment the number of arts (or "muses," as we say, with an obvious metonymic usage of the proper, mythological name in the place of the generic function). In a certain sense, photography sanctified the primacy of the descriptive system chosen four centuries earlier by Western culture; or rather, we might say that when Leon Battista Alberti, writing the *De Pictura* in 1432, spoke of an "open window" framing, or better, cutting, a pyramid of rays so that it yielded one broken ray, in some ways he was anticipating the optical criteria on which the apparatus of the camera is based. Alberti did not possess the technical capacity to make these rays cause photochemical reactions by altering a reflective surface. But the optical principles, and the facilities needed in order to render more rigorous projections (singularity of vantage point, the reduction in size of the aperture), were the same as they are now, and thus there is a strict solidarity between so-called Renaissance perspective and the results obtained by photography. The latter demonstrates, with the force of scientific and technological procedures of the "machines," that the former was correct and anticipated the very responses of nature, when this is "correctly" evaluated. It was the full confirmation of the legitimacy of illusory naturalism institutionalized by the West during the whole modern age that has remained unrecognized by other advanced cultures such as those of the Far East. In effect, there seemed to be a perfect parallel between the early attempts at photography and the axis of realism-naturalism that was then developing, especially in France, set in motion at the triumphant conclusion of impressionism.

Yet precisely because photographic techniques appear destined to assume the burden of the various illustrative tasks in the service of memory, documentation, and entertainment that had been entrusted to the manual, visual arts for so many millennia, these arts are faced with an unexpected freedom to test the potentialities of an abstract-stylized or expressionist character. These arts had already cultivated this freedom in many of their archaic phases. Finally, we come to the great chapter of contemporary art, which in its intense experimentalism generally avoids imitating those earlier solutions of a naturalistic-illusionary sort, especially because of the introduction of alternative technologies for fixing the image—for example, the "screen," which invites us to decompose into tiny particles the continuity of chromatic and chiaroscuro drafts, with a strong harmony compared with painterly divisionism and a surprising anticipation of the "electronic mosaic" that makes television possible. More generally, the great technological and epistemological revolution based on electromagnetism is knocking at the door.

From Photography to Video Recording

Photography, on the one hand, replaces manual techniques such as woodcuts and engraving in the task of furnishing faithful reproductions of preexisting images at a reasonable price, or even in that primary task of reproducing physical reality on paper. But on the other hand photography becomes a field of artistic elaborations, even if these are not entrusted to any direct exercise of manual labor practiced by the artist and are not hidden in the myth of the unique piece of work. In fact, once an impression is made on a plate or on film, it becomes possible and perhaps necessary, out of respect for its status as a matrix, to make copies or further printings of it. But nothing stands in the way of photography's intervening with a series of acts in which we can recognize the topology of every artistic operation, even if filtered through a quite sophisticated technological apparatus. The photographer who is not merely intent on reaching a goal of illustration or practical documentation will be able to play with framing, cutting a scene in odd ways, making eccentric, "useless" croppings. One can also attempt a contextual, organic embrace by including many components of harsh reality (the psychology of human beings; plastic, natural, and artificial material; lighting effects, and so on). Even rhythm or drama can be included, according to how the various motifs are played among themselves, in calculated equilibrium or disequilibrium of mass. We have not even begun to count the numerous other interventions possible in regulating the light or the exposure times. Ultimately a field of autonomous artistry is born, or rather, a new muse, who has now obtained ample recognition through an abundant literature all her own. But we should also remind ourselves that, in turn, the traditional visual artist (the painter or sculptor, according to the usual parameters) may also take control of the photographic means, preparing images of a faithful, naturalistic sort on which to conduct certain conceptual "operations." Photographic techniques can be used to emphasize the aesthetic aspects, taking the word at its most basic etymological significance. Essentially, today we can record the epidermis of things, the grain of fabrics, without any graphic or chromatic mediation, but through the high-fidelity transcription furnished by the photographic eye. A recent phase in our thinking has been characterized by that which was defined as the "death of art," in which the operators in this field decided to renounce traditional pictorial means, availing themselves primarily of the results obtainable through photography, with particular attention to enlargements and prints made on canvas, in such a way as to grant them a certain sense of "aura."

The invention of still photography was quickly followed by a mechanical application that allowed the recording of cinematic effects. Thus we entered the field of cinematography, beginning with a succession of photograms obtained first by manual and then by automatic processes of regular, predetermined velocity. Successive images at fixed intervals are flashed on the retina and, thanks to the well-known physiological phenomenon of the persistence of images, impart the semblance of continuity, of duration. Time has entered the visual field and allowed itself to be "recorded." Until the invention of cinematography, time was an aesthetic value, or perhaps the principal aspect of living existence. It was nevertheless not capable of "remaining" directly, but only through a translation into graphic and spatial forms; ultimately something was lost in the translation, hence the "inferiority" of the arts of time (literature, music) compared with the visual arts. In part this inferiority was redeemed through the recourse to various forms of writing and musical notation, and the impermanence of the arts of time was also the fundamental reason that conferred validity on Lessing's distinction between the arts of space and those of time.

The appearance of cinema problematizes this line of demarcation. This new muse (if used in an artistic way, that is, beyond the enormous advantages it provides for practical and scientific documentation) must be classified in the realm of the visual. In fact, it is through the seen, and all the synaesthetic solicitations linked to this (tactile, plastic), that we enjoy any filmic product at first viewing. In this sense we need only develop the discourse we already conducted for photography: cinema is a medium that helps the visual artist to express, to "press" as effectively as possible, the sensory values of things and of the circumstances of existence, without the abstract mediation of graphic or pictorial media. We might add that in the case of cinema, we finally find those values linked to movement, dynamism, bodies, beauty, flexibility, or the heaviness, solidity, and solemnity of actions. In effect, artists linked to the historical avant-gardes (futurism, dadaism, constructivism) wasted no time at all in grasping the enormous possibilities inherent in the exploitation of those new media, and they used cinematic techniques to produce plastic works imbued with motion: self-propelled sculptures, articulated especially in the two series addressed toward sampling either the possibilities of the inertia of inorganic bodies or the elasticity of organic bodies, of living beings. From this they produced brief films based on the proposition that one could explore the tactile possibilities of the everyday scene. This technical option has also made a comeback in recent years, when, during the 1970s, the "death of art" was declared, and with it, the end of any systematic promotion or fruition of the aesthetic. Instead, artists began exploiting the possibilities of high-fidelity recording furnished by photography and cinema (to say nothing of electronic recording, as we will soon discuss). Many painters abandoned their brushes to become filmmakers, concentrating on short subjects obtained with agile techniques.

But the passage from spatiality to temporality allowed by cinema gave new life to the classic distinction proposed by Lessing. Once cinema found its own direction or sequentiality, it became a highly adept means for the staging of myth or *fabula*, in the largest, Aristotelian sense that we met in our discussion of the literary genres. An enormous territory of artistic practices much more closely linked to dramaturgy than to visuality subsequently developed. It is evident that cinema, understood as the production of feature films, of "stories," and involving a reconstruction of characters, environments, costumes, and so on, largely diverges from the interests of the visual arts.

Let us continue to pursue for a moment the possibilities of high-fidelity recording and of multiplication that have been recently opened up by technological innovations. Along with cinematography, in the past two decades we have seen the possibility of video recording through the television camera, with apparently similar ends (even in video recording, the camera made use of brief sequences to examine aesthetic, tactile values, of the skin, of movement, of reality, avoiding the appearance of myth or narration). Nevertheless, the video recording has offered several advantages compared with cinematic work. It is immediate and specular. The artist can follow the disposition of images on a monitor while experimenting; video does not require long developing and printing times. The logic of the electronic reading of the real is by nature continuous; it does not pass through a sequence of detached photograms that invite us to think in discontinuous terms, as if it were a case of furnishing a collage of materials that are not directly successive. In other words, video shooting is much more favorable to the temporal nature of events because it avoids that degree of artificial and illusory reconstruction that weighs on cinematic editing. The "little screen" is well named: it cuts brief slices of reality and seems better adapted to close-ups or enlargements, the aspects through which we can best perceive "aesthetic values." By contrast, the big screen prefers rich and complex scenes, better adapted for narrative ends. The fact remains that the field of the visual arts, with its museums, private galleries, and markets, has by now been stabilized and enriched by this new muse of video recording, which employs, for the most part, video tapes, that is, brief scenes on "cassettes."

The enormous field of electronics is certainly not reducible to the sole aspect of video recording; rather, video recording constitutes its least innovative expression, a form easily confused with its immediate predecessor, cinematography, losing the specific element that separates the two media. Taken in this sense, electronic reproduction is of a so-called analogue type, meaning that it attempts to reconstruct the continuity of the real as if using a very close-knit "screen": in this way the analogue multiplies the points, the pixels of the electronic mosaic in an attempt to obtain "high definition" effects proper to the photocinematic image, just as the typographical screen does in order to matte the gloss of a good color photo. But these developments can also be considered a betrayal of the specific nature of the electronic mosaic, analogous to the betrayal that we already met in the true and proper mosaics executed in the third or fourth century A.D., during the final season of Greco-Roman classicism or of Hellenism (we might consider as an example the mosaic floors of Piazza Armerina in Sicily), when the number of "tiles" was multiplied to suggest shading and subtle chromatic effects. Much more appropriate is the "abstract" use of the medium during the Byzantine phase of the Ravenna mosaics. In effect, it would be more convenient for the electronic image to allow that loose-knit context of low definition that constitutes its very soul to appear without adornment, so finding a suggestive correspondence either with the ancient mosaics of antiquity and the Middle Ages, or with another mosaic sui generis—pointillism, a late-nineteenth-century movement in painting. Pointillism, like divisionism in Italy, was one of the key chapters in which contemporary art took its leave of modern perspectival illusionism, while still pretending to respect its salient characteristics (this is the reason why these movements, associated with Seurat and others, were also called neo-impressionism).

The electronic image is formed by blips of linear abstraction, of elegant stylization, of recourse to areas of intense chromatics. It is freed from the logic of industrial colors, just as the divisionists wanted to save themselves from the scourges of physical products by aiming at a fusion of tints obtained only on the surface of the retina. An image conceived in this way, thin and abstract in the true sense of the word, can easily be calculated and entrusted to computer programs. With this, then, we move to the great chapter of digital images, artificially reconstructed and not transposed reflectively from reality. Thus we find yet another new muse, computer art, which has enjoyed notable successes in recent years, and which is also the last of the processes of multiplication that we will mention here. Certainly, the artist who chooses to exploit this technological possibility must accept certain sacrifices, given that all expressive forms based on continuity and organicism must be renounced, and the artist moves rather in fields of abstraction or geometrical concretization, directed also toward decorative rather than illustrative ends. Today we have highly refined programs that can even reconstruct the fluid motions of the artist's hand and so are not defeated by organicist solutions of an informal sort. Once the piper of a certain stylization and duration of images has been paid, however, the computer artist enjoys, in exchange, the enormous possibility of conferring kinetic effects on the work, changing colors in order to obtain a perfect wash, staining or hybridizing an image, or even passing easily from two to three dimensions.

The Applied Arts

Until now the continent of the visual arts has been examined in its "highest" zones, that is, where artistic activity is configured as a beautiful or "liberal" art, to return to the definition once offered by Baumgarten: the production of rather refined objects directed toward a primarily unproductive end, for laudable social uses, celebrations, or pure enjoyment. Throughout history this has conferred a precise professional cast on the work of its respective devotees. It becomes difficult to affirm that the thousands of painters, fresco-makers, engravers, sculptors, and so on, who have succeeded one another in time, have all reached a certain critical evaluation, a positive artistic result. What can be stated with certainty is that they have occupied those areas of the career and professionalism from which one may reasonably expect an effective artistic result. This is especially true in our own age, when many of the social tasks usually assigned to the visual arts have fallen or been transferred to photomechanical or electronic techniques. Today, to be a painter or sculptor signifies less and less to belong to a professional union, and more and more to seek out the taxing role of pure artistic endeavor in the search for solutions that may be artistic in the most intense and complex sense of this word. In fact, the painter of our times is either comforted by an adequate critical recognition or appears deprived of social standing. He or she will seek to earn a living by aiming at other functions and offering him- or herself as a teacher, or as a technician for the graphics industry, for example.

This possibility of completely "missing" one's artistic success or the achievement of some aesthetic value is even more troubling for the enormous continent of "art" in the largest and most nearly originary sense of the term. Technique, to use the corresponding Greek word, once occupied the sphere of the useful and was charged with reproducing the necessary instruments for the practical needs of everyday life. This would be the chapter traditionally addressed to the applied arts, in which the aesthetic is added almost parenthetically and does not constitute the primary objective of the productive act, which is to offer us instruments that are reliably and economically functional. This is a question of leaps from the field of common experience to that of science, and technology is nothing more than the bridge constructed between the two shores. But because our conception avoids caesuras and watertight bulkheads, even the aesthetic-artistic experience, in the highest sense of the word, makes its voice heard on the issue, or rather, exercises its own attraction, creates a sphere of influence for its own purposes, while suiting itself to every essential pole of human action. Restated in more traditional terms, during the course of history, artisans asked to forge the equipment for work, for war, or for domestic life have never ceased to feel an obligation toward aesthetic categories (toward the "beautiful," if we wish to use the most conventional vocabulary) and not simply toward those of practical and scientific functionality (which we could also link with the good and the true). By invoking the three traditional categories, our discourse signifies that the artisans in question (woodworkers, carpenters, shoemakers, tailors, and so on) attempted to add some innovation, even within the limits of typical models already amply affirmed through constant use, just as they also sought to enrich the shape of the models themselves through the allocation of a certain degree of decorativeness. They thus conferred their objects with movements that were perhaps not altogether necessary according to purely functional needs, but were such that they avoided boredom and pleasantly aroused the attention of users. Yes, respect for function, but not disjointed from ingenious discoveries, reconciling use with delectation, to invoke the traditional phrasing once again. Perhaps there has always been a risk that the decorative components might appear somewhat artificial and exterior, not terribly well connected with the nexus of functions, but finally this is a common danger along the way to the completion of any work of art, even those that we term "great." In any case, this practice gave rise to a tension between crude and ornate solutions, with the possibility of excesses on either side.

The shift imposed by the industrial revolution, which was founded on machines driven by thermal energy, seemed to change entirely the terms of the question in rather brutal ways, perhaps because, in its initial phase, this shift brought about an unsustainable split between the nude and the ornate. In fact, the new tools conceived for mechanical, industrial production, and then the machines themselves, could not but be planned and executed according to schemes of rigorous functionality, entrusted to geometrical shapes, while the survival of an ornate artificiality, conceived in other times, busied itself with covering structural nudity. This is the time of proverbial artifice, when locomotives were decorated with colonnades and capitals in a Greek style, or when the essential forms of sewing machines were covered with naturalistic vines of a baroque and rococo sort. Another phase follows in which function gains the courage to exhibit itself without further tinsel; and so the season of functionalism is opened, consecrated by the movements of our century, beginning in the thirties (Bauhaus, Russian constructivism) and refined in the so-called modern movement that also invents the motto "less is more," in which the advantage of working by removing is sanctioned, in which the true, the beautiful, and the good are not different categories, but converge, until they can all be identified in a single objective. Against these canons of industrial production carried to its logical conclusions, we find, during the last decades of the nineteenth century, the prediction of someone like William Morris, who attempted to defend common sense, especially in terms of aesthetic and even moral dignity (the good and the beautiful linked) of the system of artisanal production, thereby foreshadowing the various immanent misadventures of heavy industry founded on the civilization of machines (exploitation of the proletariat, division of labor, constraining workers to heavy and repetitive tasks, dangerous divisions between the various human faculties).

Morris's prediction had utopian connotations, and he certainly lost his battle, at least in the short term. Such were the economic, quantitative advantages of industrialism that it was not possible to stop its expansion or impede its becoming the dominant technology, at least until the 1960s; therefore, two centuries of Western civilization recognize themselves in the industrial and conform to its paradigms, which inevitably influenced the other cultures of the world. But it is essential to note that this triumph was accompanied by the introduction of the vast chapter of industrial design, inasmuch as this understood that the following two extremes had to be avoided: continuing to cover the tools of the mechanical revolution with artificial decorations made to order by other eras or, the opposite extreme, abandoning any attempt at ornamentation, making tools linked strictly to the needs of productivity. The designer, who, unlike the artist-artisan, does not "make" with his or her hands, resembles the artist-multiplier who works from a matrix; the difference is that the engraver, lithographer, and photographer are expert in the production of "useless" images of a mimetic type, whereas the designer plans matrices from which to reproduce numerous multiples that are, in turn, of a utilitarian, instrumental sort (from cars to refrigerators to typewriters). The designer is bound to respect the "truth" of function, including all the calculations and instructions furnished by the most advanced technology, to say nothing of the "good" of the various economical necessities, of saving during the course of production. At the same time, the designer is faced with the usual and well-established aesthetic needs: novelty, contextuality, organicism, rhythm, and so we permit him or her to violate strict functionality, to go beyond the nudity of the tool (besides, what does such a phantom essentialism consist of?) by seeking to confer original traits in the determination of line, and by inserting allusions to mythical, religious, or historical motifs. The ingenious, well-designed tool is that which "captures" along its way references to other tools, and thus, imbued with a certain depth, puts our imaginative circuits into operation. The "less is more" credo pronounced by the modern movement seems to be an incomplete and dubious formula, linked to a specific historical period, and perhaps valid in a polemical context in confrontation with whoever pretends to make the "more" consist of exterior ornaments, stolen from preceding cycles. The fact remains that industrial design, even during the most difficult periods in modernity (the triumph of an ideal founded on mechanization), has always attempted to conquer degrees of overabundance or excess, even if in temperate ways, and has always been careful not to go beyond this function.

It is important to remember that the era of "hard" machinery has passed. Today we have seen the triumph of "soft" technologies, in which mechanical production is regulated and controlled by electronics. Products are becoming increasingly specialized, as quantity seeks an equilibrium with quality. This also leads to a strengthening of aesthetic connotations (the unproductive, the playful, the ornamental) of our tools, during an age that identifies itself more or less within the parameters of postmodernism and a post-industrial organization of work and the economy. We have recently seen the resurgence of the artisan values defended with such insistence by Morris; in fact, in keeping with this changed image we speak with great insistence of an "anti-design." The ornate has recorded a consistent victory over the plain.

This general discourse concerning tools, and the possibility and modality according to which even in such a field the categories of the aesthetic-artistic are making strides, will serve as adequate preparation for the place to be assigned to those macrotools that are works of architecture, the most honored among the muses in all times. Textbooks of the history of art usually begin the treatment of the various ages with a chapter dedicated to the respective architectural advances, thus recognizing a certain primacy in this particular figure of the artist compared with colleagues in the so-called major arts, namely painters and sculptors. An architectural edifice is not only a macrotool, but the very place that collects and orders in its internal space the entire network of tools utilized in the life (the culture) of humans. At least, this is the ingenious proposal that comes to us through the classification of the arts traced by Susanne Langer: to order our reflections on architecture by conferring on it, as a characteristic dimension, that of the basic "places," almost in the sense of archetypes, within whose coordinates our existence takes place. The place of the family (the house, the private habitation), that of the "church," that is, of the community that meets for worship and signals a divisive trace (a *templum*) between sacred space and the distracting and profane area of daily life (the place of work, of education, of political debate, and so on).

Once we have recognized the criteria that invite us to confer a maximum of dignity and importance on the macrotool of architecture, we can refer to the numerous reflections already offered for the whole group of macrotools, for the instrumental area that each culture must consider. Throughout its history, architecture has seen various disturbances develop, the attractions of the beautiful (the superfluous, the need for wasteful ornament, for excess, abundance, the inclusion of different functions, of polysemy) along with the more expected dominion of practical and scientific needs. It has even known excursions between the extremes of the plain and the ornamental, between pride and shame with regard to a blatant functionalism. A treatment like the present one cannot push beyond these generic references, for otherwise we would have to deal with the history of architectural styles, and with the fictive narration of their relation with other contemporaneous expressions of art and culture.

"Performance" Arts

Having examined the arts of space and time, we must now turn to those of movement (spectacle, theater, dance, cinema . . .). According to this sort of sequence, it seems as if movement comes after the other two dimensions, or is a result of them, existing in some sort of a dependent relationship. In a certain sense, this is true, even according to a correct physical plan where movement emerges as a dependent function of the independent, larger categories of space and time. But in terms of our general experience, and so also of aesthetic experience, which means to "insist" on this or to conform and adhere to this as much as possible, the relation is actually reversed: the full and contextual exercise of our sensory faculties certainly cannot be separated from movement. Rather, the living body is above all dynamic, the motion of arms, legs, gestures produced by the contraction of muscles and excitations of the nerves. All the other sensory zones should be seen as dependent, as the crowning achievement and integration of a similar primary motion, which can be viewed as the substratum that carries the other zones. Each of these zones consists in turn of minor muscular contractions: we might think of phonation, or even of the adjustment required of the eyes in perception, or of the aspirations necessary for smelling, of the mouth movements required for tasting. If this primacy of movement has not always enjoyed the attention and the dignity it has deserved, this is because of the usual technical reason of an impossibility of preservation.

Most cultures did not possess any legitimate means of "preserving" the values of such a field (just as the analogous possibilities for sounds, tastes, and smells were also missing). Only the graphic-visual channel existed, and this, in turn, was ready to split itself into the two or three parts of writing (in musical notation) and in the mimetic systems entrusted to the various conceptions of perspective. The virtuosity of the gestural artist and of behavior in general has been able to reach us through the rather partial and reductive instrument of linguistic description or graphic and plastic illustration. We had to wait for the introduction of cinema and electronic means, that is to say, until the turn of the century, in order to finally make use of instruments capable of preserving this whole area of values directly, or with a minimum of betrayal. Yet once the capacity for recording was introduced, this field saw an unequaled growth to the point that now it has recovered its deserved status of excellence, of primacy. It is not without reason that ours has been called a society of spectacle, precisely because this notion recognizes the vast degree of diffusion and of memorization that this form of artistry has enjoyed during the twentieth century, such that it has promoted itself as a sort of role model. We can clearly state that today all of the arts tend toward the condition of spectacle, returning to their roots in the movement that has characterized them *ab antiquo*. This, then, signifies that our culture is interested in a general process made possible by technical means that are now finally capable of assuring equal dignity, even in the area of preservation, to aesthetic behaviors. The anthropological condition of the grasshopper (waste, abundance, exploitation of the pleasures of the moment) today has precedence over that of the ant (parsimony, conservation), but this view of the ant was exactly what led us, during all the preceding cultural phases, to privilege a patiently accrued "savings account" of aesthetic values through the difficult exercise of an artistic-artisanal career (the various practices of writing or design).

We might also say that an aesthetic experience in the fullest sense is also a "performance," that is, an offering, a throwing of one's hat in the ring through the entire apparatus of the sensory and cognitive faculties. The athletic "performance" illustrates rather well this intensive sense of the word, even if in this case the task of the subject in question is too firmly linked to merely quantitative aspects (breaking the record, in terms of time and space). In fact, contrary to appearances, the apt English word "performance" is not derived from the root "form," but from a totally different root, that which we find cognate in "furnishing," present in the Romance languages. In particular, Old French (the *langue d'oïl*) made use of *perfurnance*, which then passed into the English word, and, thanks to the phenomenon of the *lectio facilior*, was changed into "performance," with the evident attraction of the better-known "form" (which has conferred rotundity and fascination on the word, contributing to its affirmation on a global scale). But even "to furnish" [*fornire*] responds well to the sense that interests us here. In fact, it is spontaneously coupled with that other word already discussed (so we speak, for example, of an athlete or any operator engaged in giving his or her best as having "furnished us with a good performance"). And how can we forget the Petrarchan "white-haired old man" who moves "from the sweet place which his age has furnished him"? In effect, the first performance to which we are called is to *vivre sa vie*, to survive the existence between birth and death. But this superperformance can be subdivided into smaller slices, although they may be even more harmonic and qualitative.

In any case, it is worthwhile to recall the advantage that Anglo-Saxon culture has assured itself in its insistence on the notion of performance, and its inscription in this term of the whole field of the arts of movement. These thus have a minimal, unifying common denominator, which was not the case in the Romance cultures, constrained as they were to assimilate largely distinct pieces (theater, cinema, dance). And we have not even considered that the concept of performance also includes gestural movements and behaviors associated with the other arts, usually linked more closely with immobile, technical means. Even literature, music, and the visual arts become performance arts when they return to their motor, acoustic, and gestural origins, origins that have been "repressed" because of the age-old affirmation of graphic means (strengthened by the dominance throughout the whole modern age of typography and Renaissance perspective in a powerful and crushing conjunction). But underneath a certain outward appearance, the inferiority of the Romance languages in not possessing the unifying term of performance in any daily or habitual use, is changed into an advantage, given that such a term ricochets and imposes itself on us with the intensified definition given it by the latest technological developments, and so by the entire material culture in which we are immersed. Performance sounds to the Italian ear like an indication of that largely intersensorial, synaesthetic performance based primarily on gestures-motion that artists of every sector can "furnish" today by letting go of their respective "artistic" privileges, consecrated by a long tradition, and by returning to the areas of a primary aesthetic exercise, which in our age can easily be recorded, thanks to film, video, and other means of preservation.

The visual artist (the painter) is thus not limited to the presentation of the result of his or her own gestures as arranged on a canvas, but can actually propose the very gestures themselves in their full fluency. When we speak of Jackson Pollock's dripping (paintings obtained by squeezing the colors from a tube), we usually also refer to the film that shows us the artist at work, as if dancing along the canvas laid out on the floor. And the poet is found increasingly in the public sphere, performing direct readings of his or her verses (which are thus enriched by acoustic effects practically untranslatable on the page). The musician accumulates in the moments of composition and execution in a presentation sound effects that are so new and contingent, so enlivened with such particular physical properties, that they cannot even be approximated by conventional means of notation. And so we truly realize the proclamation that "all the arts tend toward performance," which is also the crowning moment of the program called the "death of art." The conditions of our material culture (social, economic, technological) are so full and mature that it is no longer worthwhile to endure long and difficult trials in order to learn an "artistic" skill, which also accounts for the painful division between the few who know how to make art and the many who must content themselves with the role of patrons, after the act of creation. Today anyone can dedicate themselves to presentations and performances of an acoustic, visual, or motile nature, or better yet, can rely on a total synergy between these various channels. Anyone can be a creator, at this minimal level, without missing the comfort of the technical fixation capable of making a lasting and reproducible object. The utopian project suggested by the great prophets of 1968 (particularly McLuhan and Marcuse) also salvages, with the reassuring comfort of technological possibilities, what Schiller had prophesied concerning a humanity capable of developing the impulse to play as a reconciler and equalizer of those other impulses to know and to act, or rather, of the tiresome division between the senses and the intellect.

Spectacle and Theater

After this reference to current utopias (which may no longer exist, according to Marcuse's hypothesized "end of utopia," in current, technetronic civilization), we reenter the field of the most traditional "artistic" considerations. When corporeal performances become enriched, leaving behind their most minimal stages and moving toward the assumption of a professional consistency, we enter the field of the spectacle, or of theater. In an etymological sense, it might not be possible to find appreciable differences between the two terms, the one Latin, the other Greek, inasmuch as both return to verbal roots alluding to an exercise of seeing, contemplating, which means that both admit a verification of a division between one who furnishes the performance (the author) and a public who admires from afar, or from beyond the most limited circle, from a passive position. Finally, this division of labor imposed by the regime of the arts has already intervened. Humanity has left behind the felicitous indistinction of the exercise of a primary aesthetic (to which, however, one may hope to return, at least if the prophecies uttered along the axis that extends from Schiller to Marcuse come true). Nevertheless, we admit by convention that the term "spectacle" maintains a greater openness, regardless whether the action is staged in specially equipped or designated places. On the one hand, according to such a large and liberal connotation, even the soccer game is spectacle, as is the circus "act," or any performance played out on the streets. We thus find ourselves in a rather large and fluid environment, close to the originary meaning of the performance. On the other hand, by theater we mean a series of artistic practices that lead to a strengthening of the differences between actor and spectator. These differences are sanctioned by the institution of places assigned to the actors (the stage) and of spaces set aside for the audience (the orchestra, the seats).

An important step toward the growing complexity of the theatrical work was made when actors began to recite literary texts that preexisted their particular performance. We have already recalled the *Poetics* of Aristotle, an "ambiguous" treatise that places itself at the boundary between a phase of oral culture and one in which the primacy of writing is affirmed. In this canonical work of Greek culture, destined to exercise an incalculable influence on the civilization of the West, even literature continues to be viewed in proximity with its archaic origins. It emerges as a performance in which the *eidos* recites poetry, but by retrieving the verses from memory, and so proposing them in very schematic and repetitive forms. Moreover, this is a total performance accompanied by the sound of a musical instrument. Significantly, the poem specifically conceived for the stage, still keeping within that phase, certainly cannot be separated from its performatory complements; the recited parts will thus have to be integrated with the musical parts and accompanied by dance. Yet the premises that in the following centuries eventually lead to the "literalization" of the theater are already fixed. They will work by subjecting the musical and choreographic appendages to the primacy of the text, and, as in that other noble genre, the epic poem, there will be a simpler liberation of performatory aspects, even to the point of our arrival at silent reading. This can also be attributed to the development of the phases of classical Greek and then Roman culture, both intent on stressing naturalistic-illusory symbolic forms: the same sorts of solutions were promoted for the visual arts. The ideal parts into which Aristotle divided the typical poem thus each contribute to the overall constitution of a field that seeks to achieve verisimilitude; the characters, the ethical depth of the drama, and even the *dianoia*, seek to render a balanced and credible set of functional rules governing the emotions, also entrusting itself to a controlled *lexis* that avoids the tumult of an excessively metaphoric language, one that is too compromised by conceits, puns, or rare and unusual words. But most particularly, the essential responsibility in following this objective of credibility and verisimilitude leads toward "myth" or *fabula*, the component that becomes harnessed in the well-known Aristotelian unities, which Aristotle himself only mentioned briefly. Perhaps this was because he preached in favor of the unity of action, which could almost be called the acknowledgment of one of the fundamental peculiarities of the aesthetic experience such that today we continue to follow this unity to some degree in our artistic works. Action must be sufficiently compact and unitary to be encompassed in a single glance and retained in the memory. In fact, that which distinguishes an aesthetic-artistic product from others responding to other functions is precisely our obligation to make a "holistic" evaluation of it. It must offer itself to us in its entirety, in time and in space. Naturally, we can distinguish between the prerequisite of unity as it is placed in a theoretical context from the practical modalities of its application in a historical context. Finally, one can say that a Shakespearean chronicle play, that is, a drama following a chronological order and thus linked to history understood as a sequence of common facts, or, even earlier, an epic poem from the medieval cycle of Roland or King Arthur, through the Renaissance reworking in Boiardo or Ariosto— all of these are "successful," and, that is, unitary, in spite of a characteristically large number of digressions or lateral trails. Unity does not depend on the number of ingredients or on their quantitative presence, but on the capacity for ensuring relations of interaction, of dynamic equilibrium, which can easily be obtained by adding rather than removing details. Altogether different is the perceptual direction of style or taste, linked to the expectations of a given historical age. Both of these aspects were present in Aristotle: the correct emphasis on a still-valid theoretical need, and also the expression of a particular taste, linked to the season of ancient classicism and its need for verisimilitude.

As for perspective, we have already seen how, in the visual arts, modern Western classicism (the period from the mid-fifteenth century to the end of the nineteenth, contemporaneous with the cycle of typography and with the affirmation of the Gutenberg Galaxy) reinforced this cult of the probable until it was finally locked into a true and proper straitjacket, namely, Renaissance linear perspective, based on the scheme of the inverted visual pyramid. Analogously, as far as the theater is concerned, such a cultural cycle came to reinforce the precepts in the *Poetics*, adding to the unity of action those of place and time (action in the drama must not be displaced from a principal scene and must conclude within the arc of time established, essentially a twenty-four-hour period). These are also highly conformist shackles, which became necessary in the name of the goal of probable representation, but which also respond to the usual technical difficulties (such as rendering sudden changes of scenery credible, or constructing them with heightened detail). As a formula, we could say that Renaissance dramaturgy, which itself refers to the classical, Aristotelian source, finishes off the passage from spectacle to theater by sacrificing the performatory elements, or at least by strongly curtailing them. The spectacle can only be staged in specifically designated sites, and whoever is responsible is subjected to numerous obligations, beginning with those concerning the written text. A strong dichotomy is imposed between those who stage a drama in its actuality and fullness on the stage and those who, for example, the author, prepare the written text. This dichotomy is resolved in favor of the literary-authorial moment for the sound reason that until the advent of photochemical and electronic means of reproduction the aspects of performance, of vocal and gestural execution, could not be preserved, which led ultimately to their devaluation in comparison with the written text.

It is true that a similar dichotomy existed especially in the area of high cultural performance staged for the upper classes, who were also predisposed to sacrifice good doses of entertainment and pleasure to the needs inherent in the institutionalization of a universe of probable fictions (in painting as well as in literature, and in the appendix of the latter, which by now can be called "modern" drama). Other social classes less clearly tied to tasks of salvaging a certain ideology or a precise form of civility, or even the dominant classes themselves in moments of disengagement, remained open to the possibility of consuming rather free and uninhibited forms of spectacle, forms not constrained by the ties of the "high" precept. The great Elizabethan and Shakespearean age belonged to such a confident, post-medieval area, not yet contaminated by "modern" rules, thanks to the delay, in this case providential, with which these rules were spread from the Italian cradle toward the Germanic and Anglo-Saxon territories. But even in Italy a strong area of resistance to the legitimate theater was to be established in the commedia dell'arte. Actors did not acknowledge any

rigid controls on their performatory ability in the commedia and other out-
growths of it. They only recognized the preexistence of situations, of
"myths," of plots, which they could concretize with extemporaneous, even
if formulaic, lines, as is the case with all popular-oral literature.

In terms of the theater and spectacle in general, the nineteenth century
introduced that double-faced character we have already noticed in the
visual arts (it is useless to remind ourselves once again that these two artistic fields march to the same beat, with parallel destinies). At this time,
we saw the triumph of the probable, which, in homage to a "fiction" capable
of restoring even the strong degree of uncertainty to which its existence had
been subjected, began to liberate itself from servitude to the unities of time
and place. In the drama, episodes became more numerous, and scenes
changed with greater frequency, within certain limitations. Besides, it was
not without reason that the offspring of the epic poem, that is, of one of
Aristotle's canonical genres, took on the name of novel [romanzo] (as we
have seen), because it accepts the freedom of peripatetic acts and plots that
distinguished the medieval period and the diffusion of the new Romance
languages. But this richness of plots and characters should not be considered to the detriment of the search for the probable. The Italian writer
Manzoni is a perfect representative of such a mixture of "romantic" prerequisites, but in the name of a final triumph of the line of realism sustained
by "modern" classicism. In the meantime he once again attests to the unity
of the laboratory that oversees the construction of "poems," exactly as
Aristotle's treatise would have it. As we know, Manzoni produced two
tragedies (Carmagnola and Adelchi) to say nothing of a work in prose, I
promessi sposi (The betrothed), which is representative of those realist tendencies destined to take the upper hand during the nineteenth century.
Obviously, in Manzoni we find the predominance of the "literary," of the
sacrifice of specific, spectacular, performatory aspects of the dramatic text.
It is often said that Manzoni's two tragedies would have met a more illustrious fate if they had been verified through a silent reading, rather than
having been "executed," actualized on the stage. We are dealing, in contrast to the fortune of "the probable," with a man of letters in his revolt
against the canons of Aristotelian unity, and so apparently predisposed toward a "romantic" notion of liberty; but one pursued, when all is said and
done, in order to obtain results of a more intensely "modern" verisimilitude,
in order to investigate environmental truths relating to customs, introspec-
tion, and mass psychology, but without having to conform to predetermined
models.

Finally, the nineteenth century led to the triumph of an ideal of illusory,

mimetic theater close to the concept of a "still life." At this time we begin
to speak of the stage as a self-contained reality, perfectly executed, ignorant
of the presence of viewers who are allowed to watch the action thanks to
the miraculous transparency of a "fourth wall," viewers who are similar,
that is, to a curious and indiscreet public that observes slices of private life
through a keyhole, without itself being observed. From this, the passage is
brief indeed until we begin accusing this totally passive public of "voyeur-
ism," as Filippo Tommaso Marinetti will do during the early twentieth century in one of the most provocative manifestos directed toward the construction of a new theatrical mode, or rather, motivated by the intention to
disfigure the "theater" and to return to free spectacle, liberated more than
ever from the obligation of probable fiction.

In fact, this is the "double" of the nineteenth century, which, beginning
with its final phase (the fin de siècle), comes to disavow the "modern" ideology of conformist representation in all artistic fields. The visual arts dismiss the Renaissance perspectival system and go in search of new systems
for rendering space (putting into question even the primacy of traditional
supports, the canvas, the painting). Novels also contest the description of
characters and environments as faithful to the true, whether this is natural
or social. And theater, in its own way, does all it can to bring together the
two, or rather, three sides of spectacle: that authorial version of a production legitimized by a text, that performatory one (with actors, directors,
scenic designers), and that which focuses on the "spectators." Each of these
areas becomes conscious of the others, putting an end to the ideal of the
"still life," in which the actor had to pretend to be unaware of his or her
own recitation, sacrificing his or her own humanity to the service of a
"part," an assumed mask. Bertolt Brecht speaks of "alienation," according
to which the actor calls on the public, engages it in the action itself. Luigi
Pirandello stages a sort of systematic tension and struggle between the three
components of the parallelogram of forces in which every spectacle seems
to be engaged. The actors contest both the author and the "stage manager"
(capocomico, the predecessor, from commedia dell'arte performances, of
the modern director), but in turn they are contested by the "characters,"
the dramatis personae. Finally, the edifice of conformist and illusory fiction
crumbles on every side. The artistic symbols of the spectacle approach,
almost without limit, the material presence of the signifiers, with the consequence that the three protagonists of the entire dramaturgical operation
tend to identify themselves in a single function. In the extreme version
there is only the performer (the actor), who no longer wishes to submit to a
literary text, or rather, to a script that is conceived and realized by others

and does not faithfully aid in developing fictions. By now there is almost no more need for words, which are, in turn, ordered into syntactical constructs, into sentences and speeches. Now pure phonation or noises, as for every other gestural and corporeal intervention, become valorized to the highest degree. Or, in an even more radical move, the performer accepts the preexistence of a rather generic and indeterminate "myth," similar in this to the "plots" that served as the basis for the commedia dell'arte, as long as this allows for many possibilities of "execution" with personal, extemporaneous interventions. And it is well understood that the beautiful fluidity of this extemporaneous performance cannot really withstand the brakes, the extrinsic controls, that come from a director. The performer watches over him- or herself and the other company members who live together in the strict bonds of the daily exercises of a laboratory environment. Similarly, in the premodern organization of the theater, the stage manager was also an actor, an impresario, responsible for the organization and the circulation of collective performances, without any rigid distinction of roles.

Let it be clear, however, that this fluidity or substantial convergence of roles does not seek to promote itself to the detriment of a long and patient training period. The disappearance of overarching literary texts and other forms of external imposition does not mean that the spectacle itself is completely improvised; rather, spontaneity, the solution of the moment, comes to be assumed against the background of a long preparation of all the corporeal and gestural faculties. Even here the reference point can be the commedia dell'arte, whose improvisation flourished because of the secure career acquired by each actor. Finally, confronted with the primacy and nudity of this originary spectacle, the spectator finds him- or herself directly involved, because the exterior barriers, the topological separation between spectators and the performers, are almost all destroyed. This engagement is all the more potent because nothing prohibits the spectators from taking an active part, from their becoming actors.

At least, this is what stands at the end point of the already-mentioned libertarian utopia expressed by the lineage of Schiller and Marcuse. And the conflation of roles was enlarged by Marcuse according to the rather suggestive hypothesis of the "death of the utopia" following the imposition of the electronic revolution, with all the facilitation that this allows on the level of production and preservation. Among the various connotations of the global phenomenon of the "death of art" discussed previously, and of the return to a primary aesthetic, we must also count, evidently, a "death of the theater" to the advantage of elements of a diffused and free spectacle. It is clear that, at the very least, many decades of experimentation in this field have attempted to move toward this objective. The most important forms of dramaturgy of the later twentieth century have supplanted the phase of the production of the text, or rather, they have pushed this to an extreme of exhaustion, toward the absurd or toward a low, minimalist level (Ionesco, Beckett); and so they have replaced it with nonverbal forms (happenings, Living Theater, the Lab Theater of Grotowski; and in Italy, Carmelo Bene, and the theater of the post avant-garde theorized by Franco Quadri).

Cinema, Television

Certainly, even the theater, like the visual arts, has been spurred in its abandonment of illusory, mimetic conventions, not only by an irrepressible tendency inherent in contemporary culture as a whole, but also by the advent of a new technological means or art form that seemed to assume for itself all the prerogatives of a representation of "high-fidelity" reality, namely, cinematography. This new muse, as we noted previously, was born in the field of the visual arts, as a development of photography. It seems to wish to continue the strong reflective capabilities of this latter in its confrontation with the external world. Cinema is thus particularly apt for illuminating and recording the tactile and motor qualities of bodies; the visual arts, especially during the "hot" moments of the historical avant-gardes (cubism, futurism, dadaism, surrealism), make use of cinematic techniques in order to break the chains of immobility and in order to grasp movement, in order to pursue, with a particularly adept instrument, the examination of the structural characteristics of various objects, following them in their developments, emphasizing their plastic virtues to the greatest degree possible.

But very quickly it was discovered that this new means, besides simply appearing well suited for exploring the inert and inanimate qualities of inorganic bodies, was also adept at illuminating human actions, and so it quickly became a surrogate or a competition for theater. At the very least, it began to inscribe itself in the field of the unlimited possibilities of the spectacle. Finally, a dilemma was born around the specific nature of cinematography. Is it one of the visual arts—the arts of space—with the added complication of movement, or does it belong to the arts of time, especially those of mythopoetic investigation? How would Aristotle have judged cinema if he lived in our times? In the normative listing of his poems, would he have added "film" to tragedy and comedy? This term is nothing other than a metonymic abbreviation, a part for the whole: the thousands of meters of a roll of film, developed according to cinematographic technique in order to indicate virtual and symbolic action that only the human eye can perceive, on a screen of greater or lesser size. We have already observed that the animal eye is not able to do as much, and so the pretense made by the photocinematographic image to attain a high degree of reality is, when all is said and done, a sort of magnificent illusion, a symbolic transcription and subtraction of sensory qualities, perceivable with senses other than sight.

Aristotle probably would not have paid particular attention to this new form, not out of a sense of diffidence but because his broad perspective made him rather insensitive to the various "details" of the art forms. So, for example, he did not bother to widen the gap between the literary epic poem and the two theatrical genres developed for the stage. As we have already noted, this "ambiguity" is legible in its two versions, as a proximity to the roots, to origins, when mythopoesis was a unitary fact entrusted to every possible executive channel (and so the arrival of "high-fidelity" channels such as those assured by film should not cause any particular ripple in the system); but also, in a contrary sense, as the path toward the "classical" primacy of literature. It would not seem scandalous to Aristotle that even the elaboration of a roll of cinematic footage is a question of ability in conceiving of a long, literary text, which must be entrusted to a novelist or a playwright, or rather to a *poietès* capable of reconciling both of these roles. In fact, figures such as D'Annunzio and Pirandello were both called to contribute to the new muse during the 1920s and 1930s, but precisely inasmuch as it would be affirmed by the presence of legitimate authors.

Finally, cinema was born and raised for decades, and perhaps continues to move today, between two polar opposites: a scrupulous attention to the search for its own material, whether this is understood as a valorization of plastic and spatial effects worthy of the visual arts or for mundane, banal materials, in which it would reveal, as in an epiphany, the purest state of existence (according to the thesis of Siegfried Kracauer in a book that bears the elegant subtitle *The Redemption of Physical Reality*). Add to this the passionate appeal that Cesare Zavattini made in a similar vein during the postwar years, that we strive to uncover the revelatory character of social, quotidian, human reality using film cameras so stripped down and simplified that they could almost be considered domestic appliances. What emerges from this theory of neorealism is film of a reduced format, not the "professional" thirty-five millimeter, but the "amateur," agile, economical sixteen-millimeter or even super-eight film. A film may also be brief and may ignore the Aristotelian unities or every derivation or successor of them.

For Zavattini, a short story or diegesis is not even necessary; these will be concentrated in some "myth," in a brief, thematic, thunderous, and revelatory nucleus, full of exemplary power. This brevity of notation, inherent in a quotidian-domestic exercise of the movie camera, makes it particularly adept at grasping comic moments. Indeed, the comedy of Charlie Chaplin, Buster Keaton, and the Marx Brothers became one of the chosen territories of the cinema precisely when the checkmate of acquired habits, or vice versa, the rigidification of the puppet, the life that becomes mechanical, that is to say, the profound characteristics of comedy, were entrusted to pure plastic-visual inventions and the sound film had not yet come into existence to provoke an important strengthening of the illusionistic elements of filmic art. But after the initial confusion caused by the introduction of sound, even the cultivators of the minimalist aesthetic in film, that is, of the movie camera as an insuperable instrument for reaching the epiphany of physical values, of the real denseness of things, take it up again. There is a truth and beauty at the level of the acoustic, noise-related values that work fairly well at integrating visual, plastic, kinetic aspects. The line of thought that extends from Kracauer to Zavattini ultimately has no great difficulty in assimilating the acoustic sphere to its own agenda, in the name of a total redemption of the aesthetic dimension, that is, of a full sensory epiphany.

The Zavattini line is also one of the greatest moments in Italian neorealism of the postwar years, witnessed not only by the films in which he participated as a screenwriter and collaborator with De Sica, but also perhaps in the films of Rossellini and Antonioni. This glorification of the specific, of the dignity and excellence involved in making the "things themselves" speak, renews itself periodically through the moments of the various avant-gardes and experimental schools: the French *nouvelle vague*, American underground cinema, and so on.

But the cinema also becomes an instrument of pure entertainment linked to the field of mythopoesis through its superior status and dignity compared with the loftier media and genres to which this very productive area used to be entrusted. For one thing, it was only relatively late in its life that cinema was believed capable of sustaining "histories," myths, and emphatic or improbable characters, compared with what was considered acceptable in narrative literature or theater. In other words, cinema has gone through phases, in a sort of retarded phylogenetic development, that those "superior" forms of mythopoesis had already tried and abandoned. Finally, as we noted earlier, cinema seems to have specialized in the task of developing that illusory-naturalistic transcription of reality from which the theater of the twentieth century needed to liberate itself. Theater, which is rather less well equipped than its young rival in this mimetic-specular capacity, was just as ready to leave that task to cinema as painting had been to leave to photography the analogous task in the sector of static images. And certainly, cinematography can make itself a faithful servant kneeling at the feet of theater and the so-called bourgeois novel as these were formed in the late nineteenth century, to provide for them a faithful mimetic picture of the social scene, of environments and masses and places and circumstances, with predictable characters, well-made stories, and so on. A propensity for consumerism, for pure recreation and entertainment, is also favored by the huge economic costs of producing a film, which makes irresponsible experimentation less possible.

But between these two extremes are so many intermediary, more balanced possibilities. By coordinating a large team of specialized artist-technicians (director of photography, camera operators, scenic designers, costumers, and so on), a film director can avoid being limited to dissolving the "fourth wall" or the slice of life seen through a keyhole. In this way, we know well that even the most indulgent and commercial directors must avail themselves of the specific resources offered by the medium, which is not the case for the theater director, who must count instead on the collaboration of the spectators, free to fix their gazes on any area of the stage, to pause at a close-up or to pull back for a wide-angle view. The movie camera takes care of such work, and so establishes the exact angle of the scene (shot, reverse shot), and determines whether or not to include a wide slice of action or to limit the shot to details or close-ups. At every turn, the director is able to choose whether or not to conform to measures of the traditional story, making sure that through the camera, the spectators see only familiar sequences to which they are already well predisposed. Finally, they remain disappointed if the development of the film places this identification in question or contradicts it. The director also controls any possible epiphany of plastic and human material through close-ups, long tracks, and quick cuts, defying the expectations of the public and conferring a new weight on the ingredients of "history" so as to make them assume a rather rough quality.

Naturally, even in this case our investigation cannot be pushed too far ahead, given that it must confront specific technical knowledge (cinematography, because of its technological complexity, thus undergoes particularly accentuated and laborious developments), or rather, it must enter into a history of the styles and schools that came about after the developments of cinematic art, even in the few decades during which its whole history is played out. These tasks go beyond the scope of the present work and its goals.

It is worthwhile to develop one final reflection, a confirmation of the double-faced character that belongs to cinematography. We seem to point to that rather utopian dream, or, rather, that dream inscribed among the possibilities that we will reach at some future time, (thanks to the developments of technetronics) and that consists in a total return of the aesthetic experience, understood as a total, synergic redemption of all our best qualities. In fact, what better than a brief film to restore the organic fullness of *an* aesthetic experience, that is, of one of our global performances in which all sensory channels act at full capacity? Even in many widely distributed full-length features (which may not always find the greatest success) this epiphanic exaltation of the performatory values of the everyday, in the sense foretold by Kracauer and Zavattini, is already enacted. In certain cinematic sequences spectators can find the intense, pregnant underlining of plastic, kinetic, and acoustic effects that the other arts try in vain to approach. Their various means are always too symbolic, too abstract, and too stylized to be effective in this area.

Yet the cinematographic work places itself at the other extreme of the scale. It offers an extremely complex product, resulting from the synergy of numerous artistic competencies in a more or less broad sense, and these, in turn, vary in their effects depending on the artistic capabilities in the rather specific sense of the director, actors, and those increasingly technical or artisanal capabilities of the various co-operators. Even directors, as we well know, must suffer thousands of compromises, because film is a total work, comprehending even economic, moral, political, and technological responsibilities: a mixed and impure work that, because of such factors, inherits the impurity of other equally complex undertakings and composites characteristic of previous eras. Such was Greek tragedy, melodrama, the "work" par excellence of the nineteenth century, and escapist fiction, even if in this genre the individual responsibility of the author has a more determinate weight. But we cannot ignore the economic interests of the editor, and the control exercised over the contents of a work by dominant public opinion, always ready to intervene, and thus leaving a small margin of freedom compared with that conceded to lyric poetry, which is channeled into a small field of distribution.

It would now be appropriate to refer to that very new technological medium, television, which places itself within the sphere of cinematography just as cinematography, earlier, stood in the aura of theater. When we indicated earlier the role of a "minor" exercise for cinematographic art, perfectly adapted to the manifestation of aesthetic values, and thus a highly precise instrument for recording performances, we should have also dedicated much more space to the question of video recording. This art has no need of photochemical developing and so avoids the inevitable dead time, just as it dispenses with the obligations of editing. It is thus a perfect medium for grasping the flow of life, as long as this is seen at close range, through close-ups and "zooms" on details. Cinematography, however, emerges as the clear winner in producing long shots and the fullness of a given scene, especially if it is rich in details. To the degree that film has inherited the naturalistic and illusory vocation of theater or, in general, of nineteenth-century mythopoesis, television cannot pretend to have replaced it. The current daily transmission of programs or films on various public and private channels does not come without serious limitations to the positive fruition of film itself; the passage from the big to the small screen is easily accomplished, but also entails sacrifices, whereas the televised media reveal themselves to be insuperable in terms of "live" transmission, that is, when the director transmits events of various sorts as they happen (debates and political arguments, interviews, news and sports). In this sense video contributes in a significant way to the triumph of spectacle over theater.

CHAPTER 4

The Artist, the Patron, the Critic

Emotional Life

In the previous chapters we considered the object of our interest, aesthetics and art, in an intrinsic sense, that is, ignoring almost completely the "actors," the protagonists who make art possible. At best we threw them rapid glances, and this scarcity of attention is certainly justified in the case of aesthetic experience, in which we have if not total identification of roles between the one who does and the one who watches, apart from the enactment of the experience, then at least total interchangeability of roles. For the spectator, defined in a very limited sense, must, on the one hand, guard against the impulse to stop watching and start doing, but, on the other hand, should not feel alienated from the individual who brings the aesthetic act to completion by a difference in their relative competencies and capabilities. We also know that such a coincidence of roles constitutes the alpha and omega of the entire circle of aesthetics. We begin there, at its origins, and we end up there at the end of time. To paraphrase Marcuse, we may face the "end of utopia," and so also the "death of art," thanks to the development of technetronic civilization.

But certainly it is rather more common in this world of ours and in the different conditions of postlapsarian culture, constrained by the difficult necessities of work, to encounter artistic products that exhibit a relative distinction between one who has achieved artisanal-artistic ability and one who has renounced this path for various reasons and thus accepts the lesser role of patron of the arts or spectator. So, in the end, we find that the entire territory of aesthetics can be divided into two branches, the aesthetics of production and of reception or reading, which, brought to a significant and complex level, also gives rise to critical activity. No clear line divides the two perspectives, and the various reflections already discussed have substantially considered the possibility of inserting these partial points of view into aesthetics, sketching the knots into which each one can be tied, or designing the space for such possible developments. But it will now be useful to confront them, in a more extended and separated fashion, which will also entail a useful review of the material.

Let us begin with the aesthetics of production. From the point of view of the maker of art, we can quickly measure ourselves against the classical categories of *movere*, *docere*, and *delectare*, which gave rise to the great families of aesthetic theories, respectively linked to emotionalism (expressionism, empathy, sentiment), cognition, and the ludic spirit. We have already treated these categories, here and there, but never in any systematic way, mostly because we do not expect to choose one or the other, but rather support a healthy mix of the three. So, for example, emotions clearly concern the artist, just as they do any individual who chooses to participate in an aesthetic experience. We stated in chapter 1 that without the possibility of emotion, we cannot leave behind the realm of common sense, of a lazy and forgetful state of daily life, comforted by the first aid of habits and behavior linked to routine. It is essential that some obstacle intervene to push us beyond this, and to jolt us from the comfortable system of habit. We also know that there are certain possible paths to take in the face of rising emotions: we can abandon ourselves to irrational behavior, to the mercy of extrinsic, uncontrollable forces. Or perhaps we can channel that excess of energy to liberate ourselves from accident, to seek new modes of action that will carry us beyond our troubles; and it is at this point that the two great families of experience or coherent and knowing "discourses" part ways. The aesthetic is directed toward recomposing the totality of the situation or circumstances by enlarging contextual embrace, whereas the scientific, through the instrument of analysis, seeks to individuate and remove obstacles, to allow habit to reassert the routine.

So the artist, almost by definition, must take on emotions. He or she must be more sensitive than the average mortal to the influxes of energy of an affective-passionate nature. Today, then, we are in a position to reformulate this necessary presence of an impulse toward emotion in terms of Freudian doctrine, a great institution of contemporary culture, perhaps comparable in its significance to the passage from a civilization of machines (the modern age) to one of electromagnetism. The first age was rigid, repressive, and characterized by nonconductors, and it imposed the primacy of "weights and measures," of numbers, of a cold rationalism. The *res cogitans* demanded to establish its full domination. It recognized as its counterpart an opaque and amorphous *res extensa*, but not the possibility of a relationship with it. We might also say that the modern age was lived as a gigantic repression of the affective-passionate level. This was noticed by Freud, but also by so many of his predecessors (the great German and English romantics of the late eighteenth century, Schiller, Goethe, Schelling, Blake . . .), exactly with the arrival of various scientific and technological premises directed at "liberating" this affective-passionate level or at least reviewing the reciprocal relations between ego and id, between reality principle and pleasure principle (to adapt the Freudian terminology, which deserves the highest grade of official recognition).

But, clearly, artists and their theoreticians did not need to wait for the advent of Freudian institutions in order to accede to the reservoir of the id. Many lines of art interpretation have addressed questions of "madness" or *furor*, of the presence of god in a work of art. This latter is an ambiguous concept throughout Greco-Roman mythology, inasmuch as it was not well determined whether this presence of the divine had its location and provenance from on high or from down below. In any case, we can affirm that throughout history it has been recognized that the artist is somehow able to reach into energetic reserves "stronger than the self," at least stronger than the conscious self, in the very dialogue with other common mortals. Today, clearly, we can be explicit about the age-old notion that the artist was linked to an obscure theory, vulnerable to the accusation of irrationality. Anyone who has artistic predispositions manages to disturb, more than others, the usual equilibrium between the components of the ego and those of the id. The artist lives in a state such that he or she concedes to the drives of eros or the libido, naturally accepting the task of diverting them from the aim of direct, sexual pleasure, and of deviating along the path of sublimation. Moreover, if we believe the teachings of leftist Freudians like Marcuse, our entire technetronic civilization is now revising the equilibrium between reality and pleasure, subtracting less and less energy from the free search of the latter in order to sacrifice it to the former. Work and artisanal-industrial production cost fewer and fewer tears, absorb fewer hours, and open more and vast spaces of free time. Following this line, we encounter the utopian picture of the "death of art" in favor of a capillary extension of aesthetic enjoyment.

Nevertheless, reading between the lines, we find that not even the most contemporary and credible Freudian interpretation today takes anything away from the fact that the emotional life of the artist, although quite intense, does not take place in a vacuum. Without other contacts this life might even seem to be a waste, like that made by a geyser of a boraciferous fumarole, a geological deposit of natural gas, not conveniently piped into any container. This metaphoric pipeline in our case is given by the various operations that lead the artist to produce the work of art, to choose carefully the signifiers of the system of symbols to which artists entrust their creations. Although artists choose and treat various materials and instruments with professional mastery, they absorb the energy surplus, or rather, this is the spring that allows them to conduct those certain interventions that in themselves are uneconomical and gratuitous, and that, in turn, generally give rise to objects, to goods that we tend to consume in those moments dedicated to pleasure and free time (spectacles, novels, works of art to be viewed at shows, museums, and so on).

But speaking of this undeniable emotional factor, we must especially avoid considering it unilaterally, within its own internal space, its private life, or even worse, as understood in terms of autobiography or personal "history." The conception that we will follow in all of this is not favorable to a divisive epistemology of the inside and the outside; rather, we begin with the supposition that there is only one condition of "being-in-the-world," a penetration of self and environment, subject and object, complicated above all by the fact that "I" am many. Today the subject becomes a plural notion, "one, no one, and a hundred thousand," as Pirandello described it. The energies provided to us by nature are made *ab origine* to be emitted and released in certain circumstances, in order to then overwhelm these moments or else to be sucked in and reabsorbed by them. Clearly, in the concept of circumstance, it is also useful to include the participation of our fellow human beings in an indivisible network. Emotions, however, are neither subjective nor objective. More simply, they indicate the cessation of a state of equilibrium in our being-in-the-world and our most basic experience of living. Consequently, our emotions do not derive exclusively from the interior, just as expression, as we have observed, does not "press out" something that we have inside, but, undoubtedly, is strengthened by an impulse that does originate within us. And expression nevertheless effects its own pressure on given objects offered by the bread-and-butter experiences of the world: a pressure to which all can thus be sensitive and attentive, inasmuch as we are in a position to be able to experience this pressure with our own means of perception and comprehension.

In other words, the emotions, passions, affects, and sentiments of the artist are no different in content from those of the common mortal, but they do constitute a means, a filter, or, better yet, a catalyst, in the chemical sense of this term. These are indefinite substances, given that we cannot appreciate them in themselves but only through the volume of effects that they are able to release by their interventions, inasmuch as they are capable of obtaining syntheses, a coalescence of materials (of objective facts, meanings) that in another circumstance would not solidify or connect. In this sense, the act of artistic production continues to contain some "mysterious" variable of which the artist is never completely aware. This also justifies the emphatic term of "creation" with which we often refer to the process, especially in those aesthetic schools of a romantic lineage. But the effects of the intervention of such an unfathomable, subjective catalyst *are* objective and verifiable, inasmuch as they reflect the typical polysemy, ambiguity, and contextuality that distinguish each individual aesthetic-artistic operation.

The applications of psychoanalysis to the study of art that are most interesting to us today, however, are not those of a so-called medical type, in which an author attempts to invest the subjectivity of the artist with a displacement of interest from work to life, thus falling back on a version of "autobiographical heresy." This method supposes that the work (novel, poem, painting, and so on) is just one more symptom of the neurosis of the "great author" (the error that Freud himself committed when discussing Leonardo da Vinci). Nevertheless, it is true that through the study of the joke the founder of psychoanalysis admirably offered us another way to investigate the productive-linguistic processes by discovering the interrelationships between signifiers and signifieds, or, better, the possibility that signifiers lose their neutrality as conventional instruments when placed in correspondence with the correct signifieds, instead becoming crazed machines that "shoot" in various directions, with double entendres, echoes, elusive assonances, and so on, allowing for the drives of pleasure and libido to penetrate the fortress of serious concepts. Following this course, we throw a vital light on the reasons why the machine of artistic production obtains polysemy in the first place, by reshuffling the decks of the ego with those of the id. The emotions burst into rational processes of language, and they pervert, but they are, in turn, measurable and verifiable as deviations, differences, versions, against the background of grammatical, syntactic, and lexical institutions.

Cognitive Theories

That emotional depth is typically two-faced can easily be sustained, for along with emotions pressing on the artist, apparently from inside, there are certainly other emotions that the artist chooses to illustrate, according to various forms and artistic genres (the novel, poetry, music, painting, and so on). This is also a way of confirming the ambiguous status of the level of the passions, capable of staying within the artist, but also existing outside, as reflective illumination. Clearly, artists know about the emotions of others as they experience them in a private laboratory where they learn to see clearly their own emotional lives, according to the model of case studies. Yet even here, finally, it is impossible to establish a rigid caesura, because emotional life flows in and out of the perimeters of a single individual. In terms of emotions as objects of mimetic operation, regardless of the degree of variation or transposition, the risks of an obstructed and irrational emotionalism seem decisively reduced. Everyone admits that material of this sort is presented by the artist through the filter of a healthy critical distance; it is a case, then, of an emotional life derailed on the circuits of virtuality, mired in the laboratory, almost in a kind of "wind tunnel" that reconstitutes lived experience in the name of an experiment, rejoicing in bringing this life to the highest possible degree of irritation, the better to record the peculiarities or alternative phases of its course when faced with obstacles. Here we should recall the substantial distance that separates the meanings of a simple process of denotation from those of a more complex, symbolic operation. The former are physically present, interactive with the experimenter and capable of exercising an immediate feedback, that is, of arousing concern or excitement, or even of threatening a sense of security. The latter, more complex, meanings of some symbolic given stand solidly in a field of virtuality or presence only in appearance, in ideal form, according to that modality of "reasoning-in-absence" that is typical of humanity and that makes an *animal symbolicum* of us, as Cassirer brilliantly observed.

Finally, this is the route we must follow in leaving behind the stormy waters of emotionalist theories, to enter in the cognitive. In fact, emotional life merely reproduced with literary or pictorial symbolism, rather than being "lived," is "known," or simulated for purposes of study. But cognition in aesthetics is most concerned with the possibility (or lack thereof) that artists "know" anything in the sense of pure reason, logic, and epistemology. In chapter 1 we examined Croce's drastic separation of the sphere of aesthetics from that of logic, based on a network of distinctions: wherever a logical process (of which the sciences would be merely the utilitarian applications) is initiated, art "dies." Moreover, according to the theories of the Neapolitan philosopher, it is not for this reason that art should be left in the care of mere emotionalism, in which, justly, Croce recognizes only a blocked practicality. In order to lift themselves up to a level of aesthetic-artistic dignity, emotion and sentiment must submit to a process of formal modulation, but with a form made to measure, not comparable to the forms of the logical-cognitive processes, to which emotional life remains "other," and with which the sentimental maintains a relation of reciprocal exclusion. According to the notion put forth here, however, aesthetic and scientific (cognitive) functions are born from a single bifurcation, and so they proceed in a certain way, side by side, parallel, even if they remain apart and are directed toward entirely distinct and unequal ends. The linguistic ambiguity of the word "ends" [*fini*] is quite useful here, because it manages to capture the sense of both the masculine *fine* (end as goal), inherent in the aesthetic field (such that it follows, precisely, an autonomous end), and the feminine *fine* (end as closure, cessation), which seems more appropriate to scientific usage, in which the goal or "end" is the attainment of a conclusive finish that finds some place in the praxis of everyday life. But even if the respective "ends" of art and science diverge, according to the concept examined here, they continue to confront one another, engaged in dialogue, entrusted to poles capable of continually experiencing their respective attraction, even if they respond to different doses—more here, less there. Among the great families of operators, however, there is a continuous collaboration, a relation of equality, with equal responsibility for instituting the general presuppositions on which every cultural era is based, especially in the area of symbolic forms, or rather, the "high" valence of any culture. This is true even if there is also a division, a split, between symbolic forms of a discursive-referential type (as Langer would say) and those of a presentational type. Della Volpe, however, would play up the difference between the univocal and the plurivocal, between inorganic contexts and the opposing organic ones. This is truly a final, irreparable diversity, but of modalities of discourse that exist side by side, in a synchrony that is either idealized or historical-chronological. The relatively incarnate or corporeal forms of knowledge administered through artistic channels do not have precedence, either in terms of theory or fact. They coexist with the others, they interfere, they are nourished by exchanges and continual osmosis; and this is also valid in scientific research, which has everything to gain from maintaining a relation of reversibility with the contributions flowing from artistic research.

In the preceding chapter we encountered two typical, historically verifiable areas of a similar collaboration between artists and scientists for the purpose of instituting the general presuppositions of a determinate culture.

Renaissance perspective is a symbolic form whose foundation received collaboration from visual artists (painters, architects, with roles that are themselves already converging and interchangeable), mathematicians, engineers, astronomers, naturalists, and, in particular, scholars of optics, as Panofsky brilliantly demonstrated in a famous essay. But let us pass on to another artistic area in an entirely different age: the narrators between the end of the nineteenth and the beginning of the twentieth century also "collaborated" with psychologists (especially with those engaged in developing the specialized and revolutionary branch of psychoanalysis) in their investigations of lived experience, through discoveries of multiple personalities, deep drives, libidinal releases, neuroses, and every other psychological perversion or complication. Svevo, Pirandello, and Proust are not less important than Freud in the establishment of new parameters for contemporary ethics, in breaking down the boundaries between normal, habitual life and the mechanisms of the comic, the oneiric, the neurotic (for this latter, an essential responsibility rests with the narratives of Kafka). In all of these cases the relation between the artist and the scientist is certainly not to be expressed in the degraded and passive terms of mere "application": the writer or painter did not wait until scientific knowledge had been fully established in certain areas of interest, artists were not limited to receiving this scientific development in a secondary wave, only to introduce it into their works in some exterior way, perhaps seeking to redeem it with the added supplement of some specific trait, of some ornamental spice or emotional intensification. Artists have quite often preceded their colleagues in the scientific field, by inaugurating new postulates and then by putting them to the test, even if it was not for this that they renounced a specific means of presentation. What remains is the possibility, or even more fundamentally, the necessity, to respect a basic split between the modes of transmission proper to the cognitive-scientific function and those of the aesthetic-artistic function. The former are plain, transitive, and "inorganic" inasmuch as they are careful not to establish any relation of organic dependency with their own signifiers; the latter, however, are careful to reinforce a parallel relation of adherence or dependence. In order to facilitate the possibility of exchange between the two polarities, we have already been forced to ascertain the opportune intervention of numerous intermediary formulations, capable of assuring a bridge role, a *Mittelglied*: this is none other than rhetorical discourse, which tempers the rigors of analytic discourse, and mythopoesis, which diminishes cognitive certainties in the sequences of the myth, of the *fabula*.

Poetics

The artist, finally, assumes important responsibilities of a cognitive sort and collaborates with scientists in establishing the knowledge of an era by increasing it, renewing it, imposing on it turns and revolutions. This is the case at least as far as concerns a knowledge, a cognitive capacity turned toward content, toward the sphere of meanings. But, according to the ambiguity typical of the aesthetic-artistic operation, there are cognitive responsibilities even in the face of the dimension of signifiers: that is, a knowledge relative to the technical means of artistic production exists that is, then, a "know-how," an ability or trade. In any case, every artist is compelled to make choices, whether of means or objects, and nothing stands in the way of proceeding toward these choices with interventions of a reflective nature. That which we define as the "poetics" of any production of a work of art comes to be delineated in this same way. This notion has recently been investigated with excellent results by Luciano Anceschi. Obviously, the origin of this process lies in the *Poetics* par excellence of Aristotle, which has then been modified substantially over time by other critics. As we saw earlier, Aristotle's *Poetics* is a treatise that codifies the modalities of writing in order to arrive at the construction of several determinate literary and dramatic genres, although in present use we no longer question the specific artistic zones. There is a poetics wherever we can find an area of artistic production, including those entrusted to the new means of cinema, photography, and others totally extraneous to the interests of Aristotle (visual arts). But what counts above all is the change in subject, given that the Aristotelian treatise was laid out by a philosopher, that is, by an operator aiming for a systematic study of his object with the necessary distance between the maker and the observer who classifies from outside. Yet according to the current definition, poetics is the reflective intervention with which the "poet," the producer, or the artist accompanies the object made, perhaps proceeding in rough and abridged ways, but without ever renouncing the right/duty to contribute ideas or a "cognitive" accompaniment to the act of production. As early as antiquity, along with the *Poetics* developed by a philosopher who was not personally engaged in *poiesis*, there are many cases of poets' producing *artes poeticae* (Horace, for one) charged with personal concerns but also largely representative of a whole climate of taste. This practice has remained uninterrupted since then, so one rather frequently finds great producers of literary texts who also developed theoretical hypotheses concerning their work, sticking to more or less generalized formulas. Almost all of the classic Italian authors (Dante,

Petrarch, Boccaccio, Tasso, Manzoni, Leopardi . . .) can be considered in this light, even if they did not all produce a single treatise directly labeled as an *ars poetica*. At times one has to refer to other treatises, letters, even marginalia, that are apparently indirect compared with any explicitly declared interest of this type. And not only have the "literati" exercised such a right/duty, furnishing a performance that in their case might seem facilitated by the homogeneity between text and metatext (the product of *poiesis* is linguistic, as is the intervention of the critic into it), but so have the visual artists, musical composers, and operators in the field of drama.

This predisposition to annex opportune poetics to a more traditionally creative effort has doubtlessly grown over time through the concomitant effect of two types of factors: an increase in public opportunities that led to the release of declarations (newspapers, magazines, mass media in general, the development of information and its circuits), as well as a progressive release of artistic activities from the protective matrix of the useful or quasi-artisanal professions. To be a painter or a poet has become in our times an ever "purer" activity of high public interest, to be developed in the limelight. Artistic genius is sharpened by reinforcing the most clamorous and disturbing elements of aesthetic work (even if such aspects were certainly not unknown in previous times), such as the search for the new and the practice of polysemy (of "ambiguity"), which has further refined the degree of recklessness or the risk of art itself, thus incrementing the occasions for comments on poetics. Almost all of the visual artists of the modern period (Boccioni, Mondrian, Klee) contributed, in this sense, to forms such as essays, memoirs, lessons, interviews, and so on. But naturally, all of this is not obligatory, and so even in the current scene it is possible to find artists who, although they have proceeded to make rather difficult and even shocking turns, have expressed themselves at the level of poetics in rather sparse and contrite ways (for example, Picasso).

Naturally, even an aesthetics such as that of Croce would not seek to deny the possibility that an artist becomes both critic and theoretician of aesthetic products, including those produced by others, but such a possibility could be taken into consideration only by hypothesizing an obligatory passage through a moment of the "death of art." Thus the phase dedicated to the category of the aesthetic form (the short circuit of intuition and expression) would have to spend itself in the artist, and a new, successive phase dedicated to philosophical knowledge would begin (at least according to the logical succession of an ideal diachrony), without any organic connection between the two points of culmination. Here we encounter the risk that the one might pose an obstacle to the other, because they are not able to avoid bothersome interferences. We intend to follow a "polar" conception so that, if we cannot deny that the primary scope of any artist is to provide us with some object, a system of symbolic forms with perfect adherence between signifieds and signifiers, it seems equally indispensable that during the march toward such a pole or final goal, the artist also intersects all of the corresponding possibilities of the other poles. In other words, the artistic object is plotted with knowledge and cognition, and these constitute its very basis, so that they cannot be separated or extirpated from it. Poetry, then, carries its own apparatus of poetics, incorporated into its very depth, just as every means of transportation folds in and gathers into itself the various ramps and gangways that have allowed access to it.

More generally, the philosophical position to which we adhere is contrary to all drastic scissions. For example, we have already welcomed the opportunity for making a single system of the "inside" and "outside" of emotional life (that is, it is difficult to establish where "my" emotions end and those belonging to others begin). The same providential "making a single system" can be repeated for another of the great epistemological nodes that otherwise would remain without a solution or would find only a lacerated one, the node between individuality and collectivity. Even here, Crocean theory dives in, certainly with appreciable rigor, to block the unilateral path by which the great work of art, or rather, the synthesis between a portion of sentimental life and its relative, formative intervention (its intuition or expression) gives rise to a single, individual, personal poem, without any dependence on external circumstances (length, genres, technique).

We begin with the presupposition that the individual act and collective formation or general modality are the extremes of a single scale or, once again, the poles of a tension, itself the producer of a field in which each one of us is immersed. Every human action finds itself suspended between these two extremes and certainly seeks to express individual values, but against the background of choices that do not belong to it exclusively, but instead seem to be common to a group, to some social nucleus based on the most various criteria (generation, profession, class, educational level, language). We owe a most exemplary and convincing notion to the linguist Ferdinand de Saussure, the introducer of the felicitous, dynamic couple centered on the polar, antagonistic terms of *langue* (the collective institution in which each of us is rooted) and *parole* (the personal, subjective exercise of small or large infractions made by the individual user). We might also furnish a supplementary, persuasive analogue suggested by geology, where we find the same split between the individuality of the great peaks but also the inevitability that each of these must rest on the hard shelf of a mountain chain. Mont Blanc is distinct from Monte Rosa and other peaks, yet a level of generality makes it inevitable that they will be studied together, if for no other reason than because they belong to the same alpine arch, which assures them a common basis and acts almost like a geological "language." Yet this shared characteristic has not impeded each of them from undergoing a unique degree of erosions, slides, and millennial catastrophes, so that each has come to assume an individual profile.

Analogously, each work of art undoubtedly seeks to achieve its own distinct physiognomy, which makes it unique, almost more so than a physical person: only in it and for it do we find that certain equilibrium between signifieds, and that certain degree of incarnation of these in material signifiers, the former perfectly commensurate with the latter. Yet, to exploit the geological analogy just proposed, the work is nothing other than a swaying peak, with a particular profile, a certain mass, and yet only reaching such heights thanks to the larger chain that supports it. In the meantime, this chain links a given peak to the other peaks rising from that same shelf, each one unique and individual, yet linked together through family resemblance, subject to similar phenomena of deformation. Leaving behind the notion of naturalistic similitude, we can say that the individual work of art is not comprehensible except against the background of other works produced by the same artist, before, during, and after. These other works may appear more or less successful, just as of the many peaks rising from the same mountain chain only a few may become famous for their majesty, for their recognizable profiles. The work of a single author meshes with or branches into the works of other companions (contemporaries, students, and followers), even at times composing an entire orographic node. Just like geographic maps, maps of artistic production in relation to a certain historical era appear plotted with nerve structures or axes of continuity. Only against their background do the individual, isolated reliefs take form, and these constitute rare and partial examples, almost always referring, on closer examination, to subterranean levels still in existence even if apparently canceled. Finally, just as works of art seem to be woven with knowledge, with concepts and abilities, they now reveal to us inevitable links of a collective character, or else demonstrate themselves to be immersed in a "field" laid out between the extremes of the *parole*—of the single result—and the institution, the collective code that transcends isolated individuality.

The poetics we have just discussed belong to the family of these intersubjective choices to which each artist is called, sometimes in spite of him- or herself. Whether one practices polysemy or makes a choice of various "dramatic" strategies, the ways of innovation, in a given period, are hatched from an understanding. Human beings are fundamentally social by nature, and there exists no option that does not find adherents, sympathizers, sodality. It may also happen that during particularly adverse moments, and in the presence of exceptional destructive capabilities introduced by a single personality, these companions along the way find it difficult to emerge, but that does not take away the fact that a given action with its connected poetics, uttered by a powerful artist, contains in itself a proselytizing spirit, perhaps addressed to the future, like a message in a bottle. Certainly such a poetics is sustained by the implicit, tacit hope that someone will return to it and eventually take it up. This can happen even when the adherents might not be positioned in any strictly physical, geographical proximity, in the same city, in the same national or social area. The same set of needs may be observed by artists active in distant places. But this does not imply any diminution of the sense of a family whose scattered members might recognize themselves only later, or perhaps never, leaving to commentators and followers the task of effecting their conjunction. Similarly, to return to the useful geological metaphor, mountain chains can be broken apart, only to flourish again at a great distance in separate continents, which, however, obliges us to reconstitute their prior formations. Or, we might encounter truly diverse and noncommunicative formations, which share certain affinities of genesis and structure such that they confirm one another.

In effect, poetics are almost never isolated. Instead, for the most part, they are grouped into families such that they designate the rising and the manifestation of tendencies, movements, climates of taste. Such a classification is never extrinsic or conducted a posteriori for reasons of convenience, but is revealed in the very course of action chosen. An individual poetics boastfully asks to be systematized with similar utterances advanced by friends and members of the same group, perhaps signers of the same "manifesto" or program. Finally, we are addressing extremely dynamic realities, capable of issuing lines of force and of expressing valences that ask to be saturated and satisfied by the strengthening of alliances and collaborations.

Styles

Along with the notion of poetics, we should consider the question of style, which concerns, for the most part, the same sort of phenomena. The word "style" derives from a slight deformation and elevation of the *stilo* or pen, as we should more correctly transcribe the Latin *stilus*, which, in turn, was a technical instrument invented for the exercise of an art, but in the largest and most common sense of the term corresponding to a practical ability. This art entailed the use of a handle fitted with a metallic point for scratching the surface of wax deposited on tablets. This was the operation of cursive writing familiar to the ancient Romans. But the exercise of the stylus also allowed for expressive openings, given that there were various ways to form graphic characters by hand, with varying degrees of elegance. The stylus also opened the way to noble and superior meanings: with the application of the rhetorical figure called synecdoche (the part for the whole), material style became the indicator (style) of an entire system of aesthetic choices, at first relative only to the act of writing, but then extended to any other artistic practice.

In any case, there is more to style than the personal choices of the single operator. A given individual is also influenced by various affiliations, including those of generation, of social group, of the level of education, to say nothing of active options (in what degree one has decided to innovate, which contents or meanings of the knowledge of the era are to be accentuated, and through which strategies of sensory presentation). Even in this case, the metaphor of the mountain chain is especially valid; style is stratified reality, made of successive skins, several of which lead in a social direction and guide us toward collective options. From one act of mediation to another they flow into the great themes that belong to an entire cultural cycle, and other layers of sediment address the stylistic affirmations of a single path. The term "style" oscillates continually between these dynamic extremes. It narrows and widens, it specifies and generalizes at the same time, acting as an incessant converter.

The Normal Patron

It is now time to examine how the patron (the reader, the spectator) of the arts should behave in a normative sense before a given work. Here the patron reveals all of the utility inherent in tracing a particular group of directions (of "categories") around the aesthetic-artistic territory. From this exercise we may derive useful instructions to be addressed to a common patron, without immediately being forced onto that path that leads to the specialized and professional patron who is the critic.

The first obligation of the normal patron is to recognize the symbolic dimension inherent in all artistic works. We again take up the problem of emotional components, already encountered on the other side of the equation when we spoke of the artist. The presence of the distancing filter of the symbolic apparatus guarantees that the reader-spectator will have to avoid reacting in the "first degree" when confronting the emotional material doubtlessly agitated by the work, to avoid reacting as though in the realm of common experience, or everyday life, vulnerable to various risks and dangers, "without a safety net," without time for mediation. More generally, the patron must avoid that type of reaction that we might title "the paint of Doctor Lambicchi," a marvelous paint that immediately gives concreteness and real presence to every sort of image. Or, for example, once the reader has come to know a "mythical" sequence that releases emotions (passions, various sorts of affects), he or she will no longer be able to respond as if confronting real causes with equally powerful emotional effects. Clearly, then, a greater responsibility will also be placed on the shoulders of the author, who will have to administer conveniently a way of framing the emotional slice of life, so that this does not leave its own suspended and virtual space. This does not mean that the field of aesthetic enjoyment remains oblivious to reactions of an emotional nature or must necessarily exist in a climate of ascetic neutrality. The problem is not to avoid emotions at any cost, but to create them in a controlled space. Finally, there is some truth to the old notion, once dear to empiricist and positivist theories, according to which affectivity worthy of the aesthetic field must be weakened and attenuated. It may be acceptable to say that, in terms of a well-conceived or successfully executed drama or film, we react with shivers, goose bumps, sobs, but in the context of an "as if," almost preparing our physiological apparatus for a certain reaction without actually following through on it. Perhaps this is our way of redeeming the classic theory of the catharsis presented in Aristotle's *Poetics* (and already discussed here in an elliptical manner) in order to leave room for contrasting interpretations. Yet beyond the final and more circumscribed sense to be attributed to such a theory, its general goal is clear and irrefutable. We are alluding to the beneficent, liberating effect obtained thanks to our capacity to experience the release of passions as if in vitro, even reliving catastrophic events, or those which by now, and through the Aristotelian treatment, can only be defined as tragic. The experience is like using a vaccine, injecting oneself with a certain disease or affliction, in a controlled dosage so that it may run its complete course and be particularly ample and articulated in all of its characteristics, but remain within a regulated walled space, which then corresponds to one of the possible definitions of the proper dimension of the symbol. Through this distancing intervention, that which in real life would be bothersome or threatening to our safety or to a healthy psychic equilibrium becomes, rather, delectation, pleasure, enjoyment. This well-known property of the work of art is not only valid in terms of "mythical" affects, at the level of plot and human actions (primarily concerning literature and drama), but also in the realm of visual activity where we encounter the proverbial situation of a theme that is in itself horrifying, degrading, and repugnant, but which becomes rather efficacious if presented as image, so that it ends up controlled and carefully administered through the mediation of the graphic, pictorial, or plastic symbol.

The Heresy of Paraphrase

According to the model of a great number of illustrious precedents the theory traced here also bears a warning directed toward taking into account the organic contextual character of the artistic fact. We cannot thus rush to grasp "the" end of the sequence, of the "story," as if this were the principal objective of the work itself. As readers-spectators we must force ourselves to embrace the entire work, to retain successive passages in our memory or within our sight, weighing them carefully in a global context. Even here, the duty of the patron corresponds with an analogous duty of the composer, who, in turn, must try his or her best to slow the reading adequately, to sabotage the possibility that one may make an improper, accelerated, and transitive use of the material offered in a piece of music. Following this path, we arrive at what the American New Critic Cleanth Brooks defined as "the heresy of paraphrase": in the organic and plurivocal context that is the work (literary or otherwise), the partial extraction of a network of signifiers rendered univocal never corresponds with the "whole," it is always only a reduction of it for the sake of convenience. In the preceding lines we forced ourselves not to exclude the complicity of "knowledge," of notions, ideas, scientific conquests of an era, in the constitution of the organic body of the work of art; however, that does not mean that the "cognitive" level of the work is equal to its totality. Certainly, it is possible to "derive it" toward the field of scientific experience, but then it remains a derivation, a partial betrayal. This is valid both in terms of "knowledge" understood in a "pure" sense, related to epistemology, as well as in an ethical-political sense; the work is not equal to the so-called message, or to the ideology that conveys it, even though such an ideological component does not appear inconvenient, irrelevant, or extrinsic. It is inconvenient to extract it, discarding the contextual accompaniment and perhaps the "decorative" effects (stylistic figures, analogies, polysemy) that surround it. From this point of view it is a good idea to preach against any interpretations of art in a strictly "communicative" key. Art does not communicate, it does not transmit messages. Another of the American New Critics, Allen Tate, responded to the "communication" prejudice that pervaded Anglo-Saxon culture between the two wars (especially in theories of a neopositivistic flavor) by maintaining that art, if anything, demands a process of communion; that is, it asks that the patron sympathize with the author, making time for the work and assuming a relaxed state of mental agility for the tortuous, twisted courses imposed by the work. The patron must "live" an experience and concede a certain "duration" to it, play a game without being in a hurry to change the *fiches*, to go and verify one's winnings.

Paradoxically, it can happen that one must work at convincing the patron to accept freely this dimension of the game, of suspended and virtual space, of "as if," in which art must pull the strings, sway the values, the emotions of practical life (of moral and political behavior), without stubbornly seeking "cognitive" or edifying and consoling messages, either for or against personal ideological convictions. There is a tendency to "consume" the work of art in rather austere and serious modes, by imposing on it to respond to a pressure *cui prodest*, by rejecting any ludic dimension that does not hurry itself along the way of goals, objectives to be reached, but prefers to place the various materials of experience into tension, in a split capable of intersecting all of our interests.

At the opposite extreme, a patron may be so thickheaded, so lacking in any aesthetic education as to fail to take cognitive or generally contextual obligations into account when clearly these weigh on any work of art understood in the fullest sense. This individual hurries to "consume" the product, asking that it run without delay toward its conclusion. This nondiscriminating consumer asks only that the "myths" reach their fulfillment as soon as possible, offering a catharsis at little expense, evoked by dramas whose development must be prearranged, drawing on old, proven recipes in which only the exterior clothing of "characters" and the scenographic backgrounds change. The complex notions that the work captures along the way, enriching it and even, inevitably, "slowing" it, creating obstacles to a rapid diegesis, merely embarrass such a reader, who prefers to avoid any complications or convolutions, who believes it is better to unravel such knots, to smooth them flat, so that the transitive march toward "the" end is not interrupted.

For this same reason the patron must also be ready to invest adequately in the act of enjoyment. The work of art is located at a symbolic level, which implies the adoption of a perceptual posture capable of abstraction, stylization, or self-mastery of opportune codes of transposition (thus destroying the belief in a genuine intervention of the "paint of Doctor Lambicchi"). And then, the particular process of symbolizing proper to the work of art is inevitably accompanied by the need to search for the new, to overcome old mechanisms of habitual reception, familiar sequences of plots, stories, well-known parameters of visual representation of reality, or of the "expression" of emotions. One of the ways to recognize the presence of an authentic artistic value is to have been forced to confront and win over such resistances in the processes of reading, at the cost of recording negative responses of disappointment or irritation at first glance.

The Rights of the Reader

After having attended to these duties, our standard patron will then be called to exercise certain rights in confrontations with the author. Even in the case of a successful work of art, it is not a given that any wrongs or transgressions are to be attributed to an error in reception. The "poet" may also commit the "heresy of the paraphrase" and, that is, maintain that the value of a given work rests on the successful, full, and timely communication of a proper "message." We saw earlier how important it is to endow the work of art with an added skin consistent with the poetics of the artist, but this must be interpreted especially in modal terms. This extra skin works to furnish responses to an enormous question concerning "how" the artist reached the production of the work: through what stylistic or technical choices, what strategies and alliances, blocks of solidarity with contemporaries, scattered throughout the various disciplinary and geographical fronts of the same culture. But a poetics that expresses itself on the "what is" that the work intended to express, communicate, and transmit is less useful, or at least in such a case the patron demands full freedom and is held to verify if the "what is," or the network of ideas, is conveniently incorporated into the slowing and blocking strategies, or, even more simply, if these are present in any appreciable measure, such that they truly make an organic context of the work. It can sometimes happen, however, that the best intentions fail, either through absence or insufficiency of an adequate rhythmic or polysemic structure; or else that such a network of added values substantially modifies the intended "message" or even negates and destroys it. We frequently encounter artists who make themselves carriers of reactionary ideologies, ideologies not easily shared by others if they are uttered openly. But these artists have been able to create robust and intrinsically positive organisms, that is to say, works plotted with a knowledge or an ethics that is in step with the times. Such is the well-known case of Balzac, reactionary in his ideological proclamations, but at the same time a magnificent mythographer of the ascent of the bourgeoisie, a lucid singer of the new values affirmed by this class. On the other side of this coin, how many "good intentions," how many declarations of honest "engagement," on the part of Italian neorealist writers of the 1950s were ruined by narrative contexts destined to repeat old "stories," and linked to a naturalist nineteenth-century universe and to its subjection to fate (to make oneself the singer of a proletarian or peasant condition without perceiving the socioeconomic factors that are actually disintegrating such a condition and provoking its very supplantation, signifies a belief in destiny, in a rather natural fatality).

In other words, the author certainly has the right to pronounce judgment on the work, to accompany it with a congruous package of instructions for use that forms a constitutive part, such that the reader is obliged to consider these poetic tenets; but such a right, in turn, does not negate the right of the patron to exercise his or her own prerogatives sanctioned by aesthetic theory, in which the work is an organic, polysemic, "ambiguous" context containing associations, references, and linkages not necessarily considered by the author. In addition, in a psychoanalytic regime such as ours we cannot establish the location of the author with any certainty. Should we look for the author at the level of the ego or the id? We now refer to the classic conflict in Pirandello's drama, which places the various characters and the author at odds, precisely because the former come from within the latter, from primary and unconscious choices against which the author for various professional, social, and opportunistic reasons seeks desperately to resist, out of fear that one of their crude and courageous insurrections may alienate the public, editors, directors, and theatrical producers. The "superficial" author may be less valid than the subterranean producer emanating from the id; in any case the final result of the work does not belong to the author, who can only say, through a "journal entry" corresponding to a declaration of poetics, "how," according to what procedures, a particular end was pursued.

Obviously, throughout this work, we have refuted the prejudice according to which the work of art speaks or expresses the subjectivity of the artist. This subjectivity could almost be considered a catalyzing substance favoring the aggregation of materials that are neither internal nor external, neither subjective nor objective, but seem to be positioned in a "polar" tension between the two extremes in a continual, reciprocal exchange. It is useful to know the biography of a writer or of a successful artist as an interesting addendum to the poetics of the individual in question; such ideas released on the work may help to explain the plot, as long as the work is not overturned or made into an instrument or an accessory for the glorification of the author. In the field of psychoanalysis, a greater heresy leads us to consider the work as a useful symptom for reconstructing the neurosis from which an author suffers. If that is our aim, we must limit ourselves to clinical cases and with an application of psychoanalysis understood as medicine, as therapy. This method cannot be extended to aesthetic interpretation.

So the field of rights extended to the patron of the arts seems ample and articulated; however, this patron also runs against a limit imposed by the unitary criterion that stands between the most valid attributes of a successful work of art as such. The author of the work in question cannot veto any given interpretive process or denounce any largely associative readings brought to light by apparently distant ideas; therefore the declaration that the author claims not to have considered a particular direction, not to have possessed certain notions that are attributed to him or her is largely worthless. The interpretive game is truly open and limitless, and can be extended to any historical or cultural context. The author does, however, have the right to defend the contextual character of his or her work, to demand that the patron presents it in its entirety and does not arbitrarily separate it into sections, concentrating on certain parts and ignoring others. Systems of reading can or rather must be open, plurivocal, aggregate, but they must conform to an internal coherence that leads them to confront in the same measure all of the materials placed within the perimeters of a single work.

Critical Discourse and Rhetorical Discourse

After the reactions that can justly be expected of a reader or of a generic patron of a work of art, we arrive at those rather more circumstantial ones, which we may expect directly from a critic. Not that there is a break between one figure and another, but, if we wish to make a philosophical question of it, an exercise of categories or functions, there is no point at which the common patron, almost installed at the heart of a system of transcendental forms, decides to return to the prerogatives of either the aesthetic-artistic or the scientific pole. From this point of view we can give some credit to the Crocean version, for without doubt, the types of activity undertaken by the producer of a work and by the one who judges the work are different, or at least they seem to be on different sides of the fence. More particularly, during the moment of the intervention of a critical evaluation, it is of little import, from the categorical point of view, if such an intervention is entrusted to a few verbal expressions or to a long and complex discourse. But there are notable differences in the practical act, even here, between interventions of a simple, general nature to which we are all subject, if for no other reason than our membership in the human race (and the duties to which we are subject are transformed, in turn, into a power or a right), and the more shrewd, repetitive interventions that fulfill the purposes of the professional sphere. Finally, this is the very difference we have already noted, but in a productive field: whoever can aspire to art is open to the primary result of an aesthetic nature, but in order to have a solid result in the field of art, and produce successful works with a high degree of probability, it is necessary to hypothesize the rise of professional artists (writers, painters, composers, and so on), who assume strong responsibilities in such a sense by predisposing themselves to the expectation that something relatively positive will result from their work. In other words, the configuration of some professional competence divides the subject of a vague and diffuse aesthetic experience, on the one hand, from the producer, the artist in the fullest sense, on the other. Analogously, this possible configuration of a field of critical professional performances establishes a distinction, for our present purposes, between the normal patron of works or artistic goods, called to make use of latent talents centered around humanity, education, and culture, and the one who, instead, makes him- or herself into a reader or spectator almost out of obligation, for career reasons.

The cultural phase in which we now live, rich and complex as it is, has led us to develop every competence and professional area. Our era has seen a multiplication of opportunities for the career of criticism: we might think of the various columns in newspapers, journals, weeklies, or of programs on radio and television as examples of this, even if merely for a criticism reduced to the recitation of facts and limited to a particular area of technical production (cinema, theater, music, or the arts, perhaps with more recent specializations concentrating on painting, sculpture, architecture, or design). But academic modes of exercising critical judgment today are on the rise thanks to the extension of instruction, especially into the ranks of high schools and universities. The teachers of these advanced courses are potentially also critics by profession, even aiming toward competitive or careerist ends. Criticism, finally, through its various modalities, is today a flourishing genre. Some may even draw a negative conclusion from this, affirming that this increase in a critical spirit will only inhibit creativity itself. But once again, this sort of response presupposes an inauspicious idealism, of which the distant and guiltless progenitor can actually be considered to be Vico, reexamined and developed by Hegel and later by Croce, with the opportune passage from a diachronic conception to a synchronic one. According to a certain conception of diachronic historicism, humanity will experience "hot" ages dedicated to the sentimental-creative impetus, followed by "cold" ages in which art "dies," yielding to logical reasoning. Croce, in particular, transports a similar scheme from diachrony to the a-chrony of a purely logical succession of moments of the Spirit, which, however, continue to exclude each other from time to time. But certainly those who let themselves be influenced by schemes of this sort are destined to return, perhaps against their very will, to a vitiated historicism, according to which our age sins precisely in an excess of reason. We write too many books on aesthetics and criticism, which results in reduced creativity. The response, instead, can be more comforting: we live in an era that has not yet experienced sterility on the productive front, but rather has developed various functions and professions in the name of an "abundance" capable of manifesting itself in every direction, perhaps even yielding an embarrassment of riches. Ours is, then, an era that is far from the poverty and schematization of other, previous eras, in which there was space only for the essential functions, exercised in crude and elementary ways. And if other historical moments have already known a similar abundance and flourishing, it still does not seem opportune to reiterate the historical-romantic judgment, retaining them guilty of creative sterility.

Returning to questions of a theoretical nature, it is true that between the production of texts (of works) and the critical intervention made on them there is a certain hiatus, but even so we find certain great intermediaries furnished by an articulation of the types of discourse. More specifically, we can return to the benefit of rhetorical discourse, which in effect functions egregiously as a "converter." Rhetoric assures that copenetration of fields from which the present conception arises, according to which the various functions (categories) exhibit a polar nature. In the meantime, even the field of scientific function presents itself as divided, as broken up by the traditional conflict between the physical-mathematical disciplines, which are primarily quantitative, and the humanistic, qualitative ones, or in any case, those dependent on descriptive-valuative parameters. Rhetorical discourse functions primarily as an excellent *Mittelglied* between art and science, because it is engaged not only on the front of *docere* (of knowledge, consciousness), but also on those of *movere* and *delectare*. We can neutralize the passions and affects if we limit ourselves to a field of mathematical theorems and consequent demonstrations, but it is difficult and, in fact, even harmful or counterproductive to strive toward this in the field of political or juridical debate where the layer of emotional life forms part and parcel of the material under investigation. This process is not without some fallout, spread from the object of study to the subject who conducts the examination, and then to the audience. Where there is no mathematical, rigorous, univocal truth, but only probability or opinion, the mode of presentation becomes an important weapon for "persuading" one's own public, and so we return to the virtue of *delectare*: the valid rhetorician must know how to pepper speech with a pleasing semantic and syntactic redundancy. Variation, hendiadys, and every other stylistic figure that might seem inopportune in a strictly logical sense are welcome in a rhetorical one, and there is no discourse regarding human material that can do without rhetoric. This is well known by political orators, the leaders of various parties, and prosecuting and defense attorneys involved in trying cases, even if the degree of eloquence depends, finally, on the means of peroration itself, on the channel chosen to bear the message: an acoustic channel invites redundancy, whereas a graphic-visual channel, resting on written texts, must be more sober and measured.

So critical discourse belongs to the great family of rhetorical discourses, which treat human materials and for which there are no indubitable criteria of "truth" (formal or experimental as they may be), but only greater or lesser degrees of persuasion. It is then a case of exercising an impact on the audience (whether present or absent, near or far) with the subtlety of one's arguments, appealing to "common opinions" accepted by all (or at least by that certain audience to which we are directed), and with the capacity for reconstructing facts in a way advantageous to one's own cause, placing into evidence the points that are most favorable, spicing the whole with felicitous and abundant eloquence. We are still in a field that is primarily subject to an attraction of the scientific pole, but that does not take away the fact that we feel a strong pull toward the aesthetic pole as well. At the extreme, nothing prohibits the properly aesthetic-artistic prerogatives from becoming so strong and valuable that a slippage from one field to another is indicated. It can happen that a discourse born as critical, during some occasion linked to the exercise of the corresponding profession, is equally adept in its use of polysemy and excites the passions or exploits dramatic construction so convincingly that it merits, in turn, a positive evaluation as a work of art *tout court*, in a splendid and successful literary context.

Nevertheless, even if this possibility cannot absolutely be excluded, it cannot become obligatory. At the very least it remains true that artistic production and critical judgments about that production are based on two distinct variants. We will not grant credence to the voices that insist on the equally creative character that must belong to good critical prose, almost according it the privilege of projection toward an autonomous end so as to construe the text as being subjected to judgment almost like a pretext, like material that is itself susceptible to free variations.

Yet it is also true that the inclusion of critical discourse in the great scheme of the rhetorical discourses relativizes it enormously, making it the place of quite fluid, plastic interventions, susceptible to various and unpredictable results. We must confront this place of criticism with the utmost discretion, taking it in its etymological sense (linked to discerning, to a capacity for division, analysis), but in its more ample derivation related to the use of common sense, which knows how to evaluate the pros and cons in each circumstance, avoiding unilateral positions. If this complexity and discretion of judgment is required in every rhetorical occasion (political, judicial, laudatory, general), it is even more so in the case of valuative discourse referring to a work of art, one of whose constitutive characteristics, as we know well, resides in a fundamental "ambiguity," or rather in polysemy. In this arena, the chase is on for surprising possibilities of meaning that had eluded previous interpreters and perhaps even the author. A source of doubts and contrasting judgments can be found in that other obligation connected with the search for the new—but what constitutes successful innovation as opposed to a frozen, superficial pretense to surprise the public? To what degree should novelty be allowed? When should it be considered excessive and gratuitous?

Militant Criticism and Historical Criticism

There are thousands of different ways to undertake a critical-valuative intervention, as Luciano Anceschi has demonstrated in his *Phenomenology of Criticism*; it is impossible to rigidify the course of criticism according to fixed schemes, with, at best, few exterior variants. All of the numerous divisions and disjunctive considerations to which we were constrained in the analysis described in the previous chapters can be changed into distinct, corresponding modalities in the critical exercise. There will thus be many sliding axes between extreme and opposite poles. We will be able to bring the concrete praxis, here and now, of the single artist into proximity with his or her own poetics so that they form a single, common system. The result of this identification can be called militant criticism, concerned initially with giving birth to new works, and then constrained by a similar heuristic obligation to forget all of the rest, to make a tabula rasa of preceding solutions. These solutions must inevitably take on the semblance of a preestablished profile, almost a caricature, however unjust it may be. In such a case, the critic is somehow gaudy, becoming part defense attorney, ready to malign any prior solutions or those that seem to take a different road from one's own, and part priest, who celebrates, together with the artist engaged in new solutions, a sacrificial rite, by symbolically "killing" the fathers, even if they had been loved and venerated a day earlier. In this sphere of action, aesthetic theory must behave like the well-known proverb: "If the people lead, the leaders will follow." It is important for the "people" of art to run ahead, to occupy new positions: too bad if the old theories seek to negate our efforts or fail to communicate. Certainly, the militant critic is often the same *poietés* engaged in the effort of imposing a "new style" and, with outstretched arms, demands solidarity with companions along the way. In effect, we know that in this "hot" sector of works-in-progress, the emergence of an original tendency that seeks to destroy the past is never entrusted to a single artist, but is incorporated in a rather generational front. It is difficult, but not impossible, for the militant critic to act as the baptist for a single Savior. In general, however, this critic fights for the common cause of a group of adepts, even bringing them together as signers of a canonical manifesto (of symbolism, futurism, surrealism, and so on). How many manifestos have we encountered throughout history, even if the term is relatively recent? The manifesto is typical of a society that is largely directed toward extroversion and mass communications; we might think of the Dantesque "sweet new style," or of the Pléiade of Ronsard and friends.

At the other extreme of participatory anxiety demonstrated by the militant critic, and by that critic's partiality and partisanship, we have the distance of the historical critic, who "has understood the game," and knows that various generations succeed one another through the ages, each one directed toward fulfilling its own symbolic sacrifice of fathers, toward extending a destructive manifesto towards prior proposals. But the various generations compose a line, they give rise to the river of history that may not be continuous, but rather may proceed by jumps, with ruptures, oppositions, lacerations; or perhaps, if we like, the river will demonstrate that it does not flow in a rectilinear manner, but winds about. This varying dynamic will come to compose a regularized cloth, capable of foreseeing the changes, and of organizing the rhythm of variation, for example, through recourse to the scheme of polar couples: classic and romantic, Apollonian and Dionysian, closed and open, static and dynamic. Naturally, there must be a way to redefine the historical axis itself by considering such couples as if they returned at periodic intervals, just as a comet reenters the solar system from time to time, giving rise to certain predictions. In order to fulfill the basic vocation, the historical critic must be able to admit multiple variations, but always returning them to a canvas where the same couple encounters recurring patterns. History improvises, but according to a script to be modified with contemporary solutions.

Remaining within the scheme traced by Anceschi, we must still consider the philosophical critic who fearlessly seeks to remain on the track of extreme phenomenology, as presented by the field of artistic manifestations. Below the phenomena we must seek out the permanent functions and general categories at the cost of sacrificing the movable and multiple characters of the sector. In order to arrive at the economical syntheses proposed in chapter 3, we were forced to proceed by way of this ruthless and even heroic path, simplifying, flattening, and leveling; but basically, it is also a question of optical distances, and one can even defend the utilitarian merits of panoramic views such as those recorded by artificial satellites that orbit the earth. We might think of cartography, which knows how to utilize various scales effectively, conscious of an inverse proportionality between intensity and extension: the more we continue to embrace vast sectors of land, the less we retain of local detail. Maps made on a grand scale tell nothing to a tourist interested in visiting local spots. Analogously, both the reader involved in some artistic practice on the production side and the patron on the other side of reception may draw some modest profit from this book. But surely a greater degree of profit might be had in the general realm of education, by a polyvalent patron not constrained by professional or personal choices to cultivate a single area of expertise. This individual is able to express a system of organic responses corresponding to different opportunities arising from contemporary society.

Critique of Form and Critique of Content

Instead of a scale running from the intensive to the extensive, we could operate along a different axis: from the particular to the general, from the internal to the external, considering the dialectical nature of artistic symbols on which we have already insisted numerous times. Symbols seem to us like points of conjunction or intersection between reasons purely inherent in the physical level of symbols, and those inherent in the signifieds that lead outside, toward the knowledge of the era, until they flow into pure reason and practical reason, into the great epistemological and ethical-political choices.

From the "internal" part there can be various disciplinary fields of philological criticism, that is, fields directed toward ascertaining or establishing works in their originary consistency by liberating them from the betrayals of different means of diffusion and publication. We might also say that these are areas of purely auxiliary intervention, almost pretextual, aimed at flattening or making navigable the ways for confronting a critical-valuative judgment, which must in any case presuppose a text in order to be able to confront it as an "organic context." But rhetorical discourse teaches us that one of the first tasks of the orator is to establish the facts on which to base an argument. Facts are often uncertain and confused; their description is already an organic part of the procedure itself and cannot be left to others.

The gap separating the critic-philologist from the critic interested in issues of style is small indeed. Style is conceived in such broad terms that it is difficult to exclude those components that are relative to content. Yet, when we spoke of stylistic criticism, we referred to scholars especially drawn to literary works and interested in microtextual components (grammar, rhetoric, considered with particular attention to syntactical movements or elementary choices of lexicon). When we refer to stylistic criticism, we think of individuals coming for the most part from linguistics and Romance philology, such as Karl Vossler or Leo Spitzer, and, in Italy, Giacomo Devoto, Gianfranco Contini, and others. These critics all are interested in the Crocean scheme, yet they resist the broad short circuit desired by the author of the *Aesthetics* between linguistic facts and expressive facts, that synthesis so powerful that it excludes every possible tension between a public-institutional moment and a personal-creative one. Instead, these thinkers accept the existence of a common basis, of a *koiné* that allows them to evaluate, through difference, individual "swerves," aberrant choices, the expressive tics capable of revealing the presence of an "author" predisposed to that opportune thickness (that is, of those deviant, retarding elements) that must be recognized as facts of art.

Yet we know that in our own times, so-called structuralist linguistics founded by Ferdinand de Saussure has received broad affirmation within this area of linguistic-stylistic interests stemming from definite "historical" schools. And it is precisely to Saussure that we owe several of the most influential binary couples of the past several decades. These have circulated far beyond the particular disciplinary field in which he was versed: the couple of *langue-parole*, which borrows a simple and efficacious terminology to define the external dialectic between the public moment and that of the individual, tenaciously subtended to every human action. As we saw earlier, not even the visual arts are immune to this, although Saussure was quite far from applying this binomial to such a field of interests: he limited himself to examining its validity in the field of common sense (in which "speech" exercises its full right), and this helped it slip equally into a scientific field, that is, linguistics understood as a specialist discipline. But we have repeatedly maintained in these pages that even the making of art cannot avoid certifying itself along this axis; and such notions of poetics and style are valid in their equipping the entire field of artistic production in such a direction, to say nothing of the connected critical evaluation.

The other highly effective couple advanced by Saussure (and we have even made ample use of it here) is that which sees the dialectical (polar) opposition between the signifier and the signified. As the arrows of so many successive interpretations have been staved off by the fortress of this couple, so many interpretations have attempted to untie that Gordian knot by placing the accent on one or the other of the faces of the symbol. Again, to return to the current argument, the stylistic criticism of our times is primarily interested in the face of the signifier, which has seemed preferable to examining that of the signified for various reasons. For one thing, it is more within reach of the very competencies of the critics (for the moment let us speak of literary critics), who certainly are more versed in linguistic-grammatical-rhetorical facts than in psychosocial or political-economic "contents." In other words, there is a choice of poetics in this tendency, a more or less conscious reaction against other seasons in which the external/content-related faces of works of art were privileged (such as the conjuncture of positivism and naturalism during the second half of the nineteenth century).

Along this path we meet another of those dialectical couples that are revealed as so useful, almost indispensable, for equipping the field of critical investigation, that which sees the polar opposition between the autonomy and the heteronomy of art (Luciano Anceschi, throughout the course of his career, has maintained this insistence). Naturally, even in this case an aesthetic theory like that of Croce would opt for peremptorily untying the Gordian knot by declaring the privilege of the pole of autonomy: either art is constituted and recognized in its autonomous status, or it is *not* (hence the famous Crocean distinction expressed drastically by the title of a volume of his essays conceived in just this sense: *Poetry and Non-poetry*).

Let us not forget the "removing" methodology that subsequently follows. The good critic must proceed by excluding from consideration any elements of another nature (ethical, cognitive, ludic), according to personal judgment, inasmuch as this faculty is aesthetic. The act of leaving open a congruous space to the pole of heteronomy instead means many things. First, to recognize, in a historical context, that art may have prospered among other cultures in a position of subordination compared with ends and interests that are extraneous to it (religion, magic, public utility, or entertainment); but certainly in a proper topology of the complete picture of human activity (or rather, to use more traditional terms, in a valid and exhaustive philosophical system), and, especially with reference to a mature and complex society like ours, it will be better to guarantee absolutely a convenient autonomy (autotelia, intrinsicness) to the facts of an aesthetic-artistic nature, as we have done here since the beginning. We have also insisted on the polar character that must have the affirmation of such a principle, as the place of an emanation of influx, of a field of lines of force that intersect those of other fields. The contexts of single works must remain open to capturing multiple interests, and only in this way do they also guarantee their organic (polysemic, totalizing) character.

It is thus extremely difficult for those "internal" or formalist approaches of stylistic (or structuralist, semiotic) criticism to play the card of intrinsicness exclusively. Context is open, porous, discontinuous, and hemorrhaging. The stylistic criticism of Spitzer gave access to the fantasies of the unconscious, to the manifestation of a supercontent, furnished by the life of the libidinal drives giving rise to various deviances, swerves, and expressive tics. The linguistic instruments are transformed into extraordinary symptomatic apparatuses through the tapping of the repressed, as long as these symptoms are not used to diagnose illnesses or neuroticism of the author. In other words, we can immediately consider these aberrant conducts of the individual author as catalysts for expressing the collective neuroses of a whole society. Certainly, the most refined instruments of contemporary semiotic-structuralist-formalist analyses (for example, those of Stefano Agosti) will also exhibit this leak of billowing subterranean energy, even if it is to be identified with the signifying body of the words. From classic and limpid Freudian doctrine we then pass to one more dark and tortuous, but more attentive to inserting linguistic facts into the analysis, as elaborated by Jacques Lacan.

Without going all the way to the insurrection of the vertical axis of the id, to violating a definition that is too closed by autonomy and by formalist criticism, the very forms of linguistics and rhetoric will be enough. From internal constructs, from the brief syntagmas that give rise to single phrases, we pass to those more complex constructs that regulate discourses, the longest and more laborious textual strategies leading to genres: rhetorical genres (the political, the judicial, the laudatory, in which critical discourse itself is positioned), or else literary genres (brief, long, narrative, lyric, and so on). Little by little as the spectrum of materials is enlarged, the operation becomes more difficult to maintain from inside, limited to an exercise of autonomy and formalism; the critic will almost inevitably want to "capture" extrinsic interests or establish relations of collaboration or synergy with them. The needle of the scale oscillates toward the pole of heteronomy, until it raises concerns on the opposite side. If, while we are moving in an "internal" field of stylistic criticism understood in a strict sense, it is better to save the exits and overcome a pretense of "doing by oneself," now on the contrary it will be better to remain alert so that the opening to the other will not provoke yielding or submissions to the extreme case of an art resigned to the destiny of "sounding the trumpet" for the revolution. This proverbial expression is used correctly by Elio Vittorini to denounce the climate of "engagement" during the years immediately following the Second World War when intellectuals were ashamed of the aspects cultivated in their own sector (all the worse if they were artists or writers) and dreamed of contributing to the "revolution," or at least, in the absence of any concrete possibilities for action, to the formation of a block of solidarity with the oppressed classes. But at the same time there was an enormous *trahison des clercs*, a betrayal by experts who renounced any notion of holding the channels of innovation open and active—in short, this ample, totalizing, liberal reexamination constituting the "game" of art and also its contribution to the knowledge of the era.

Relations with the General Cultural Context

In the areas most sensitive to the attraction of the heteronomous and content-related pole we find those figures that Anceschi, among others, would place under the rubric of the scientist-critic. Perhaps this would include those who, during the second half of the nineteenth century, saw in art just one more instrument for conducting an experimental study of nature, directed toward trying out optical and chemical reactions in the case of the visual arts, or physiopathological ones in the case of the novel. Even in a conjunction of this type we might find the confluence of criticism and poetics, and so we have the example of Emile Zola, who honestly believed in his *Roman expérimental*, and even more in the direct responsibility of the writer to create a work of social medicine, or to make of art an edifying and instructive monument, an informative resource.

These choices or hypotheses obviously bear the color and flavor of their time, of that phase of civilization in which they were made, and which, as perhaps was inevitable, place too much faith in the myth of heteronomy and engagement. Such works maintain their engagement in the face of radically innovative tasks, in the face of a nascent branch of knowledge, but they provide no margins of autonomy or "play" for the arts. Yet, who will ever be able to speak of "long genres" (the novel, theater, cinema) without having to deal with certain "ethical" depths (the component of the characters) or with questions of "mentality," of ideological values conveyed by the characters? How then will the critic who has decided to confront such works be able to avoid some "knowledge" of the very sciences that in some way "arm" or aid their areas of interest, such as psychology, psychoanalysis, and sociology, this latter articulated in thousands of different forms and at numerous levels?

As if all of these possibilities of enlargement or collaboration that link criticism and the various more or less contiguous disciplines were not enough, there still remains the possibility for a more risky enlargement. It will have been noted that in all of the preceding pages we have made frequent gestures toward technological factors that have been decisive in giving a face and an order to the various cultures throughout history. But where are we to position such factors? What status should be granted to technology? Does it belong within the scientific function? On the one hand, it must, because scientific experimentation takes on the task of technological innovation, assuring advancement for itself. But, on the other hand, once instituted, technology becomes an instrument of daily use, and so flows in the riverbed of common experience, or rather, is the most characteristic manifestation of it. We live, we consume the praxis of every day by entrusting ourselves to an indifferent and nonchalant use of the prevalent technology, which functions like a *langue*, like a habit of work, transportation, communication (alimentation, recreation, hygiene), and which thus contributes powerfully to shaping us. We are all children of this dominant "language" (which, then, can articulate itself clearly in so many sublanguages and distinct families). Scientists are like each one of us in the moment when we undertake such a direction, come to effect our own enactments of the *parole*, that is, studies and research directed toward ameliorating or toward abrogating or modifying the dominant technological attitude. The field of the arts is even more engaged there, if possible, because the arts involve an exercise of technology, thus conditioned by this technology while at the same time art must refine technology, bringing it to qualitative and "final" results. Here the ability of the technical exercise to construct determinate objects is the goal of the activity, and not the instrument for acquiring some useful practice.

Even following this path we notice an entanglement and confusion of the ways, a thickening of the forces that cause the great technological options (where we realize the fusion of the three channels, common, aesthetic-artistic, scientific) to appear as the most adept at characterizing the various historical-cultural cycles. Throughout this book we have sketched the data characteristic of the "Gutenberg Galaxy" (the modern age; the primacy of typographic writing; naturalistic, "high-fidelity" perspectival representation) as well as to a later, technological age (transmission and recording entrusted to electronic means, finally capable of treating acoustic and behavioral values; space understood as a symbolic form of electromagnetism; a return toward the original territory of the "est," precisely because today there is the possibility of assuring its survival). All of this is consonant with the large and full meaning, today, of the very concept of culture, which cannot be limited to the "high" levels of the arts and sciences, but, as its etymology suggests, must also address the lower levels, when culture is also cultivation, related to concrete labor and productive practices. Among the most recent humanistic disciplines are cultural anthropology (which does not differentiate between the various levels, also because it is primarily concerned with elementary societies in which these diverse functions are interwoven, in which these differential traces are barely pronounced) and the science of culture, or culturology. This latter, highly ambitious field seeks to effect the same conjunctive-disjunctive examination, that is, accords the same level of attention to the low-material level of technology as to the ideal-symbolic level of the arts and sciences. Culturology is especially interested in the interrelations of these two levels in questions of feedback or reciprocal nutrition that continually links them.

This is also the maximum amplification conceivable in the realm of heteronomy or the confrontation with the "other," of the location of art in a totalized context. It is a particularly arduous and demanding path for the scientist-critic who intends to follow it, especially because a sort of ineluctable postulate emerges from all of this treatment we have offered. This postulate suggests an inverse proportionality between intensity and extension: the wider the embrace, the more the artistic work is considered within general coordinates of theory and linked within a particular historical-disciplinary context, then the less it is valorized in its specificity, in its individual existence. The present map or cartographic undertaking sketches a broad system of organic responses. In its pretense to completeness, this project takes for granted a certain inefficiency in its analysis or local characterization within the various sectors of the truly enormous field covered here.

Bibliographical Essay

Like the text itself, this bibliography avoids specialization. The works indicated here were present in the mind of the author, and he was more or less directly engaged with them as he wrote. Each work mentioned, in turn, also furnishes suggestions for further reading. An attempt has been made to indicate texts that are currently available, with a few rare exceptions. Where possible, the English version of the work has been cited.

1. Aesthetic Experience

For the concept of historical relativity followed here, see A. Banfi, *Vita dell'arte. Scritti di estetica e filosofia dell'arte*, in *Opere*, ed. E. Mattioli and G. Scaramuzza, vol. 5. (Reggio nell'Emilia, 1988). A similar conception is reexamined and developed by Luciano Anceschi in *Progetto di una sistemazione dell'arte* (Milan, 1960), and generally throughout his work, as we will see in the following paragraphs. A position of relativity based on a distrust of the possibility of reaching any useful definition of art was put forth, in a highly polemical context, by A. Plebe, *Processo all'estetica* (Florence, 1965); also see E. Garroni, *La crisi semantica dell'arte* (Rome, 1964). A critique of the concept of art developed in an Anglo-Saxon context between the wars, with analytic criteria of language and humor traceable to the so-called later Wittgenstein was made by Virgil C. Aldrich, *Philosophy of Art* (Englewood Cliffs, N.J., 1963). The positions of the "death of art" and then of aesthetics can be linked with, among others, Harold Rosenberg, *The De-definition of Art* (New York, 1972). A commonsense, pragmatic position is taken by Umberto Eco in *La definizione dell'arte* (Milan, 1968); a flexible definition, positioned against the background of ontology, is offered by Gianni Vattimo, *Poesia e ontologia* (Milan, 1967).

Once we have overcome the question of a definition of aesthetics, we can consider more general works on the history of aesthetics and its primary theoretical problems. Various authors contributed to the anthology *Momenti e problemi di storia dell'estetica*, 4 vols. (Milan, 1961), and some of the contributors will be mentioned in the following paragraphs. Other works to consider are Wladyslaw Tatarkiewicz, *History of Aesthetics*, 3 vols. (The Hague, 1970–74), especially vol. 1, *Ancient Aesthetics*; G. Morpurgo Tagliabue, *L'esthétique contemporaine* (Milan, 1960); D. Formaggio, *L'arte* (Milan, 1973); *Estetica moderna*, ed. Gianni Vattimo (Bologna, 1977); L. Rossi, *Situazione dell'estetica in Italia* (Turin, 1976); and S. Givone, *Storia dell'estetica* (Bari, 1988). General contributions in which personal theoretical positions are also taken include Theodor W. Adorno, *Aesthetic Theory*, trans. C. Lenhardt (London and Boston, 1983); M. Bense, *Estetica* (Milan, 1974); and Hans Robert Jauss, *Aesthetic Experience and Literary Hermeneutics*, trans. Michael Shaw (Minneapolis, 1982).

After these indications of a general nature, we pass onto the single historical components that are linked in the concept of aesthetics. Concerning poetics, everything obviously begins with the eponymous treatise of Aristotle; for the fortune of this work throughout the centuries, see A. Plebe, *Origini e problemi dell'estetica antica*, in *Momenti e problemi*, vol. 1; B. Weinberg, *A History of Literary Criticism in the Italian Renaissance*, 2 vols. (Chicago, 1970), and edited by Weinberg, *Trattati di poetica e retorica del '500*, 2 vols. (Milan and Naples, 1970); R. Bray, *La formation de la doctrine classique en France* (Lausanne, 1931); see also Renato Barilli, *Poetica e retorica* (Milan, 1984). For rhetoric there also is an originary, eponymous Aristotelian treatise; see A. Plebe, *Breve storia della retorica antica* (Bari, 1968), as well as Roland Barthes, *La retorica antica* (Milan, 1972). See also C. S. Baldwin, *Ancient Rhetoric and Poetics* (Gloucester, Mass., 1959), and D. L. Clark, *Rhetoric in Greco-Roman Education* (New York, 1957). For a general history of the development of rhetoric, see V. Florescu, *La retorica nel suo sviluppo storico* (Bologna, 1971); Renato Barilli, *Rhetoric*, trans. Giuliana Menozzi (Minneapolis, 1989); and A. Battistini and E. Raimondi, *Retoriche e poetiche dominanti*, in *Letteratura italiana*, ed. A. Asor Rosa, vol. 1 (Turin, 1984). Other references will be linked later with the contextual character of poetic discourse. For theoretical rather than historical accounts of rhetoric, see G. Preti, *Retorica e logica* (Turin, 1968), and Paolo Valesio, *Novantiqua: Rhetorics as Contemporary Theory* (Bloomington, Ind., 1980).

As for aesthetics, properly speaking, it seems important to begin with the work that officially introduced the term destined to dominate the field, the *Aesthetics* of A. G. Baumgarten. An earlier text by the same author, *Reflections on the Poetic Text*, has more recently been discovered. In Italy this was published by Aesthetica of Palermo, a publishing house that issues work of the lively International Center for Studies of Aesthetics, led by L. Russo. The Center also published the proceedings of a conference linking the great aesthetologue of rationalism with his "empirical" counterpart, *Baumgarten e Burke* (Palermo, 1986), with contributions by various authors, including Renato Barilli, "Baumgarten, Kant e Leopardi." Also see Barilli, "La rivincita dell'estetica," in L. Rossi, *Situazione dell'estetica in Italia*, and F. Fanizza, *Variazioni dell'estetico* (Naples, 1982). Edmund Burke's masterpiece is *A Philosophical Enquiry into the Origin of Our Ideas of the Sublime and Beautiful*, 3d ed. (London, 1761). To understand this work in the context of the aesthetics of empiricism, see L. Anceschi, *Le poetiche del Barocco letterario in Europa*, in *Momenti e problemi*, vol. 4, *L'estetica dell'empirismo inglese* (Bologna, 1959).

Also, G. B. Vico (see his *Opere*, ed. F. Nicolini [Milan and Naples, 1953]), according to the perspective taken here, must be seen as engaged in a dialogue with empiricists and rationalists rather than simply anticipating Crocean idealism. In particular, he anticipates Baumgarten in his notion of *gnoseologia inferior*. For this, see Barilli, *Poetica e retorica*. The "inferiority" of aesthetics ends with Immanuel Kant's classic, *Critique of Judgment*, trans. J. H. Bernard (New York, 1951). His best follower is Friedrich Schiller, *On the Aesthetic Education of Man*, ed. and trans. Elizabeth M. Wilkinson and L. A. Willoughby (Oxford, 1986). A classic figure in the encounter between the equilibrium of various faculties is J. W. Goethe, especially in his maxims. Another follower of this line, in the key of desperation and regret, is Giacomo Leopardi, *Zibaldone di pensieri*, in *Tutte le opere*, ed. F. Flora, 2 vols. (Milan, 1957). For Leopardi, see also Barilli, *Poetica e retorica*, chap. 7; C. Luporini, *Leopardi progressivo* (Rome, 1980); and S. Timpanaro, *Classicismo e illuminismo dell'Ottocento Italiano* (Pisa, 1969). For theories of romanticism in general, see M. H. Abrams, *The Mirror and the Lamp: Romantic Theory and the Critical Tradition* (New York, 1953), and Philippe Lacoue-Labarthe, *The Literary Absolute: The Theory of Literature in German Romanticism*, trans. Philip Barnard and Cheryl Lester (Albany, N.Y., 1988).

The conception of diachrony in an ideal sense, that is, of an aesthetics that precedes logical and mature adult activity, is established and finds its most important proponent in G. W. F. Hegel, *Aesthetics*, trans. T. M. Knox

(Oxford, 1975). This concept is taken up again by Croce, whose most important contributions to this material appear in *Aesthetics as Science of Expression and General Linguistics*, trans. Douglas Ainslie, 2d ed. (1902; London, 1922); *Breviario di estetica* (Bari, 1951); and the *Aesthetica in nuce*, written in 1928 for the *Encyclopedia Britannica*. His essays in *Poesia e non poesia* (Bari, 1960) furnish an example of a critical definition that earlier I characterized as proceeding "by removal," that is, as directed toward excluding from any value judgment all elements not specific to aesthetics; however, his *La poesia* (1936; Bari, 1963) represents an attempt to admit mediating elements, such as "literature." The prejudice that poetry and logic cannot exist simultaneously is again encountered, under a different, perhaps more rigorous theoretical formulation in that other protagonist of idealism, or rather, of the Neo-Hegelianism of the Neapolitan school; see Giovanni Gentile, *Philosophy of Art*, trans. Giovanni Gullace (Ithaca, N.Y., 1972). For both Croce and Gentile, see A. Attisani, *L'estetica di F. De Sanctis e dell'idealismo italiano*, in *Momenti e problemi*, vol. 3.

I assign maximum importance to the classic work of John Dewey, *Art as Experience* (New York, 1934). I also considered other works of Dewey, not only for their reflections on aesthetics but also for their various philosophical positions: *Logic: The Theory of Inquiry* (1966; New York, 1983), *Conoscenza e transazione* (Florence, 1974), in collaboration with A. F. Bentley, introduction by M. Dal Pra, which I have followed for its dynamic conception of cognitive problems, and *The Quest for Certainty* (1929; New York, 1960). For the aesthetics of Dewey and the debate surrounding them, especially in North America, see Barilli, *Per un'estetica mondana* (Bologna, 1964), which makes a bridge between the concept of experience as it is found in American pragmatism and that found in the field of European phenomenology, especially in France (J. P. Sartre, M. Merleau-Ponty); for this, see Mikel Dufrenne, *The Phenomenology of Aesthetic Experience*, trans. Edward Casey (Evanston, Ill., 1973). Another work by Dufrenne is also quite useful, *The Notion of the A Priori*, trans. Edward S. Casey (Evanston, Ill., 1966). A more recent attempt to link Dewey with certain developments in European phenomenology, including the thought of Martin Heidegger, is suggested by Richard Rorty, *Consequences of Pragmatism* (Minneapolis, 1982). Another key moment in the present discussion is constituted by Jan Mukařovský, *Aesthetic Function, Norm and Value as Social Facts*, trans. Mark E. Suino (Ann Arbor, Mich., 1970, 1979). For Mukařovský, see A. De Paz, "Semiologia e sociologia nell'estetica strutturalista di Mukařovský," in *Lingua e stile* (December 1979).

Another classic work that includes contributions to the definition of a "group" of properties to be recognized in aesthetic experience is Eliseo Vivas, *Creation and Discovery* (New York, 1955). For the concept of the presentational, see S. Langer, *Philosophy in a New Key* (New York, 1958). See also chapter 2 herein and Barilli, *Per un'estetica mondana*, chap. 8. To these contributions of a philosophical nature we should add those of the New Critics, for example, Cleanth Brooks, *The Well Wrought Urn* (London, 1968); J. C. Ranson, *Poems and Essays* (New York, 1955); and Allen Tate, *Essays of Four Decades* (Chicago, 1968) and *Formalismo americano* (Bari, 1969). In collaboration with W. K. Wimsatt, Brooks also wrote a brief history of literary criticism worth consulting, *Literary Criticism: A Short History*, 2 vols. (Chicago, 1983). Another author who is usually linked with the New Critics is William Empson, *Seven Types of Ambiguity*, 3d ed. (London, 1963). We should also mention I. A. Richards, *The Philosophy of Rhetoric* (New York, 1965), and also Barilli, *Poetica e retorica*, chap. 7. In partial agreement with the approach taken in these works is the aesthetic thought of Galvano Della Volpe, *Critica del gusto* (Milan, 1964). This "group" of properties is also treated in the work of L. Pareyson. Another path to the same conclusion is suggested by the art historian C. Brandi; among his numerous publications of a theoretical nature we include *Segno e immagine* (Milan, 1960) and *Teoria generale della critica* (Turin, 1974). See also the contribution to *Brandi e l'estetica* (Palermo, 1986) by Barilli, which attempts to bring Brandi into a "Kantian" line of thought.

2. From Aesthetics to Art

In terms of the sign and symbol, the most important work on a behaviorist aesthetics is Charles Morris, *Writings on the General Theory of Signs* (The Hague, 1971). The best Italian scholar of Morris's thought is F. Rossi-Landi, *Charles Morris* (Milan, 1953) and *Semiotica e ideologia* (Milan, 1972). I have also echoed Dewey's critical reservations against this line of thought, from his *Conoscenza e trasazione*, chap. 9 (laid out by his collaborator Bentley). The concept of the symbol sustained in a cultural anthropological context can be found in Leslie White, *The Science of Culture* (New York, 1949) For an articulated concept of culture that takes account of both the material and symbolic dimensions, see *Il concetto di cultura* (Turin, 1970), ed. Pietro Rossi, and Marvin Harris, *Cultural Materialism: The Struggle for a Science of Culture* (New York, 1979). The concept of cultural materialism I have followed is indebted to Marshall McLuhan, *The Gutenberg Galaxy: The Making of Typographic Man* (Toronto, 1962) and also *Understanding Media* (New York, 1967). In the field of German culture, but as transplanted to the United States, the importance of the symbol is defended by Ernst Cassirer, *The Philosophy of Symbolic Forms*, 3 vols., trans. Ralph Mannheim (New Haven, Conn., 1953–57). Cassirer is essential for the work of Langer, whom we have already referred to on many occasions. The struggle to safeguard the dimension of formations of a general character, without "reducing" them to the level of mere phenomena, but also without separating them from the global field of praxis, is also at the center of the logic of E. Husserl, who, in this, shares with Cassirer a Kantian heritage; see his *Ideas Pertaining to a Pure Phenomenology and to a Phenomenological Philosophy* (The Hague, 1982–89). This multidimensional conception, according to which there is a level of ideal entities in an aesthetic field corresponding to the level of physical phenomena, is followed by several scholars who more or less directly refer to phenomenology. See, in addition to Dufrenne, *The Phenomenology of Aesthetic Experience* and *The Notion of the A Priori*, Roman Ingarden, *The Literary Work of Art*, trans. George Grabowicz (Evanston, Ill., 1973), and *The Cognition of the Literary Work of Art*, trans. Ruth Ann Crowley and Kenneth R. Olson (Evanston, Ill., 1973). Also see Aldrich, *Philosophy of Art*.

After American semiotics of the 1930s, based on behaviorist theories and conceived in a climate of neopositivism, during the 1960s in Italy we saw a semiotics based on linguistics that corresponded to work in the United States. The origin for all of this is, obviously, Ferdinand de Saussure, *Course in General Linguistics*, trans. Wade Baskin, 3d ed. (New York, 1966), the basis for the now famous couple of signifier-signified. And yet Saussure's views can be linked with the pragmatist position; see Barilli, "Alcuni problemi epistemologici relativi al 'Cours,' " in *Lingua e stile*, no. 3 (1968). A foundation of linguistics that is primarily "analytic" (understood, that is, as rejecting the dyarchy between internal and external, form and content, and so on, and thus no longer Kantian) is found in Louis Hjelmslev, *Resumé of a Theory of Language*, ed. and trans. Francis J. Whitfield (Madison, Wis., 1975). As far as the enormous mass of recent semiotic studies, it is worthwhile to refer to Umberto Eco, *A Theory of Semiotics* (Bloomington, Ind., 1976). For zoosemiotics in particular, see Thomas Sebeok, *Perspectives in Zoosemiotics* (The Hague, 1972). For more complex and dialectical semiotic positions, see E. Garroni, *Semiologia ed estetica* (Bari, 1968); L. Nanni, *Per una nuova semiologia dell'arte* (Milan, 1980) and his recent *Contra dogmaticos* (Bologna, 1987); and Robert Scholes, *Semiotics and Interpretation* (New Haven, Conn., 1982).

A closer examination of the field of interrelationships between semiotics, linguistics, and aesthetics (literature) must refer to the historical "islands" represented by the Russian formalists and the Prague functionalists. See Victor Erlich, *Russian Formalism*, 4th ed. (The Hague, 1980), and J. P. Faye, "Le cercle de Prague," *Changes*, no. 3, which includes a discussion of Mukařovský. These schools, however, were forgotten in the immediate postwar years, only to be rediscovered in the 1960s. American New Criticism, by contrast, has undergone a complete reversal. The most representative author of the linguistic-literary, critical-aesthetic synergy in contemporary semiotics is, without doubt, Roland Barthes, *Elements of Semiology*, trans. Annette Lavers and Colin Smith (1968; New York, 1977). The Saussurian term "semiology" was popular in Europe before the English word "semiotics" was adopted. Of Barthes, see also *Criticism and Truth*, trans. Katrine Pilcher Keuneman (Minneapolis, 1987), and *The Fashion System*, trans. Matthew Ward and Richard Howard (New York, 1983). This contribution records Barthes's moment of greatest radicalism after the manner of Hjelmslev; after this the French critic changed his attitude, returning to the vague and removed ("weak" thought, deconstruction, and so on), as is clear from *Pleasure of the Text*, trans. Richard Miller (New York, 1975). An analogous move can be seen in the work of other French critics, including Gérard Genette, from *Figures of Literary Discourse*, trans. Alan Sheridan (New York, 1984), to *Palimpsestes* (Paris, 1982). T. Todorov, also departing from a study of the Russian formalists, attempted to transpose the linguistic categories of Hjelmslev to literary criticism in his *Grammaire du Décameron* (The Hague, 1969), but then turned to the notion of the symbol in romanticism, and reached a conception of broad critical relativism in *Literature and Its Theorists*, trans. Catherine Porter (Ithaca, N.Y., 1987). Julia Kristeva has always been interested in the notion of *difference* developed by Derrida; see *Revolution in Poetic Language*, trans. Margaret Waller (New York, 1984). For a discussion of these various topics over a critical range from an initial analytic-formalist rigor toward hermeneutic and deconstructionist viewpoints, see Barilli, *Tra presenza e assenza* (Milan, 1981). The enterprise of reaching a science of culture, but only following linguistic indications (also for a predominant interest in literary texts) is undertaken by the Russian semiotician J. M. Lotman. See my objections, in the name of a culturology that considers the material-technological level, in the anthology *Estetica e società tecnologica* (Bologna, 1976).

More specifically, addressing the sections of chapter 2 titled "Equivocal, Univocal, Plurivocal," "Signifier-Signified," and "The Acoustic Symbols of Literature," we must repeat certain indications already furnished in the first chapter, that is, pertaining to the general categories of aesthetic experience (Della Volpe, American New Criticism, Empson and his concept of "ambiguity"). Along the line of semiotic interests we should also add the work of J. Cohen, and Michael Riffaterre, *Semiotics of Poetry* (Bloomington, Ind., 1978). The confluence between rhetoric, linguistics, and literature emerges in the classification undertaken by Gruppo μ, *Retorica generale* (Milan, 1976) and *Retorica della poesia* (Milan, 1983). We add now B. Mortara Garavelli, *Manuale di retorica* (Milan, 1989). The attention to microtextual components is opened by the two great classicists of our time, F. Saussure, the author of the already-mentioned *Course in General Linguistics*, whose interest in paragrams is reconstructed by Jean Starobinksi, *Words upon Words: The Anagrams of Ferdinand de Saussure*, trans. Olivia Emmet (New Haven, Conn., 1979), and S. Freud, *Jokes and Their Relation to the Unconscious*, trans. James Strachey (New York, 1963). From both of these authors, I have developed certain hypotheses around a possible interverbal project for our times, *Viaggio al termine della parola* (Milan, 1981), also based on the experience of Joyce with *Finnegans Wake*. For this, see Umberto Eco, *The Aesthetics of Chaosmos: The Middle Ages of James Joyce*, trans. Ellen Esrock (Tulsa, Okla., 1982). For the interverbal project and its links to the fields of concrete, visual poetry and "new writing," see M. Bense, *Estetica*; as well as L. Pignotti and S. Stefanelli, *La scrittura verbo-visiva* (Rome, 1980); A. Spatola, *Versa una poesia totale* (Salerno, 1967); L. Ballerini, *La piramide capovolta* (Padua, 1975); and V. Accame, *Il segno poetico* (Milan, 1981).

For the theoretical problems involved in translation, see G. Mounin, *Teoria e storia della traduzione* (Turin, 1965), and E. Mattioli, *Studi di poetica e di retorica* (Modena, 1983).

For the musical symbol, the basic work for the considerations developed here is Langer, *Philosophy in a New Key*; another classic is Eduard Hanslick, *The Beautiful in Music*, trans. Gustav Cohen (New York, 1974); a valid approach by various Italian authors can be found in *Musica e filosofia* (Bologna, 1973); another contribution, directed toward rejecting the ineffability of music, is that of E. Eggebrecht, *Il senso della musica* (Bologna, 1987); also relevant is the essay by M. Pagnini, *Lingua e musica* (Bologna, 1974).

The problem of the existence of an iconic sign is confronted by Eco in *A Theory of Semiotics*. Also see the anthology *Semiotica della pittura*, ed. O. Calabrese (Milan, 1980), and Calabrese's *Il linguaggio dell'arte* (Milan, 1985). One of my own interventions in refuting the iconic sign in favor of an approach in terms of descriptive codes can be found in *Culturologia e fenomenologia degli stili* (Bologna, 1982). Such an approach finds its basis in the classic contributions of Rudolf Arnheim, *Art and Visual Perception* (Berkeley and Los Angeles, 1974), and *New Essays on the Psychology of Art* (Berkeley and Los Angeles, 1986). Also fundamental are the contributions of Erwin Panofsky, whether for the study of the historical-cultural character of Renaissance perspective in *Perspective as Symbolic Form*, trans. Christopher S. Wood (New York, 1991), or for the revelations made on various other planes, which in linguistic terms would be similar to syntax or semantics, or to the signifier and signified, in *Studies in Iconology* (New York, 1972).

3. The Multiplicity of the Arts

Two authors who discuss the question of artistic technique, especially its richness and variability, are D. Formaggio, *Fenomenologia della tecnica artistica* (Milan, 1953), and G. Dorfles, *Discorso tecnico delle arti* (Pisa, 1958), *Il divenire delle arti* (Turin, 1967), *Nuovi riti nuovi miti* (Turin, 1965), and *Artificio e natura* (Turin, 1968). For a historical account of the problem, see also F. Bollino, *Teoria e sistema delle belle arti* (Mantua, 1979).

The classic essay by Gotthold Ephraim Lessing is *Laocoön: An Essay on the Limits of Painting and Poetry*, trans. Edward Allen McCormick (Baltimore, 1984); a more recent discussion of the sensory classification of the arts is undertaken by A. Baratono, *Arte e poesia* (Milan, 1945). The present discussion owes much to S. Langer, *Feeling and Form: A Theory of Art* (New York, 1953) and also *Problems of Art* (London, 1957).

For the question of the literary genres, one of the best known historical contributions is F. Brunetière, *L'evoluzione dei generi nella storia della letteratura* (1890), a work that reflects its positivist context. A more phenomenological approach is suggested by L. Anceschi, *Le istituzioni della poesia* (Milan, 1968). For the relation between rhetorical discourse and lyric genres, we can also mention several contributions of a historical and theoretical nature: *Les arts poétiques du XIIe et du XIIIe siècle*, ed. E. Faral (Paris, 1923); P. Bagni, *La costitutzione della poesia nelle "artes" del XII-XIII secolo* (Bologna, 1968); R. Tuve, *Elizabethan and Metaphysical Imagery: Renaissance Poetry and Twentieth-Century Critics* (Chicago, 1957); and F. Croce, *Le poetiche del Barocco in Italia*, in *Momenti e problemi*. In our period, the affinities between poetry and publicity in general have been addressed by Roman Jakobson, *Essais de linguistique générale* (Paris, 1963–73). Also see L. Pignotti, *Il discorso confezionato* (Florence, 1979).

A good introduction to narratology is R. Scholes and R. Kellogg, *Nature of Narrative* (Oxford, 1966). For oral literature, see P. Zumthor, *La presenza della voce* (Bologna, 1984), as well as the now-classic Walter Ong, *The Presence of the Word* (New York, 1970), and his *Orality and Literacy: The Technologizing of the Word* (New York, 1982). Narratology based on a more semiotic foundation finds its distant ancestor in Vladimir Propp, *Morphology of the Folktale*, trans. Laurence Scott (Austin, Tex., 1971); another follower on more solid ground is Algirdas Julien Greimas, *Structural Semantics: An Attempt at a Method*, trans. Daniele McDowell et al. (Lincoln, Neb., 1983). We should also mention Barthes, Genette, and Todorov for the theory and history of narrative, as we already observed in the bibliographical notes of the preceding chapter in the general discussion of poetic discourse: they begin as a kind of unit (linked to Hjelmslev's linguistics), but part ways. The divergence is perhaps most radical in Barthes, already visible in *S/Z*, trans. Richard Miller (New York, 1974), which pays particular attention to psychoanalytic motifs. Tzvetan Todorov, *The Fantastic: A Structural Approach to a Literary Genre*, trans. Richard Howard (Ithaca, N.Y., 1975), is also important in this context. As for Genette, in addition to the already-mentioned *Palimpsestes*, we should recall *The Architexte: An Introduction*, trans. Jane Lewin (Berkeley and Los Angeles, 1992), which opens up the problematic of citation and rewriting, which in turn are brought together in the notion of postmodernity, for which see I. Hassan, *The Dismemberment of Orpheus: Toward a Postmodern Literature* (Madison, Wis., 1982) and *Paracriticism: Seven Speculations of the Times* (Urbana, Chicago, London, 1975). For the postmodern in general, see Barilli, *Tra presenza e assenza* and *Il ciclo del postmoderno* (Milan, 1987), as well as the anthology of essays, *Postmoderno e letteratura*, ed. P. Carravetta and P. Spedicato (Milan, 1984). In this key we might also read the *Lezioni americane* of Italo Calvino (Milan, 1988). Also see Umberto Eco, *Lector in fabula. La cooperazione interpretativa nei testi narrativi* (Milan, 1979). At this point we should also cite Eco's two novels: *The Name of the Rose*, trans. William Weaver (San Diego, 1983), and *Foucault's Pendulum*, trans. William Weaver (San Diego, 1989). The formation of a tradition of nineteenth-century realist novels finds its culmination in Emile Zola, *The Experimental Novel*, trans. Belle Sherman (New York, 1964). The great defender of such a tradition in our own century, who also denounces the evils of contemporary narrative, has been Georg Lukács, *The Historical Novel*, trans. Hannah Mitchell and Stanley Mitchell (Lincoln, Neb., 1983); *Realism in Our Time: A Literature and the Class Struggle*, trans. John Mander and Necke Mander (New York, 1964); and *Theory of the Novel*, trans. Anna

Bostock (Cambridge, Mass., 1971). A more dynamic methodology, with greater attention to later developments from the first wave of the twentieth-century avant-garde to the second, can be found in Lucien Goldmann, *Towards a Sociology of the Novel*, trans. Alan Sheridan (London, 1975). An excellent outgrowth of Russian formalism, with an intelligent hybridization of rhetoric and theory in general is Viktor Shklovsky, *Theory of Prose*, trans. Benjamin Sher (Elmwood Park, Ill., 1990), and *Letture del Decamerone* (Bologna, 1967). Today, the work of Bakhtin is attracting a great deal of attention. See his *Esthétique et théorie du roman*, trans. Daria Oliver (Paris, 1978). A classic often forgotten these days is Erich Auerbach, *Mimesis: The Representation of Reality in Western Literature*, trans. Willard R. Trask (Princeton, 1953). The critique of the centrality of the realist-naturalist novel, conducted in the light of the first and second waves of the avant-garde, is found in Barilli, *La barriera del naturalismo* (Milan, 1980), and his *L'azione e l'estasi* (Milan, 1967) can be considered as a sort of introduction to the aspects of narrative of the later twentieth century. For these various problems, see also the anthology *Gruppo 63. Critica e teoria*, ed. R. Barilli and A. Guglielmi (Milan, 1978); R. Giovannoli, *La scienza della fantascienza* (Milan, 1982); M. P. Pozzato, *Il romanzo rosa* (Milan, 1982); and R. Barbolini, *Il detective sublime* (Rome, 1988).

For the origins of art, see Franz Boas, *Primitive Art* (New York, 1955), and André Leroi-Gourhan, *The Dawn of European Art* (Cambridge, 1982). For general relations between art and society, see Arnold Hauser, *The Social History of Art*, 4 vols. (London, 1962). For perspective and its cultural implications, see Panofsky, *Perspective as Symbolic Form* and *Studies in Iconology*, as well as P. Francastel, *L'arte e la civiltà moderna* (Milan, 1957), and *La figure et le lieu* (Paris, 1967), and H. Damisch, *L'origine de la perspective* (Paris, 1987).

For the nexus of expression-abstraction, the most important work is Wilhelm Worringer, *Abstraction and Empathy*, trans. Michael Bullock (New York, 1963). Fundamental are the positions of several of the major artists of our century, including the complete writings of Umberto Boccioni, Wassily Kandinsky, Paul Klee, K. Malevich, and Piet Mondrian. For contemporary art in general, see G. C. Argan, *L'arte moderna* (Florence, 1970); R. De Fusco, *Storia dell'arte contemporanea* (Bari, 1983); and R. Barilli, *L'arte contemporanea* (Milan, 1984).

For the reproduction of the image, see Walter Benjamin, "The Work of Art in the Age of Mechanical Reproduction," in *Illuminations*, ed. Hannah Arendt, trans. Harry Zohn (New York, 1973). See also, in *Storia dell'arte italiana* (Turin, 1980), part 3, vol. 2, F. Mazzocca, *L'illustrazione roman-*

tica, and M. Miraglia, *Note per una storia della fotografia italiana*. Also see P. Pallottino, *Teoria dell'illustrazione italiana* (Bologna, 1988). On experimental photography, see Laszlo Moholy-Nagy, *Painting, Photography, Film*, trans. Janet Seligman (London, 1969). For the history of photography, see A. Scharf, *Art and Photography* (London, 1991); A. Gilardi, *Storia sociale della fotografia* (Milan, 1976); I. Zannier, *Storia della fotografia italiana* (Bari, 1986); F. Alinovi and C. Marra, *Fotografia: illusione o rivelazione?* (Bologna, 1981); Beaumont Newhall, *The History of Photography* (New York, 1982). For the relation between photography and other systems of technical reproduction, see G. Celant, *Artmakers* (Milan, 1984); D. Palazzoli, *Fotografia, cinema, videotape: l'arte nell'età dei media*, in *L'arte moderna* (Milan), no. 119; L. Patella, *I presupposti tecnici e teorici della stampa e della grafica*, ibid., no. 117; *Semiologia grafiche e fotografiche sperimentali*, ibid., no. 118. Also see contributions by Barilli, "Il video-recording," in *Informale oggetto comportamento* (Milan, 1988), vol. 2, and "Arte e computer," in *Il ciclo del postmoderno*.

For the critique of methods of industrial production, the key texts are John Ruskin, *Complete Works* (New York, 1897); William Morris's writings on architecture; and on Morris, see *William Morris e L'ideologia dell'architettura moderna* (Bari, 1975). Also see E. Castelnuovo, *Arte, industria, rivoluzioni* (Turin, 1985). For the opposing tendencies in rationalism, see Hans Maria Wingler, *The Bauhaus*, trans. Wolfgang Jabs and Basil Bilbert (Cambridge, Mass., 1969); G. C. Argan, *W. Gropius e la Bauhaus* (Turin, 1974); and N. Pevsner, *Pioneers of Modern Design* (London, 1966). T. Maldonado returns to this thematic in light of more recent polemics in *Avanguardia e razionalità* (Turin, 1974) and *Il futuro della modernità* (Milan, 1987). The opposite point of view, in favor of postmodernism, is taken by C. Jencks, *The Language of Postmodern Architecture* (London, 1977). Also see Paolo Portoghesi, *After Modern Architecture*, trans. Meg Shore (New York, 1982), and the writings of Philip Johnson. For industrial design, see G. Dorfles, *Introduzione al disegno industriale* (Turin, 1972); V. Gregotti, *Il disegno del prodotto industriale* (Milan, 1986); and G. Anceschi, *Monogrammi e figure* (Florence, 1981). Concerning the postmodern perspective in industrial design, see A. Branzi, *La casa calda* (Milan, 1984). For a sort of historical and theoretical summary of the decorative arts, see Ernst Gombrich, *The Sense of Order* (Oxford, 1979).

As an introduction to the performance arts, the phenomenological approach of Maurice Merleau-Ponty, *The Structure of Behavior*, trans. Alden Fisher (Boston, 1963), may be useful. For links with the characters of contemporary society, see *Il teatro nella società dello spettacolo,* ed. C. Vicentini (Bologna, 1983). For the concept and practice of performance, see *La performance oggi* (Macerata, 1978). The climate of the "death of art" in which this problematic situates itself is discussed by Herbert Marcuse in *Eros and Civilization* (Boston, 1966) and in his essay "The End of Utopia," in *Five Lectures,* trans. Jeremy Shapiro and Shierry Weber (Boston, 1970); F. Menna, *Profezia di una società estetica* (Rome, 1983); M. Perniola, *L'alienazione artistica* (Milan, 1971); and F. Alinovi, *Dada, anti-arte e post-arte* (Florence, 1980) and *L'arte mia* (Bologna, 1984). The great founder of the notion of the convergence of the arts is R. Wagner. For naturalist theater, see Emile Zola, *Le naturalisme au théâtre* (Paris, 1889). For the critique of naturalism, see Adolphe Appia, *Oeuvres complètes* (Lausanne, 1983–91), and F. T. Marinetti, *Teoria e invenzione futurista* (Milan, 1968). On Brecht, see Frederic Ewen, *Bertolt Brecht* (New York, 1967); on Pirandello, see Barilli, *Pirandello: una rivoluzione culturale* (Milan, 1986). On the problems of the later twentieth century, see M. Kirby, *Happening* (Bari, 1968); F. Quadri, *L'avanguardia teatrale italiana* (Turin, 1984), and *Il teatro degli anni settanta* (Turin, 1984); M. De Marinis, *Il nuovo teatro* (Milan, 1987); and L. Bentivoglio, *La danza moderna* (Milan, 1977).

On cinema in its relation to the visual arts, and during the years of the historical avant-gardes, see J. Mitry, *Storia del cinema sperimentale* (Milan, 1971), and the anthology *Il cinema d'avanguardia 1910–1930* (Venice, 1983). On the theoretical level, in this same perspective, see Rudolf Arnheim, *Film as Art* (Berkeley and Los Angeles, 1960), and C. L. Ragghianti, *Cinema* (Turin, 1970). For cinema as narration, see Georges Sadoul, *Histoire générale du cinéma* (Paris, 1946–75), and G. Aristarco, *Storia delle teoriche del film* (Turin, 1963). The theory addressed here is indebted to Siegfried Kracauer, *Theory of Film: The Redemption of Physical Reality* (New York, 1960); also see C. Zavattini, *Diario cinematografico* (Milan, 1979), *Basta coi soggetti!* (Milan, 1979), and *Neorealismo, ecc.* (Milan, 1979). On the contemporary avant-garde, see P. Bertetto, *Il cinema dell'utopia* (Salerno, 1970). On one of Italy's major protagonists, see the anthology *Michelangelo Antonioni,* ed. G. Tinazzi (Parma, 1985); for a theoretical point of view in accordance with semiotics, see G. Bettetini, *Cinema, lingua e scrittura* (Milan, 1968), *L'indice del realismo* (Milan, 1971), *Produzione del senso e messa in scena* (Milan, 1975), and *La conversazione audiovisiva* (Milan, 1984), with sections on the question of television.

4. The Artist, the Patron, the Critic

The emotional aspects of aesthetic and artistic experience today are greatly influenced by the question of psychoanalysis. The "medical" approach, directed primarily at analyzing the biography of an author, is addressed by the writings of Marie Bonaparte. A classic for correct interpretations of Freudian doctrine is E. Kris, *Psychoanalytic Explorations in Art* (n.p., 1962). An intermediary position between stylistic criticism and biographical attention can be found in C. Mauron, *Dalle metafore ossessive al mito personale* (Milan, 1966). Among the best Italian contributions, correctly addressed to questions of the work rather than the author, is Francesco Orlando, *Towards a Freudian Theory of Literature*, trans. Charmaine Lee (Baltimore, 1978). See also A. Trimarco, *L'inconscio dell'opera* (Rome, 1974) and *Itinerari freudiani* (Rome, 1979); Barilli, *Comicità di Kafka* (Milan, 1982); L. Russo, *In margine alla nascita dell'estetica di Freud* (Palermo, 1982); and the very useful S. Ferrari, *Psicoanalisi e letteratura, bibliografia generale 1900–1983* (Parma, 1985).

For the notion of poetics proposed here, see L. Anceschi, *Progetto di una sistematica dell'arte*, and the more recent contributions of two of his students, R. Pajano, *La nozione di poetica* (Bologna, 1970), and C. Gentili, *Poetica e mimesis* (Modena, 1984). For a notion derived from the Crocean "openings" in *La poesia*, see W. Binni, *Le poetiche del decadentismo italiano* (Florence, 1968), and L. Anceschi, *Fenomenologia della critica* (Bologna, 1966). For the method of bipolar couples, see Anceschi, *Autonomia e eteronomia dell'arte* (Florence, 1959). Classics of this method are Heinrich Wölfflin, *Principles of Art History* (New York, 1950); Henri Focillon, *The Life of Forms in Art* (Cambridge, Mass., 1989); and his follower, George Kubler, *The Shape of Time* (New Haven, Conn., 1962). Several traces of Wölfflin's approach recur in the classic postwar text by Umberto Eco, *The Open Work*, trans. Anna Cancogni (Cambridge, Mass., 1989). For stylistic criticism, see Leo Spitzer, *Essays in Historical Semantics* (New York, 1968), and G. F. Contini, *Varianti e altra linguistica* (Turin, 1970). For an approach to formalist criticism with instruments of a semiotic nature, see M. Corti, *Principi della communicazione letteraria* (Milan, 1976); C. Segre, *I segni e la critica* (Turin, 1969) and *Le strutture e il tempo* (Turin, 1974); d'Arco S. Avalle, *Tre saggi su Montale* (Turin, 1970) and *Modelli semiologici nella Commedia di Dante* (Milan, 1975); and S. Agosti, *Il testo poetico* (Milan, 1972). Passing on to a larger frame of interests, see E. Raimondi, *Tecniche della critica letteraria* (Turin, 1967), and *Teoria della letteratura*, ed. E. Raimondi (Bologna, 1975); also see *Sociologia della letteratura*, ed. G. Pagliano (Bologna, 1972). Current interest in overcoming the semiotic perspective and returning to hermeneutics (deconstruction) are documented by M. Ferraris, *La svolta testuale* (Pavia, 1984); Jonathan Culler, *On Deconstruction* (Ithaca, N.Y., 1982); and A. Trione, *L'estetica della mente* (Bologna, 1987). With reference to the visual arts, a broad panorama of critical methods is found in A. Hauser; also see A. De Paz, *Sociologia e critica delle arti*, ed. E. Mucci and P. L. Tazzi (Milan, 1979). On the connections with material culture and technology, aside from the contributions of McLuhan, also see the work of H. A. Innis in this field. An ample reconstruction of the nexus between cultural activities and one particular aspect of technology (printing) is conducted by Elizabeth Eisenstein, *The Printing Press as an Agent of Change* (Cambridge, 1979). Also see M. Costa, *Teoria e sociologia dell'arte* (Naples, 1974).

Index

Renato Barilli is professor of the phenomenology of styles at the University of Bologna, Italy. His areas of study include literary and art criticism and aesthetics. He has published numerous books in Italian on poetics, cultural theory, and contemporary art, including *Culturologia e fenomenologia degli stili* (1982), *L'Arte contemporanea* (1984), and *Il ciclo del postmoderno* (1987). Minnesota has also published a translation of his work *Rhetoric* (1989).

Karen E. Pinkus is currently assistant professor of Italian at Northwestern University. Her interests include psychoanalysis and the relation of visual and verbal arts. She translated Giorgio Agamben's *Language and Death* (Minnesota, 1991).